"Simply the best book ever written on crisis communication."
— **Tom Casey,** vice president of public relations
and marketing, Solaris Health System

"Steve is a media expert, a street-smart guy with powerful insight that makes this book so relevant for our time."
— **Ernie Anastos,** anchor, FOX 5 New York

"Read this book now before you have to ask yourself, 'What was I thinking?' Steve's sage advice definitely beats 'on-the job-training!'"
— **Lucia DiNapoli Gibbons,** regional president, Wachovia

"Heaven forbid you should find yourself or your company with a public relations crisis on your hands. But if you do, Steve Adubato has a wealth of common sense for how to weather the storm with a minimum of damage."
— **Jim Willse,** editor, *The Star-Ledger*

"This book should be in every leader's library and on every communications professional's desk . . . an excellent guide to how to use communications to our advantage in times of crises."
— **Laurence M. Downes,** chairman and CEO, New Jersey Resources

"Steve Adubato gets right to the core of crisis communications.
. . . Honesty, engagement, planning, and training are the tools you need to deal with a crisis."
— **Bob DeFillippo,** chief communications
officer, Prudential Financial, Inc.

"Steve Adubato is one of my favorites. He has a clear point of view and isn't afraid to share it, particularly when it comes to media issues and media coverage of important stories."
— **Joe Scarborough,** host, "Morning Joe," MSNBC

"Steve's book contains tons of valuable advice on the importance of a proactive crisis communication plan. Plus he shares practical ways to sharpen your leadership skills in this process. A great read!"
— **Jack Mitchell,** author of *Hug Your Customers* and
Hug Your People and CEO of Mitchells/Richards/Marshs

"Steve Adubato continues his role as the perpetual teacher by reinforcing that there are lessons to be learned from every circumstance, lauded or loathed. The fact that he had no trouble finding content for this entertaining and instructive book proves how important and necessary it is. Read it to insure you are not a chapter in the sequel."
— **Thomas Marino,** CPA, partner and CEO, J.H. Cohn LLP

"The truth will out. My parents and grandparents used to say it. And now, from his own unique perch—having seen life from both sides of the camera and both sides of the typewriter—Steve Adubato is saying it, too. We can only hope that those who need to read this book carefully, will."

— **Bill Ritter,** anchor, ABC/7 in New York

"Who will you call first in a crisis? My answer, unequivocally: Steve. Dr. Adubato provides a commonsense approach to dealing with every senior executive's nightmare, a crisis. His readable, entertaining book is a must for every exec's desk. Sooner or later we all will need it!"

— **Patricia Costante,** president and CEO, MDAdvantage

"The responses in the lonely minutes in the wake of a crisis separate great leaders from mediocre ones. Steve's hard-hitting book will be your Survival Guide. We are including *What Were They Thinking?* as the textbook in our Rutgers Executive MBA program."

— **Dr. Farrokh Langdana,** director, Rutgers Executive MBA Program (http://EMBA.Rutgers.edu)

"Through carefully selected, often riveting actual events in *What Were They Thinking?* Steve Adubato drives home powerful communication lessons across the board. Individuals as well as corporations will be well served by these insightful analyses."

— **Ronald J. Del Mauro,** president and CEO, Saint Barnabas Health Care System

"Steve makes the art of communication into a 'science' by presenting real-life situations that challenge your thinking. Great resource for anyone that makes his or her profession communicating in the twenty-first century!"

— **Annette Catino,** president and CEO, QualCare, Inc.

"In every big story or scandal we ask, 'What were they thinking?' And so often, the answer comes: 'They weren't.' Steve Adubato does better than that, detailing why headline-grabbing stories stayed in the spotlight." — **Contessa Brewer,** news anchor, MSNBC

"Steve Adubato is a national treasure! In *What Were They Thinking?* he offers a brilliant collection of riveting stories designed to teach the reader how to communicate quickly and effectively in a crisis. A must-read if—in your personal or professional life—you need to let others know that you are sincere, that you are competent, and that you care." — **John E. Welshons,** author, *When Prayers Aren't Answered* and *Awakening from Grief*

"*What Were They Thinking?* is a must-read for anyone who wants to know how to handle a crisis. This practical guide to the dos and don'ts of crisis management uses real-life examples of how communication strategies can help or destroy us in the process."
— **Patricia Pilas Kuchon, Ph.D.,** Graduate Faculty, Strategic Communication and Leadership, Seton Hall University

"A great communicator, Steve Adubato once again delivers his advice in a way that is adaptable to any crisis communications situation. Realistic advice from one of today's best crisis communications professionals." — **Mike Slusarz,** vice president of marketing and public relations, Saint Barnabas Health Care System

"From the introduction revealing his own PR calamity as a young legislator to the chapters detailing how corporations, politicians, and other individuals have publicly addressed their various ordeals, national media analyst Steve Adubato, Ph.D., explains why certain 'messages' made in times of crisis have succeeded or failed. Whether you are a CEO, a PR pro, or simply a person in a serious predicament, this book provides key insights into human expectations and offers reliable communication techniques to implement whenever disaster strikes and reputation, image, or honor is at stake." — **Marlene Browne Chamberlin,** author of *Boomer's Guide to Divorce* and Forbes.com expert on money and divorce

"People want to hear the truth in an authentic way. In *What Were They Thinking?* Steve Adabato guides us through how to plan and deliver a strong message in any crisis situation."
— **Keith H. Green,** president and CEO, United Way of Essex and West Hudson

"*What Were They Thinking?* is the classic crisis communication book that is a must-read for any professional in any arena. I'm making it required reading for our entire sales force and management team." — **Nick Matarazzo,** executive vice president, Integrated Marketing and Sales, Hachette Filipacchi Media

"Steve Adubato's new book *What Were They Thinking?* answers perhaps the most pressing question for every leader or aspiring leader under fire—How do I avoid a media nightmare? This perceptive and timely book offers the right answers for crisis communication because Steve Adubato gets it. A real winner."
— **Joe Watkins,** political analyst, MSNBC

"Steve Adubato reminds us that in a media-saturated environment like ours, public perception is reality; if you are in the public eye, your response to a crisis can either sustain or bury you. By vividly recounting a series of public crises faced by various organizations and individuals, Steve concisely and persuasively draws out the lessons of their (mostly unsuccessful) responses to those crises and underscores how a strong crisis communications plan could have salvaged their situations." — **Patrick C. Dunican Jr.,** chairman and managing director, Gibbons P.C.

"I've known Steve for years—he's the right guy to have around during a crisis." — **Bobbi Brown,** founder, Bobbi Brown Cosmetics

What were they thinking?

CRISIS COMMUNICATION: THE GOOD, THE BAD, AND THE TOTALLY CLUELESS

STEVE ADUBATO, PH.D.

RUTGERS UNIVERSITY PRESS
New Brunswick, New Jersey, and London

LIBRARY OF CONGRESS CATALOGING-IN-PUBLICATION DATA

Adubato, Steve.
What were they thinking? : crisis communication—the good, the bad,
    and the totally clueless / Steve Adubato.
        p. cm.
    Includes bibliographical references.
    ISBN 978-0-8135-4361-1 (hardcover : alk. paper)
    1. Crisis management—United States—Case studies. 2. Public
relations—United States—Case studies. 3. Communication. I. Title.
    HD49.A34 2008
    658.4'056—dc22

                                                        2007048328

A British Cataloging-in-Publication record for this book is available
from the British Library.

Visit our Web site: http://rutgerspress.rutgers.edu

Manufactured in the United States of America

Writing a book about crisis communication is one thing. But living through a crisis is quite another. This book is dedicated to all the victims of 9/11, and to the survivors, family members, and the courageous rescue workers who put their lives on the line at Ground Zero in New York City.

To the victims of the Virginia Tech killings, their family members, and loved ones, as well as those who perished in the West Virginia Sago Mine and those they left behind.

It is also dedicated to all the innocent victims of the crises and tragedies described in this book who did nothing to deserve their fate.

We should never forget that in many crises and tragedies there are real victims with names, lives, and families who suffer so much more than any public relations fallout or loss of market share. Far too often, once the crisis is over and the cameras are gone, for many, the pain and the heartache just begins to set in.

For all of these victims and their loved ones—may we never forget.

CONTENTS

ACKNOWLEDGMENTS

This book would not have been possible without the help of a great team, including:

Theresa Foy DiGeronimo, who once again helped edit, organize, and put the finishing touches on these cases. She is a writing partner I am fortunate to have. As for partners, you couldn't find a better one than Mary Gamba, vice president of marketing for our firm Stand & Deliver. I'm not exactly sure how Mary found the time to run our company, focus on our clients, and keep this book on track (not to mention manage her own family life), but once again, she did it and I am forever grateful.

There are two newcomers to our writing team who added a great deal. Lisa Marie Latino is young, but always eager to learn. Her research was particularly helpful and her always positive attitude kept things in perspective. Laura Amerman is also a great researcher who did much of the early work, helping to determine which cases warranted inclusion in this book.

To Marlie Wasserman and the team at Rutgers University Press—once again, they have been a pleasure to work with. Marlie never lost faith that this project would get done and that the final product would make a significant contribution to the crisis communication arena. I want to thank Colleen DiGeronimo for her creative ideas in connection with the cover of this book. I also want to thank my colleagues at a variety of venues where I "contribute." These colleagues include my editors at The Star-Ledger of Newark, where my weekly column continues to challenge me to write about things that matter to those who care about leadership, communication, and business. They also include those who have helped me as I talked about many of the cases in this book while on the air both at MSNBC (where I've contributed as a media analyst) and the TODAY Show, and when writing columns on media issues for both MSNBC.com and TODAYshow.com.

In addition, in the academic world, where I try to keep one foot firmly planted and teach several courses on such topics as media, crisis communication, and leadership, I want to thank my colleagues and students in the Rutgers University Executive MBA Program, the Montclair State University Department of Broadcasting, and the Seton Hall University Stillman School of Business and its College of Education and Human Services.

I also want to thank my colleagues in public television, where I have worked as an anchor for nearly two decades, particularly those at Thirteen/WNET (PBS) in New York.

To my colleagues at the Caucus Educational Corporation, thank you for your patience and support.

Finally, I want to thank my wife, Jennifer, who once again listened to and read countless drafts of chapters of this book when they were far from completion. And to my three sons, Stephen, Nicholas, and Christopher, who were patient with their dad spending so much time "writing in his office." A writer couldn't ask for a better, more supportive family.

What
were
they
thinking?

Introduction

My personal introduction to crisis communication is burned in my memory of events I would like to forget. In 1984, I was a twenty-six-year-old New Jersey state legislator who had quickly learned how to use the media to my advantage. But I was naive and unprepared for my first public relations crisis. During my second year in office, I found my photo on the front page of the *Herald News* with a caption and a few lines that made it clear that Steve Adubato not only made laws in the statehouse, but apparently broke them when it suited him.

That's what you get when you're stupid enough to park your car—with official government plates bearing your initials and the gold seal of the state—in a parking space reserved for handicapped drivers. (I told you it was stupid.) What was I thinking? I wasn't. I was running late to deliver a brief speech to a local community group, and there was no parking spot available. I knew I would be in and out in just a few minutes. That's my lame rationalization.

The fallout from the news article was embarrassing and humiliating. Angry calls flooded into my legislative office. I deserved all the criticism I got and more, but I didn't know what to do. When would it stop? Was my political career over so soon after it had just begun? I started to feel sorry for myself, which is of no use when facing a crisis or an embarrassing event. This was about public perception, and it didn't take a genius to figure out that a state legislator with official government plates parking in a handicapped spot clearly identified by a very large blue sign would be perceived as dumb and insensitive.

I needed a crisis communication strategy. Should I ignore the bad press? Respond to it? Defend my actions? Take the blame? Blame somebody else? No matter what I did, I was sure that some voters in the next election would, no doubt, remember that picture of my car in that parking space. But whether or not I got their vote would depend entirely on how I communicated to the public in this crisis.

Every Crisis Offers a Lesson

That's what crisis communication is all about. It's a strategy or plan that helps you respond to an out-of-the-norm problem, event, or situation that cannot be handled through standard operating procedures, smart management, and commonsense leadership. It is a strategic method of response that allows you to reach out to key stakeholders—customers, clients, sponsors, stockholders, and the general public—and inform, reassure, and ultimately cement their loyalty and support, or at least get the benefit of the doubt.

Some corporations spend millions of dollars on crisis communication plans. Others ignore the subject entirely because when they think "crisis" they think stop-the-world catastrophic incidents that are not a part of their business and beyond communication response—the 1996 TWA Airline crash, the Exxon *Valdez* oil tanker fiasco in Alaska, and the events surrounding 9/11.

But as too many business, organizational, and political leaders find out the hard way, a crisis can happen any time, anywhere, and to anyone. It can happen to the guilty or the innocent, a "victim" or a "villain." It can happen to people (Don Imus, Alberto Gonzales, Christie Whitman), or to organizations (CBS, Jet Blue, Virginia Tech), or to both. When it does happen, crisis communication is largely about public perception, which many in this media-driven world confuse with objective, factual reality.

That's why we're all open to potential communication and PR crises or scandals. We're talking organizational mergers or downsizing of a workforce; a CEO involved in some salacious sexual or financial scandal that jeopardizes stock price, organizational reputation, and internal morale; union strikes; violent employees or students; bankruptcy or other financial problems; an inflammatory e-mail that inadvertently finds its way to the broader cybersphere and the media. Any of these circumstances and so many others can produce a crisis that is then made worse by the lack of preparation and by the poor execution of a response on the part of those involved.

The cases in *What Were They Thinking?* represent a cross-section of experiences involving organizations and individuals. Some you will recognize from national headlines, while others will be less well known but no less powerful in the lessons they can teach us. In the following chapters, we'll explore a variety of cases—the good, the bad, and the clueless—in which organizations and individuals faced some sort of challenge or crisis that required them to communicate to a variety of critical audiences in an articulate, effective, and timely fashion.

We'll also study the communication plans of some who got it right. The way CEO James Burke of Johnson & Johnson handled the Tylenol tampering case in 1982 continues to be the gold standard in crisis communication, and the 2004 case of CEO Art Ryan at Prudential Financial gives us insight into how modern technology can be effectively used to support crisis communication. We'll also look at National Football League Commissioner Roger Goodell's masterly handling of several high-profile scandals in his sport. Ironically, FOX News talking head Bill O'Reilly got it right by "shutting up." The problem, however, is that such examples are few and far between.

You will find that in most cases presented in this book, the communication fell woefully short and sometimes terribly flat. To name just a few, we'll talk about individuals such as Rudy Giuliani and Jon Corzine, who made the mistake of thinking that the problems in their private lives did not require the same level of crisis communication skills as those in their business/public lives. (Yet in the chapters on Giuliani and Corzine, we also explore how both public officials handled other crises extremely well.) We'll analyze the Duke lacrosse team "rape" fiasco, in which Prosecutor Mike Nifong and the Duke University administrators and faculty mistakenly thought they could gain public support by rushing to judgment and pandering to public opinion. In our study of crisis communication plans, we'll also look at organizations such as Major League Baseball, which tried to ignore and then deny dangerous and unethical practices by their employees for their own economic gain. Of course, we'll dissect stories of less-than-forthright public figures such as Defense Secretary Donald Rumsfeld, who made the crisis involving the death of Army Ranger Pat Tillman worse through a combination of arrogance and stupidity.

Others who got it wrong under pressure include the executives and top editors at the *New York Times* who tried to ignore the Jayson Blair "problem" until it blew up in their faces. One of the scandals that I was personally and profoundly impacted by, which I examine in the book, is the pathetic and hypocritical response of the Catholic Church to the crisis involving numerous dangerous priests who preyed on innocent children—in some cases for decades.

Some cases in this book explore self-inflicted wounds and crises such as Dick Cheney's ridiculous mishandling of his accidental shooting of longtime friend Harry Whittington on a Texas hunting trip. Other cases examine how organizations and individuals deal with what happens to them. Among these are the response to the Virginia Tech murder spree that took place on April 16, 2007, and Rudy Giuliani's extraordinary leadership in New York City in the days and weeks immediately following September 11.

While most of the cases in this book involve high-profile people involved in much-publicized controversies, a few explore people whose names you may not recognize. One of those people is Rose McCaffery, the superintendent of the Glen Ridge New Jersey Pubic Schools. In 1989, the small, suburban, and wealthy community of Glen Ridge was confronted with the horrific and violent rape of a seventeen-year-old retarded girl by a number of admired school athletes. The case of Rose McCaffery graphically demonstrates how a nationally publicized scandal or crisis can happen to anyone, anywhere, at any time. As you will see, Superintendent McCaffery was in no way prepared for what she and the tiny town of Glen Ridge were about to face. From these and many others we will learn how not to communicate in a crisis.

Learning on the Job

Since my initial introduction to the value of a well-planned response, via the parking-in-a-handicap-space calamity, my view of crisis communication has been greatly influenced by my work as a journalist, university lecturer, communication coach, and media analyst for MSNBC, MSNBC.com, Todayshow.com, and previously on the FOX News Channel.

As a media analyst, I focus on how people handle and communicate in challenging circumstances. I have provided commentary and analysis on how President George Bush communicates under pressure and why he so often misses the mark. Given the many press conferences in which he often appears confused when being asked a direct question, it is obvious that President Bush is not an eloquent public speaker or polished orator. But being a polished speaker is not a prerequisite for being a credible crisis communicator, nor is it the primary focus of this book, which attempts to examine how leaders of all stripes and speech abilities respond and react to crises. Speech-making is but one piece of a comprehensive and effective crisis communication strategy or plan. Handling a crisis or scandal with poise, dignity, and in a calm and controlled fashion is what is critical to a leader's ability to lead when others around him or her are confused and afraid. On so many counts, President Bush consistently failed this test by any reasonable standards.

Although President Bush and his consistently poor crisis communication performance warrant an entire book in itself, you will see that there is not a single case study in this book dedicated exclusively to him. Instead, his varied communication gaffs are featured in the Katrina/FEMA case and are also discussed in the Whitman/EPA, Alberto Gonzales, Dick Cheney, and Pat Tillman cases.

My work at MSNBC and MSNBC.com, as well as my appearances on NBC's *Today* show, have also focused on "pop culture" crises including those involving Rosie O'Donnell, Donald Trump, Barbara Walters, Michael Richards, Britney Spears, Mel Gibson, Don Imus, and countless others whose names are not important, but whose experiences under pressure instruct us.

Also, in countless interviews that I have conducted as an anchor for Thirteen/WNET (PBS) in New York, and in my work hosting a variety of news programs on both public television and the Comcast Network, I have seen what happens when individuals under fire are ill-prepared. I have seen people on the other end of a question implode before my eyes. In fact, I can see it in their eyes—the fear, the anxiety, and the desire to be any place other than where they are at that moment, all because they aren't prepared to answer some tough questions about a difficult situation. I've seen so many seemingly innocuous situations turn into crises because of how they are mishandled by individuals and institutional representatives.

As a long-time columnist with New Jersey's *The Star Ledger* newspaper writing on the subjects of communication and leadership, I have profiled hundreds of cases and scenarios involving one crisis or another. In all of these columns, I have sought not only to explain what has gone wrong, but why and more importantly what the rest of us can learn in the process. Writing this weekly column has reinforced my view that the vast majority of us don't communicate nearly as well as we think we do or as well as we are capable. The good news is that with some coaching and candid feedback, we can dramatically improve our performance, even in the most difficult of circumstances.

That is my role as a communication coach. Through my firm, Stand & Deliver, I have tried to help organizations and executives proactively develop strategic communication plans that anticipate a crisis or a problem and then I help them execute that plan when needed.* This work with some of the finest organizations and corporations in the country has taught me a great deal about this challenging and often complex process. I've learned, for example, that effective crisis communication isn't about winning or about turning a bad situation into a good one. Rather, it is about knowing what, how, and when to respond to a problem so that major constituents (be they employees, stockholders, customers, organization members, or even one's own spouse) feel we are being truthful, forthright, and contrite. Crisis communication is sometimes about minimizing the damage or the "hit" you are sometimes going to take.

The Clinton Effect

Speaking of "taking a hit," let's talk about the "Clinton effect." I had numerous friends, colleagues, and others who, when they heard that I was writing a book about handling a crisis or a scandal, suggested I write about one case or another. Among the many cases suggested were: former New Jersey governor ("I am a gay American") Jim McGreevey, Merck/Vioxx, former U.S. senator Larry Craig of Utah and his bathroom sex scandal, former

---

*Full disclosure: In this book, I do not provide media analysis or commentary involving any client or organization that I have coached through a crisis.

Evangelical preacher Ted Haggard, Martha Stewart, CBS and Dan Rather, the Abu Ghraib Prison scandal, the NSA illegal wiretapping controversy, Enron, author James Frey and his tearful apology to Oprah, New Orleans Mayor Ray Nagin, Rush Limbaugh's incredibly insensitive mocking of Michael J. Fox, publisher Judith Regan and the O.J. mess, to name just a few. All these cases were potentially interesting and informative, but the twenty-two cases that were ultimately selected for inclusion in *What Were They Thinking?* hopefully represent the most diverse and relevant cases for any professional who may face a serious challenge or problem, and in turn a potential crisis.

However, one case that was suggested more than any other was the Bill Clinton–Monica Lewinsky scandal. I thought a lot about it and did extensive research on this highly publicized and significant event in presidential and American history. I'm not talking about the actual "sexual relations" between Clinton and Lewinsky (that never really interested me), but rather the aftermath. Then it hit me—the irony of the Clinton/Lewinsky episode is that in so many ways Bill Clinton broke virtually every rule and contradicted every "lesson" that I espouse in this book and yet, as of 2008, he still comes out smelling like a rose.

Think about it. I'm not saying everyone likes Bill Clinton. In fact he has many detractors, including many conservatives and others who really dislike him. But we're talking about a guy who can still raise more money (particularly for the William J. Clinton Presidential Library and the Clinton Global Initiative) and gets paid more money to deliver a one-hour speech than any president in American history or probably any human being on the face of the earth. It's uncanny.

In this book I argue that it's important to proactively disclose your mistakes and not try to deny, stonewall, or cover up. But that's exactly what Bill Clinton did as it relates to his sexual relationship with White House intern Monica Lewinsky. Clinton lied to everyone. Not just his wife and his family, but to the media, a federal grand jury, and ultimately the American public. In this book I describe strong leaders as those who do not "lawyer up" and use legal jargon to parse the meaning of words. Yet, Bill Clinton is the guy who made famous the expression: "It depends upon what the meaning of is, is." He was anything but candid and forthright in his public comments. He often lost his cool, showed his anger, and most importantly, avoided taking responsibility for his actions.

I have said that the best way to handle a crisis is to get out in front of it and deal directly with the media. Instead, Clinton had his wife Hillary go on the *Today Show* to defend him (with no knowledge that the Lewinsky story was actually true) and blame the "vast right-wing conspiracy" for going after her husband. I've said that blaming others for your actions is a stupid and dangerous approach to crisis communication that is bound to come back to hurt you. Yet, that is exactly what Bill Clinton did, but he didn't have the guts to do it himself; rather, he had his wife do it on national television. Pretty low, huh?

There are so many lessons highlighted in this book about how to handle a crisis that Bill Clinton ignored and contradicted, yet, he is still beloved by so many. So what gives? I can think of only one explanation: Bill Clinton is one of the most charming, charismatic, and disarming public figure one will ever meet. Many who hate him and everything he stood for as president (including former GOP House Speaker Newt Gingrich) say they still like being in his company. Clinton's smile, his handshake, his famous eye contact, his knack for remembering your name and your face, and his ability to connect with people on a powerful, human, and personal level allows him to overcome the leadership and character flaws he exhibited in connection with the Monica Lewinsky scandal.

This fascinating paradox became particularly clear to me just a few weeks before I finished this book. I happened to be at the Sheraton Hotel in New York City, where the Clinton Global

Initiative was holding its annual conference. By chance, as I was walking out of the hotel's gym with my longtime friend and lawyer Nick Grieco, Bill Clinton happened to get out of a nearby elevator surrounded by the Secret Service. Without missing a beat, Clinton walked up to me and introduced himself, and of course I responded, "Hello, Mr. President" while shaking his hand. Over the years I've written countless columns and have done numerous on-air commentaries blasting Clinton for his handling of the Lewinsky matter. Still, it was hard not to be struck by his presence—his aura, the powerful first impression he makes. But what especially struck me is that Clinton went out of his way to introduce himself to Nick, who wasn't directly in his path, adding, "I love that T-shirt." Nick was wearing a Bruce Springsteen T-shirt (the Boss was doing his most recent tour in the New York area). As Clinton walked away, Nick, who is a life-long Republican and who twice voted against Bill Clinton for president, turned to me and said, "That guy is amazing. It is like meeting a rock star. Now I know what everyone is talking about."

So there you have it. Of course some of Clinton's personal charm and appeal has to do with being a former president. But there is more to it. Neither George H. W. Bush nor his son has this kind of appeal. Jimmy Carter didn't have it and no one talks much about Gerald Ford or Richard Nixon's personal charm and charisma. Ronald Reagan had it, but not nearly to the degree of Bill Clinton, who seems like the kind of guy who could get away with just about anything. Bill Clinton has something so unique when it comes to the ability to make a human connection both in person and on television that he is able to break virtually every rule of crisis communication and not only live to tell about it, but to prosper, flourish, and still be a powerful and credible national force in a way that even Hillary Clinton cannot match.

So what is the lesson for the rest of us in all of this? It is pretty simple. Unless you believe you posses that rare combination of natural-born and highly developed skills and tools that make you as dynamic, charismatic, and charming as Bill Clinton, you should play it by the book—more specifically, the crisis communication lessons in this book—because Bill Clinton is one of those larger-than-life "Babe Ruth"–type figures who can break all the rules of the game and still wind up on top. Unfortunately, the rest of us have to play by a more traditional set of rules.

So read on and let's get to work. I am confident this book will help you sharpen your communication skills so that when a crisis or serious challenge strikes (and eventually it will), you will not be paralyzed by fear and confusion. Instead, you will be prepared not only to survive it, but also to improve your standing as a person and a leader.

Johnson & Johnson's Tylenol Scare

GETTING IT RIGHT

What were they thinking? ——————————
The multinational corporation was thinking that if
they could face their sudden crisis in a proactive,
honest, and timely manner, they could save the
long-term viability of the company.

The Lesson ——————
They were right.

When it comes to crisis communication, virtually every organization's performance under pressure is measured against Johnson & Johnson's handling of the Extra Strength Tylenol/cyanide-lacing scare in October 1982. Although it occurred in a very different media environment than our present one, this case is still a valuable example of how a company should communicate when its reputation, as well as its financial survival, is on the line. Johnson & Johnson not only survived the original publicity surrounding the seven deaths tied to the cyanide-lacing of its product, but the company's public image was actually enhanced by the episode. None of this was an accident. While Johnson & Johnson's actions were not flawless and mistakes were made, its superior communication strategies are a model of crisis management that all business leaders should study.

A Model of Proactive Action

To begin, it's worth noting that the idea of an over-the-counter medication being tainted with cyanide was unprecedented in 1982. There was no prototype showing how to handle this kind of public relations and public-health nightmare. Americans were understandably concerned and afraid when word got out that seven people had died after taking Tylenol. No one knew how widespread the problem was or whether it was an inside job. The government had little ability to regulate the situation or "protect" the public. The pressure was squarely on Johnson & Johnson, a company with a solid national and international reputation as a producer of baby products, shampoo, bandages, and drugs, but also a company with no official crisis communication team or plan. However, it did have a group of smart, proactive executives and mangers who understood the critical nature of the situation.

Working in its favor, Johnson & Johnson had built up tremendous goodwill among millions who were inclined to give the company the benefit of the doubt. But cyanide in Tylenol? This was a seemingly insurmountable PR disaster. Still, company executives recognized that in a crisis, even one of epic proportions, the window of opportunity to gain public support is a narrow one. So, within hours of realizing that a potential problem existed, Johnson & Johnson set up a seven-member "crisis team" lead by one person, Lawrence Foster, who had the skills, the experience, and the reputation to set the tone and have it executed and supported by everyone at Johnson & Johnson, including CEO James Burke. Johnson & Johnson's lawyers were obviously involved, but it was Burke, Foster, and Johnson & Johnson's senior management and communication team that were dictating the company's internal and external communication. They decided immediately that full and timely disclosure was critical to surviving this crisis.

Without knowing the extent of the Tylenol contamination problem or how the tampering had occurred, Johnson & Johnson decided to be proactive. They immediately recalled all Tylenol capsules from stores in the Chicago area, where the original deaths occurred. This move demonstrated that Johnson & Johnson's top priority was protecting the public, even at a tremendous financial cost to the corporation's bottom line. The crisis team quickly decided that the company's long-term reputation was more important than any immediate fiscal impact.

Identifying Key Stakeholders

When the recalled capsules were examined, two were found to contain cyanide. At that point, Johnson & Johnson's crisis communication team decided to be consistently out front and accessible. They identified the company's most important stakeholders and worked to communicate, share information, and respond to questions and concerns from these various publics, including:

THE NEWS MEDIA. J&J immediately informed the *Chicago Sun Times*—no cover-up here. Burke then conducted a press conference that was transmitted to nearly thirty different sites where reporters had gathered from around the country to ask him questions about the situation. He answered every question as directly as he could. He was poised and confident and was media savvy. Johnson & Johnson's communication team also sought high-profile network opportunities for James Burke on such programs as *60 Minutes, Nightline,* and *Donahue.* Johnson & Johnson also took out full-page ads in major newspapers across the country informing consumers that they could exchange Tylenol capsules for Tylenol caplets, which had been cleared of any tainting.

Clearly, the company's top priority focused on warning the public about the dangers that might exist with Extra Strength Tylenol still in stores across the country. This in turn caused most media organizations to see themselves as conduits of this information to a fearful and extremely anxious public.

THE GENERAL PUBLIC INCLUDING LONGTIME CONSUMERS OF JOHNSON & JOHNSON'S PRODUCTS. Johnson & Johnson immediately set up a twenty-four-hour hotline with twenty-three telephones operated by well-informed Johnson & Johnson medical and health experts to answer any and all questions related to Tylenol, cyanide, or any related topic. This hotline received over 200,000 calls, a fact that was widely reported in the news media, which again reinforced Johnson & Johnson's reputation for being responsible and responsive.

JOHNSON & JOHNSON EMPLOYEES. This group was obviously concerned, and they too were being pressed by friends and family as to what the "real story was" about the Tylenol/cyanide scare. Burke held forums with employees, answering their questions and keeping them in the loop, and inviting them to share information with their friends and family.

THE GOVERNMENT. Johnson & Johnson was quick to notify and engage the cooperation of federal regulatory bodies like the FDA and law enforcement agencies like the FBI. This further secured their place as an aggrieved party seeking justice in this tragedy.

MEDICAL PROFESSIONALS. Working through national organizations, Johnson & Johnson sent information as it became available, knowing medical professionals were being inundated with questions and fears from people all over the country who were seeking answers to their questions.

Johnson & Johnson was not forced or pressured into taking any of these steps. Rather, the crisis communication team understood the need to be proactive in its communication as well as in setting up a mechanism to facilitate a dialogue with interested and concerned parties. By taking this "we're all in this together" approach, Johnson & Johnson was able to gain the cooperation of many of these key audiences.

Of course this cooperation did not come cheap. All of Johnson & Johnson's efforts are estimated to have cost $100 million during this period, but clearly was a very smart and prudent investment on the part of the company.

The Power of Trust

Largely because of the way Johnson & Johnson handled the Tylenol/cyanide incident, the company was seen as a corporate "victim" of some sick, dangerous killer who was targeting the company and its customers for no apparent reason. It was also important that the media accounts quoted independent medical experts involved in the case who were convinced that the tampering took place "after leaving the manufacturer's plant in Pennsylvania."

Johnson & Johnson's willingness to be open and honest—even when it came to mistakes and misstatements—was critical to gaining the trust of the news media and the general public. An excellent example of this full-disclosure communication approach was evident in the way that Lawrence Foster, Johnson & Johnson's chief crisis communication spokesperson in the Tylenol case, handled his misstatement regarding the presence of cyanide in the manufacturing plant.

Foster initially issued a statement to reporters that there was no cyanide in the manufacturer's plants. A few days later, the Associated Press heard that there was cyanide in the plants and called Foster to confirm the report. "After checking again, Foster discovered that indeed a small amount of cyanide was used in the manufacturing plant for quality-assurance testing of some kind. However, the cyanide was kept in a completely separate facility from the production line, and none of it was missing. There was no way that it could have gotten into the capsules accidentally. Even if it had, it would have been so dispersed as to be harmless."[1]

Still, Foster realized that he had made a mistake and reached out to the Associated Press and clarified the situation. This was essential if Johnson & Johnson was to continue to be seen as trustworthy and reliable. Further, as Watergate and other well-publicized crises remind us, it is usually the cover-up that is much worse than either the crime, scandal, or the mistake that an organization is involved in. Foster clearly understood this. Interestingly, initially Foster had asked several news organizations not to run with that story about the cyanide in the Johnson & Johnson plants and they agreed because it was understood that there was no direct connection between its presence in the plant and the cyanide lacing of Tylenol.

Later, when the New York Times got access to the information and told Foster and Johnson & Johnson that they were running with the story, he immediately contacted such publications as The Star-Ledger (which is based in New Jersey, the home of Johnson & Johnson's corporate headquarters) as well as the Associated Press. He told them that the Times would be running the story about the cyanide in the plant, but asked these additional members of the media to "use their discretion." Interestingly, when the stories ran they were not sensationalized and Johnson & Johnson was not portrayed as the corporate villain. There was little public reaction to them, which in many ways was part of Johnson & Johnson's reward for acting in such an open and accessible fashion. Foster's solid reputation and track record with the media was paying off.

Doing It Right

It is important to note that when the first press accounts appeared regarding the deaths associated with Extra Strength Tylenol, Johnson & Johnson was operating in a very different media environment than companies must deal with today. In 1982, there was no easy-access Internet. There were no 24/7 highly competitive cable news networks like CNN, MSNBC, or FOX News. There was no YouTube, no Google, no bloggers, no cell phones. Yet still, there are several key elements that Johnson & Johnson incorporated into their crisis response plan that are remarkably notable *because* of their effectiveness in the intense media environment we must all now respond to.

The key lessons from the Johnson & Johnson cyanide scare that we can all learn from include the following:

1. Establish a solid crisis communication team led by one person. Like Foster, that person must be a strong communicator who can convey a clear message and must have the unequivocal backing of all company bigwigs.

2. Act quickly and proactively, even if all the facts are not yet in. This quick action portrays a sense of responsiveness to the public that will protect you from charges of cover-up down the line.

3. Identify key stakeholders and then create an effective communication system that consistently allows for a dialogue between the company and these important members of the media and the public. Show a willingness to share any and all information.

4. Proactively seek out appropriate and tough media opportunities. Instead of ducking hard-news outlets such as *60 Minutes*, go to them. Who does that unless it is a company that believes in what it is doing and isn't afraid to communicate its message in the toughest media environment?

5. Show that you and your company are trustworthy and reliable. This will sometimes require a willingness to expose mistakes or errors, while resisting the temptation to cover up.

6. Don't ever hide behind lawyers. Of course we must all consult with our lawyers in times of crisis, but they should have limited public involvement in the crisis communication process. We all know that future liability and litigation are legitimate concerns, but it cannot be apparent that they are the company's paramount concern.

7. When mistakes or misstatements occur, own up to them. Foster did. Doing so increases your credibility and reputation as a "straight shooter" who can be trusted. It may also build goodwill with key stakeholders when new "issues" arise.

The testament to the effectiveness of these communication guidelines culled from the annals of Johnson & Johnson's handling of the Tylenol/cyanide incident is the fact that shortly afterward, Johnson & Johnson's market share not only recovered, but Extra Strength Tylenol and other Tylenol products remained one of the strongest sellers in the pain-relief market. This proves once again that it's not what happens, but rather how you deal with it, that matters most.

The *Exxon Valdez* Oil Tanker Spill

THE INVISIBLE AND CLUELESS CEO

What were they thinking?

Lawrence G. Rawl, the chairman of Exxon Corporation, thought he could minimize the extent of a massive problem by being detached, impersonal, and arrogant.

The Lesson

You can often minimize inevitable public relations fallout when faced with a sudden and unexpected disaster by planning for an honest, well-timed, and empathetic response from the top player in the company.

Nearly two decades after it happened, the response by Exxon executives to the *Valdez* oil spill disaster remains a prime example for how not to handle a crisis. It was March 24, 1989, when the nearly 1,000-foot oil tanker was moving through Prince William Sound in Alaska headed for California. There was no storm, no wind, no ice, and no rough seas. With such calm waters there was little reason to think that anything terrible would happen when Captain Joseph Hazelwood put the massive tanker on auto pilot—but it did.

Captain Hazelwood put the vessel in the hands of third mate Gregory Cousins, who had little experience navigating the narrow strait that was known as Bligh Reef—one of the most challenging areas of Prince William Sound. Moments after midnight, the tanker hit submerged rocks that ripped a hole in nearly the entire length of the ship. Eleven million gallons of crude oil spilled into the pristine waters off Alaska, creating a 1,300-square-mile oil slick and killing an estimated 100,000 animals.[1] Within hours, word got out locally in Valdez. Soon, national and then international media would converge on the small Alaskan town. It was the worst oil spill in U.S. history. This event called for exceptional response strategies from Exxon executives. The people of Valdez who made their living off these waters; the U.S. government, which would demand answers; the citizens of the United States and environmentalists from around the world who would be angered and worried— all would be looking to Exxon to explain what happened and what the company was going to do to make amends.

A Pathetic Response

From the beginning Exxon executives made a series of mistakes that would make a very bad situation a lot worse. At first they tried to minimize the extent of the problem by implying that environmentalists and the media were exaggerating the severity of the situation. They also focused virtually all of the company's efforts on the operational side—the cleanup. Exxon's leadership mistakenly believed that if they "cleaned up" the expanding oil spill, they could minimize the public relations fallout. They did not realize that an immediate cleanup was impossible. In fact, after a massive and multifaceted effort, it would take nearly ten years for scientists to conclude that Prince William Sound was remotely back to normal.

Exxon's efforts to clean up the site should have had nothing to do with meaningful crisis communication. With the world's media showing graphic images of devastated wildlife and with Alaskan fisherman accusing Exxon of destroying their livelihood, Exxon needed to communicate empathy and compassion and do it on a timely basis. This did not happen.

Then more bad news for Exxon. Numerous reports asserted that Captain Hazelwood had been drinking the night of the accident. Word also got out that Exxon knew that Hazelwood had previously had his driver's license revoked for drunk driving and had been hospitalized for alcohol treatment. Yet another crisis for Exxon and yet again no adequate response.

Finally, ten days after the incident, Exxon took out a full-page ad in numerous newspapers to announce its commitment to cleaning up the spill. Even this was a bungled communication opportunity. For starters, the ad was nine days too late. Then to further hurt the chances of gaining the public's trust, the ad made no mention of culpability and offered no direct apology to the people of Valdez.

This was a stance Exxon would continue to take throughout the months and years of investigation that followed. As a full-blown PR crisis was unfolding in the national and international media, Exxon execs were looking around for someone else to blame. In fact, the day before the ad appeared, Lee Raymond, Exxon's president, told ABC News that he blamed "ultimately the Coast Guard" for delaying the use of dispersants. But a chronology of the first four days after the spill—assembled from state and Coast Guard official reports and dozens of interviews with company spokesmen, fishermen, and others—sharply contradicted this assertion.[2] Clearly, the Exxon plan was to duck and cover, hoping the public would swallow its attempts to divert the blame.

Not only was the tone of Exxon's communication plan off key, but its most important messenger was nowhere to be seen. CEO Lawrence Rawl made the fatal mistake of delegating all significant communication responsibilities to his PR team. Exxon's "spokesperson" in Valdez kept changing, which made the company look weak and disorganized. CEO Rawl said he didn't go to Valdez right away because he felt "technologically obsolete," demonstrating how little he really understood about the CEO's primary leadership responsibility in a crisis. Rawl reluctantly put out an unemotional statement on video that communicated little if any empathy and compassion for those whose lives and livelihood had been devastated by the Valdez fiasco. Rawl didn't say a word about the wildlife and ecosystem that had been destroyed. Only after nearly three weeks of constant criticism and pressure did Rawl finally go to Alaska.

Let's Count the Ways Exxon Got It Wrong

Lawrence Rawl's handling of the *Valdez* fiasco gives us a classic example of a CEO who just didn't get it.

To begin, when an incident even remotely as big as the Exxon oil spill happens, time is a precious commodity. Everything Exxon did in this crisis came too late. The fact that Exxon waited ten days to run a newspaper ad and three weeks to send their top CEO to the scene made absolutely no sense. According to Paul Shrivastava, who at the time of the *Valdez* incident was the director of the Industrial Crisis Institute: "All crises have a window of opportunity to gain control of 45 minutes to 12 hours."[3] It is critical that organizational leaders understand this narrow window of opportunity; Rawl clearly did not.

Rawl's own comments demonstrate the difference between someone who sees him- or herself as simply an operational manager and someone who is a real take-charge leader. He tried to excuse the fact that he didn't immediately go to the scene by saying: "Getting me up there would have diverted our own people's attention; I couldn't help with the spill; I couldn't do anything about getting the ship off the rocks." What was he thinking when he said this? Gerard Meyers, a former chairman of the American Boaters Company and who at the time of the *Valdez* incident was a crisis management consultant, commented on Rawl's delayed visit by saying: "What we have here in my opinion, is a classic unmanaged crisis. As phony as it sounds, sending the chairman to the scene would have shown genuine concern for what happened there."[4]

The other piece of the equation in this communication disaster is that Exxon executives didn't seem to understand or appreciate the public outcry against both the incident and Exxon's handling of it. Many Americans joined a campaign to boycott Exxon and showed their displeasure by cutting up their Exxon credit cards. Instead of empathizing, some Exxon executives, such as Frank Iarossi, president, Exxon Shipping Company, said several years after the incident: "Exxon is a very, very proud company that has done a lot to protect the environment . . . the public's reaction [in connection with the *Valdez* incident] is totally irrational . . . how much good is this really doing? We're not willing to make [the commitment] to go anywhere and do anything anybody says."[5]

Limiting the PR Fallout

If not for this kind of arrogance, there is compelling evidence that Exxon could have minimized the public relations fallout if the company leaders had acted in a more reasonable, empathetic, and timely fashion. Clearly, Exxon was going to take a hit on this no matter what it did. Any time the media latches onto a story this big and this visual, a corporation (even one with a great reputation) is going to be raked over some coals. Yet, the key to a solid crisis communication operation is to understand that even though the organization is going to be vulnerable to legitimate and in some cases even unfair criticism, if the execs at the top are committed to planning and executing a timely and personal response, the fallout can be limited. But on every level, CEO Lawrence Rawl's delayed response, bumbling comments, insensitive actions, and shift-the-blame accusations set Exxon up for a corporate disaster.

Surprisingly, even with time to rethink his bungled response after his retirement from Exxon, Rawl still did not get it. To the end, he thought he could duck responsibility and protect the company by blaming others. At the time of the crisis, he told the national media and testified before two congressional sub-committees that Captain Hazelwood was drunk when he ran the Exxon *Valdez* oil tanker aground. But then, in 1994, he gave a different version in federal court as he testified in a multi-billion-dollar lawsuit against the company and Hazelwood. He told the court he had made those earlier comments based on bad information he got from the news media and the U.S. Coast Guard saying, "I told the truth totally, but I had bad dope. I wasn't careful at that period of time, I was under a lot of pressure. I said some things that if I had more time to get information, I wouldn't have said." Now Exxon and Hazel-wood were contending that alcohol had nothing to do with the grounding; that Hazelwood was closely monitored following his 1985 treatment, and that the Coast Guard botched the blood-alcohol tests of the Exxon *Valdez* crew.[6] Rawl is right about not being careful at that time, but he obviously doesn't see where he went wrong. Even in a court of law, under oath, and years after the event, Rawl is looking to avoid responsibility by blaming others.

For so many reasons, the Exxon *Valdez* oil spill continues to be the case we can point to as a glaring example of what not to do in a crisis.

Don't Let This Happen to You

It happens. Sometimes with no warning, business leaders find themselves in the middle of a disaster. The first step in dealing with this reality is to acknowledge that unforeseen problems will happen and then plan for them before they happen.

Secondly, everyone in positions of influence must know what that plan is and be trained in how to implement it. Inter-estingly, Exxon had a 250-page containment plan, approved by the state of Alaska, specifically for responding to potential spills in Prince William Sound. Yet, this plan was ignored when the crisis actually hit.[7]

What's your crisis communication plan? Who will you call first? Who will be the company spokesperson? How will you communicate with your employees, clients, customers? With stockholders? With the public? What timeline will you follow? What media outlets will you turn to?

If you don't have the answers to these questions documented in a written policy, read on. Each of the cases explored in this book will illustrate how you can proactively prepare to deal with a crisis in your life or your company or organization that, if not handled correctly, could bring you down for good.

The New York Knicks

KNOW WHEN TO FOLD 'EM

What were they thinking?

James Dolan, Isiah Thomas, and the entire MSG / New York Knicks management team were thinking that they could go into court, where lurid details become national headlines, and still win the PR battle.

The Lesson

You can't. When the PR cost is not worth it, do all you can to stay out of court (and quietly settle if possible) when facing volatile, salacious, and embarrassing charges involving an alleged racial, ethical, marital, or sexual matter.

Sometimes when you or your organization faces an embarrassing incident (often the precursor to a crisis or scandal) the best crisis response plan includes actions to get the situation behind you as quickly as possible. In cases involving explosive charges such as sexual harassment in the workplace, it is often advisable to settle the situation out of court and avoid potentially awkward and even more embarrassing details and allegations that are sure to become public through the media—or at least in your professional and personal sphere. The more visible or high-profile the party involved, the more the organization and that individual have at risk in terms of image, credibility, and reputation—whether the party charged is guilty or not. Therefore, there is a greater incentive to settle a legal case before it even goes to court, thereby avoiding unwanted media attention and intense public scrutiny. It may not always be fair, but these are the "rules of engagement" when it comes to the high-profile crisis communication game.

Let me be clear. If you are accused of something that you believe to be patently false—if there is no factual foundation for the charges against you or your organization—then respond and fight with all the passion and intensity you can muster. However, in many cases, especially those involving charges connected to events motivated by sexual, ethical, or racial factors or those involving morally inappropriate behavior, there is at least some factual basis for the allegations. Simply put, sometimes things happen in life that you'd rather not have others find out, which often has absolutely nothing to do with the law or a courtroom.

This isn't about a legal definition of guilt or innocence. In fact, you may have a very good chance of "winning in court" if you opt to fight. The problem, however, is that in the process of trying to "win" in the courtroom, it is very likely that you will lose the battle—sometimes very badly—in the court of public opinion and perception.

The Knicks and MSG Are Out of Bounds

As several cases in this book show, pursuing a legal strategy often directly conflicts with a smart and appropriate crisis communication strategy. Through much of 2007, Madison Square Garden and its marquee team, the New York Knicks, as well as its chairman James Dolan and coach Isiah Thomas, faced and lost an embarrassing and highly publicized court case involving charges brought by former vice president of marketing Anucha Browne Sanders. Browne Sanders charged that Thomas, in cooperation with MSG and the Knicks, promoted a hostile work environment where she was subjected to numerous verbal assaults as well as unwelcome sexual and romantic advances. Browne Sanders sought $10 million in her suit against the Knicks and MSG. She won $11.6 million, and that was before compensatory damages were awarded.

Specifically, she accused Isiah Thomas of repeatedly calling her a "bitch" and a "ho." Further, Browne Sanders said Knicks' star player Stephon Marbury called her a "black bitch" and one of Marbury's relatives who worked for the Knicks called her the "n word." This was just the beginning of the foul and profane language that Browne Sanders alleged was used toward her in her sexual harassment charge. Once Browne Sanders brought the charges, she was fired from her high-paying marketing job by Knicks and MSG chairman James Dolan, who argued that her suit was not only distracting the team and MSG, but that she was also seeking witnesses within the MSG corporate family to testify in the court case, further disrupting the company.

Clearly, proving sexual harassment in a court of law is not easy. The alleged pattern of conduct must be consistent and must be witnessed by others to corroborate this information. Apparently, Isiah Thomas and James Dolan (Dolan says without the advice of counsel) decided to fight Browne Sanders's charges in open court and take their chances. Soon, however, it became clear that no matter what verdict was reached in the courtroom, the Knicks and MSG had already lost the crisis communication game in the public relations effort to limit the damage to the organization's reputation and credibility.

Because they chose publicly to fight Browne Sanders's charges, much of the evidence in this explosive case became public, especially in the New York tabloids that live for such scandals. Everything about this case was tailor-made for both the front and back pages of publications like the *New York Daily News* and the *New York Post*.

Additionally, the national media jumped all over the case, including national television news programs as well as countless Internet and Web-based media sources. Video transcripts of depositions taken for the case were released to the public through the media, which produced more embarrassment and scandal for the Knicks and MSG. Later efforts to explain or clarify these depositions in open court or in media interviews made the situation worse. All of this was being played out as a juicy "he said, she said" soap opera, except the characters were real and the reputation of the organization was at stake.

Airing Dirty Laundry in the Press

Protestations of innocence aside, if the case had been settled out of court, we would not be talking about it today and certainly would not be privy to details such as the following, reported in the *Daily News*:

A former Knicks assistant coach took the witness stand today at the sex harassment trial that has rocked the NBA and backed up many of Anucha Browne Sanders claims against team boss Isiah Thomas. Jeff Nix, who worked for the team for 15 years until he was fired last month, testified he was present when Thomas called her a "bitch" and "ho." He recalled a 2004 meeting in which he quoted Thomas as telling Browne Sanders: "Don't forget, you f——— bitch, I'm the president of this f——— team." Nix, who served under eight head coaches including Thomas, said Browne Sanders told him of an incident that same year in which Thomas allegedly hugged Browne Sanders and professed his love for her. He said Browne Sanders pulled away from Thomas at "the end of a hug" which occurred in a hall off the Garden floor and later told him: "I saw Anucha pushing away from Isiah," Nix testified.[1]

In the same vein, the *Post* reported that Jeffrey Nix testified in open court that Browne Sanders told him repeatedly that Thomas consistently used foul language when speaking directly to her; " 'What the f— is your job? What are your job responsibilities, you f—ing ho?' "[2] This is the kind of information that will cause Thomas to lose the PR war even if he wins the battle.

Isiah Thomas's deposition, played in open court and reported by the media, produced an embarrassing glimpse into his racial attitudes as well as his view of women. This is character suicide that can't be undone. Thomas actually said in his depositions that while it may be wrong for a black man such as himself to call a black woman such as Anucha Browne Sanders a "bitch," it would be worse if a white man called her a "bitch." This got tremendous media attention and was a major topic on talk radio, both on sports programs and those not connected to sports but fascinated by Thomas's asinine analysis. Thomas's explanations of his tortured logic on race and women only exacerbated the situation. (Later, activist and racial provocateur Al Sharpton would publicly criticize Thomas for his comments.)

MSG and Knicks boss James Dolan's videotaped deposition on December 11, 2006, was also played in court and widely reported in the media. Still images of Dolan were published in numerous newspapers and Web sites—they showed an executive who was often smirking, scoffing, and, according to many, not appearing to take Browne Sanders's sexual harassment charges seriously. Dolan also boasted in his deposition, "All decisions at the Garden I make on my own."[3]

Another of Dolan's statements in his deposition was replayed and reprinted in countless media outlets (which, again, would never have been made public if this case had been settled). As characterized by *New York Daily News* columnist Jane Ridley:

Slumped in a chair, sighing deeply and looking like a bored Knicks fan in the fourth quarter, Madison Square Garden boss and wanna-be blues star James Dolan wanted his deposition over as quickly as possible. Perhaps, the $10 million suit brought by his former marketing chief Anucha Browne Sanders was getting in the way of much-needed voice practice. His indifference was reflected in his oh-so-funny comment after he agreed that calling "anyone a bitch or a black bitch at the Garden" was "not appropriate." "It is also not appropriate to murder anyone. I don't know that that has happened, either," he quipped."[4]

One wonders what James Dolan could have been thinking making such an insensitive, inappropriate, and stupid comment in a deposition that was bound to become public because he determined that this case should be fought in open court. It was juicy material like this as well as a variety of other embarrassing pieces of information that caused the *Daily News* to establish a daily feature entitled, "New York Knicks Court Report" that chronicled the Browne Sanders case against the Knicks. Every day that the newspaper feature appeared, the more embarrassing it became for James Dolan, Isiah Thomas, and their team.

Take a look at some of these damaging headlines and excerpts:

Dolan's Other "Frat" House: He Ran Cablevision Like a Wild Child, Say Former Employees

"He [Dolan] admitted to firing Browne Sanders after she lobbed sex-harassment allegations at Thomas and Knicks star guard Stephon Marbury. He also nonchalantly dismissed allegations she had been cursed to her face."[5]

Garden May Get Pruned: Isiah Clues Dribble Out from Jury

During his videotaped deposition, Dolan nonchalantly admitted to firing Sanders without consulting his lawyers while her sexual-harassment claims were still under investigation by the Garden. "All decisions at the Garden I make on my own," Dolan said, claiming he believed she'd attempted to tamper with the internal probe. "I specifically did not consult with counsel."[6]

Sleaze Play in Stephon Marbury's Back Seat

MSG's vice president for human resources, Rusty McCormack, talked in a court testimony deposition about star Knicks guard Stephon Marbury, who testified in open court about having sex with a twenty-two-year-old Knicks intern. The intern was compelled to be a witness and testify in court about her sexual encounter with Marbury in his limousine after a night of partying at a New York strip club. McCormack's deposition tape also presented testimony claiming that Marbury allegedly called Browne Sanders a "black bitch" when she fired his cousin Hassan Gonsalves in 2005. Marbury claimed in court, "I didn't call her a black bitch . . . I called her a bitch."[7]

James Dolan's Indifference Shows Anything Goes at MSG

Surely it's not every day that a Knicks captain makes racist, sexist slurs against a top female African American executive, wondered Browne Sanders's lawyer. "McCormack said it was up to his subordinate, John Moran, to follow through. Moran said, 'It slipped my mind.' Talk about a bad day for the HR department. If these guys had only done their job, a whole lot of money could have been saved and bad publicity avoided. Not that Dolan seems to give a damn."[8]

Please End This Game of Ugly Ball

Not to be outdone in reporting the growing scandal, *New York Post* columnist Andrea Peyser also went after Rusty McCormack for what many perceived to be a cavalier attitude regarding Stephon Marbury's outrageous behavior toward Browne Sanders as well as exactly what McCormack considered to be sexual harassment, saying:

The absolute low moment came yesterday. Garden vice president Rusty McCormack, an elderly gent with a complexion the approximate shade of ripe cheese, was seen on videotape discussing how he convinced owner Jim Dolan to fire Sanders.

McCormack was asked if referring to a person as "n——" was contrary to Garden policies.

The correct answer would be, "Yes." Fatally, he said, "Again, it's not harassing a person. That's a pretty serious term! They would be reprimanded and told not to refer to that person again."

He was asked, again, by Sanders' incredulous lawyer—"Is calling a person "n——" a violation?

"No. I don't think so," he struggled. "It would not be a very nice thing to do."

Oh, it got worse. He was reminded that player Stephon Marbury had referred to Sanders as a "black bitch." Was that OK?

"It could be, depending on the severity of it. All that stuff is by degrees. How many times, if it's not said directly to the person. . . .

"The 'black' has racial overtones," he finally stammered. "And the bitch part."[9]

So there you have it. If James Dolan, Isiah Thomas, and the entire MSG /New York Knicks management team had only settled this case and made sure it never went into a courtroom, they would not have to deal with the PR problems created by all this drama and amazingly embarrassing media coverage. Even if they believed themselves totally innocent of the charges, it didn't take a genius to realize that all this ugly and nasty racist garbage was going to become fair game in the media, and then in turn in the minds and hearts of millions of news media consumers.

In fact, in the end, it doesn't really matter that the New York Knicks and MSG lost this case in court and that Browne Sanders was awarded $11.6 million. They lost this case the minute they decided to fight it, well before the jury verdict. They lost in the court of public perception as well as in the critical PR battle in the media as every lurid and embarrassing tidbit and detail became public. The longer this case went on, the more of this garbage came out and the worse it got for Dolan, Thomas, and company. The crisis was dragged on needlessly when they actually appealed the verdict and received additional negative media coverage until the Knicks and MSG ultimately decided to reach a settlement with Browne Sanders in the amount of $11.5 million. To make matters worse, several new sexual harassment suits were brought against MSG in the days after the multimillion-dollar jury verdict in October 2007. What were Knicks management and MSG thinking?

Think Long and Hard

This case gives us all a number of valuable lessons when facing a potentially reputation-damaging court trial.

1. Seriously consider whether you and/or your organization are prepared for what going to court means. This is a time when you've got to know when to hold 'em, and know when to fold 'em, particularly when it comes to being accused of something as embarrassing as sexual harassment. Simply put, sometimes you "just can't win" certain battles because in the process of attempting to win, the dirty laundry involving you and your organization are likely to be introduced into the court case and ultimately into the media and exposed to the general public. Once you go to court, everything becomes fair game. And remember, all of us have "dirty laundry" or at least the appearance of it.

2. Don't attack the victim. Attacking the "victim" may work as a part of a particular legal strategy, but when these actions are reported in the media, it can make you or your organization look petty and mean-spirited. When the Knicks went after Anucha Browne Sanders, it may have been necessary in order to have any chance of winning the case, but it backfired in the media and in the court of public opinion. Remember that in certain situations it is nearly impossible to fight on two fronts successfully: in a court of law and in the court of public opinion.

3. Everything is a presentation. Once you opt to go to court, depositions will be taken. In this particular case, James Dolan's December 11, 2006, videotaped testimony became the source of significant public ridicule. Dolan's slumped posture, black T-shirt, and widely reported smirking and scoffing were not good for Dolan or MSG and the Knicks on many levels. He made a terrible appearance and his presentation screamed "unprofessional" and "sloppy."

In contrast, the appearance of Anucha Browne Sanders had a great deal to do with the positive way she was perceived by the jury, the media, and the general public. She came across as professional, likeable, and credible. That was not by accident. Unlike others in this book (see the case of Rose McCaffery and the Glen Ridge rape scandal) Sanders and her advisors clearly understood that what she said was important, but how she said it and what she looked like while saying it was just as important. How you appear and comport yourself has a great impact on how people perceive you. Your demeanor and presentation matter a lot.

4. Quibbling over the details doesn't work. Consider Stephon Marbury's absurd testimony when he said he didn't call Anucha Browne Sanders a "black bitch," but rather he only called her a "bitch." He may have been technically accurate (who really knows?), but he sounded like an idiot saying it—as if he gets some kind of medal if he called her only a "bitch." Further, consider Isiah Thomas's just as ridiculous videotaped deposition in which he said that it would be wrong for a black man such as himself to call Browne Sanders a "black bitch" but it would be worse if a white man were to do the same thing. Again, it may have been what Thomas was thinking, but hearing and seeing him say it was a totally different story. The media seized on his confounding comments, which caused him, the Knicks, and MSG only more embarrassment. The risk of having your own words turn against you is one of the many pitfalls of fighting a crisis in open court, which often requires you to answer some difficult and challenging questions.

Regardless of what verdict was reached in this case, everyone associated with the Knicks and MSG looked terrible—except for Anucha Browne Sanders, who carried herself in a professional, dignified, and appropriate fashion. It is inconceivable that James Dolan and Isiah Thomas, as high-profile figures based in the media capital of the world—New York City—didn't realize that nothing positive could have come from fighting this case in open court. Again, one must ask: What were they thinking? So many things could have and should have been handled differently. With all their financial resources, the Knicks and MSG should have consulted with media and image experts who could have helped James Dolan present himself in a more positive fashion. Both Dolan and Thomas (who at the time this book went to press was in serious jeopardy of losing his job as Knicks coach) should have been coached and trained for their respective depositions and open testimony in court. Their legal team's advice needed to be combined (and, if necessary, contradicted) by a smart, responsive media/communications strategy. Yet ultimately it is unclear if Dolan and/or Thomas would have accepted such advice and feedback, given their apparent desire to fight this battle their own way.

Chaos in a West Virginia Coal Mine

"THEY'RE ALIVE!"

> **What were they thinking?** ────────────
>
> International Coal Group executives and West
> Virginia Governor Joe Manchin were thinking
> that they could postpone the inevitable hit the
> company and all involved were going to take by not
> immediately clarifying "good news" rumors while
> they figured out how to deliver the "bad news."

> **The Lesson** ────────────
>
> Wishful thinking and being paralyzed by fear
> is a dangerous combination in a crisis.

Company and government leaders called it a problem of "miscommunication." Others called it a "communication breakdown." Any way you look at it, what happened on January 2, 2006, to the Sago miners and their families in West Virginia after a coal mine collapse was unimaginable, unconscionable, and incredibly insensitive. It was a communication nightmare of epic proportions, and some say it could have been avoided.

This case study is not about blame. It is about understanding why so many companies and organizations are woefully unprepared to handle serious communication challenges involving a major incident. There is no way of knowing whether what actually happened to the West Virginia miners inside that mine could have been avoided. But what happened after the mine collapse was inexplicable.

After the collapse, the first unconfirmed reports were that all twelve miners were alive, not dead as had been presumed. It was a miracle. No one could believe it. Everyone's prayers had been answered. Families rejoiced and the country exhaled deeply as the news media erroneously reported the unbelievable news. But forty-five minutes later, at about 12:15 A.M., officials of the International Coal Group along with the West Virginia governor realized that the miners were in fact dead. Virtually everyone in a leadership capacity became paralyzed. No one knew what to do, how to communicate, and with whom to communicate. No one took charge. Chaos ensued.

International Coal Group executives should have known better, but were clueless as to how and when they should proceed. There was no plan. No strategy. No standard operating procedures. A lack of systematically considered options or choices is what causes people to freeze in such moments of crisis. We never imagine anything like this ever happening to us or our organization. But planning for the "worst case scenario" is really the only way to plan, especially in the dangerous field of mining. Wishful thinking or naively hoping for the best is no substitute for a strategic plan. So what did the participants involved ultimately do in this case? Company and government officials, including West Virginia Governor Joe Manchin, waited almost three hours after the "alive" reports circulated before gathering the families of the miners in a local church and informing them that the original reports were wrong.

Company officials, led by CEO Ben Hatfield, apologized for what was called a "miscommunication." Hatfield was right to apologize, but the words of remorse couldn't begin to undo the pain and suffering these grieving relatives were experiencing. *Washington Post* media critic Howard Kurtz said the mining company's communication was "inexplicable."[1] The *New York Daily News* headline on January 5, 2006, called it the "mother lode of misinformation."[2] Kurtz and the *Daily News* were being kind. The three-hour delay was also terribly insensitive and unfair to the families involved. I don't question the motives or the intent of the Sago Mine officials, but you have to seriously question their judgment. What were they thinking? The West Virginia miner case provides powerful lessons for any organization involved in an activity that could turn into an accident, disaster, or potentially a full-blown crisis.

What Should Have Happened?

First, company officials should have immediately held a press conference at 11:45 P.M. or soon thereafter to make it clear that the initial "unconfirmed" reports were just that—"unconfirmed." This would have lowered expectations. Company officials knew that rescue workers were on cell phones instantly communicating to family members and other concerned people that the miners were alive. The inaccurate rumor spread like wildfire.

Instead, company officials opted to engage in wishful thinking, not wanting to dampen the spirits of those understandably celebrating. They wanted to believe the miracle. But again, wishful thinking is not a strategy—rather, cautious, disciplined communication is. This pattern of "wishful thinking" is a consistent problem in a variety of organizations and institutions profiled in this book. Otherwise smart, thoughtful, and even articulate professionals seem inclined to stick their heads in the sand and hope the storm blows over. Yet, every time, the storm only gets worse.

In the Sago Mine case, the communication storm really began once it became clear that the miners were dead. Company officials, as well as representatives from the West Virginia governor's office, needed to quickly gather family members together to candidly and compassionately share the bad news. I admit that there is no exact "right" amount of time one should wait to break this kind of news. And it's understandable that those breaking the news need some time to gather their own emotions and feelings. But certainly, within thirty minutes of knowing that the miners had died, the families should have been told. Difficult? Undoubtedly. But every second that they waited allowed the rumor mill to take over and feed the hopeful families positive but inaccurate information, making the pain that much more difficult to bear when they found out the horrible truth.

Because company and government officials weren't sure how to communicate about the miners' deaths, they waited approximately three hours after they knew the miners had died before they brought family members to a local church and broke the terrible news at 3:15 A.M. By then it was way too late. Their credibility was shot. Eyewitnesses reported that pandemonium broke out as grief turned to anger at this complete reversal of the miners' fate, and the delay in this information, and some family members tried to physically attack mine company executives. There was screaming and shouting along with charges of coverup and incompetence and, of course, many tears. A bad situation had just turned worse.

To his credit, International Coal Group CEO Ben Hatfield said that if he could do it over again, he would have communicated to family members immediately upon finding that the miners were dead. Again, he apologized profusely. But apologies aren't enough in a crisis. You must have a clear communication plan and a timely, concise, and coherent message. You need to understand the many pressures of communicating to family members, concerned citizens, as well as a news media hanging on your every word. None of these things are likely to occur just in the midst of a crisis. By then, it's often too late.

Today's Technology Changes Everything

Technology is a powerful factor in the crisis communication equation today. In the West Virginia miner tragedy, someone "on the inside" used a cell phone to talk directly to families and other concerned parties. The problem is that what they communicated was inaccurate. It wasn't confirmed. It was a rumor.

There was an initial, unconfirmed "report" that said the miners were "alive," which became interpreted as a "fact." What happened next was similar to the telephone game we played in school, where you tell one kid something and he tells it to the next and she tells it to the next. In the end, the message received is usually a far cry from the initial message that was sent.

Fast forward. With cell phones and other instantaneous communication technology, the "telephone game" is sped up dramatically. Add to the mix the fact that dozens of media organizations and crews were camped out very close to the mine and you've got a potential communication powder keg. In the Sago case, misinformation was communicated live to millions of households across the country by 24/7 cable news organizations like CNN, the FOX News Channel, and MSNBC. Add to that the Internet stories and blogs that broke as soon as the "they're alive" rumor started, and you've got millions of media consumers convinced that a "miracle" had taken place in the mine. But in a crisis like this, the problem is that you can't put the genie back in the bottle once it's out.

Dealing with the Initial Stages

One lesson we should take from this aspect of the Sago Mine case is that you must be especially careful in the initial stages of dealing with a disaster or serious problem. Everything that is said in the most informal or innocuous of settings has the potential to be communicated to millions within minutes, if not seconds.

Once the inaccurate rumor or unsubstantiated fact is out there, the involved party has an absolute responsibility to correct the misinformation. The International Coal Group officials didn't do that. By their omission, by not acting, they perpetuated "miscommunication," which caused more pain and suffering for family members. It also seriously hurt the company's reputation.

Officials at the Sago Mine were fearful of being criticized for allowing the initial "they're alive" information to become public, so they did nothing. They said nothing. In any crisis or scandal, it is essential to understand that you are going to take a hit. You are going to be criticized no matter what you do, but you can greatly influence how bad the hit is and how long it lasts. No matter what their intentions were, International Coal Group executives would not have been blasted in the mainstream media or in the eyes of millions of Americans if they had clarified the "they're alive" inaccuracy within the first hour. Time is a critical factor in managing a crisis. Apparently, they knew that the miners were dead. It had been confirmed. They needed to communicate that hard-to-hear "news" within minutes of learning it. Obviously this still would have been extremely painful and difficult for families, as well as the nation, to hear, but waiting the three hours only made it worse. It raised hopes that shouldn't have been raised.

Additionally, the International Coal Group had no crisis communication plan. No one was really in charge. There was no chain of command and no one managing the flow of information. There was no organized process for sharing as well as communicating information.

Think about it. Mine officials knew that a media horde was gathering as soon as word got out about the collapse. The CEO, or the head of communications (it is unclear that such a role or person even existed in the company), should have organized the key players and led a discussion on how, when, and what the company would communicate to key audiences and how they would deal with the media. Of course the operational side of managing the mine collapse was critical—trying to save the miners was paramount. But these two objectives were not mutually exclusive. Organizations must pursue operational efforts while at the same time strategically and smoothly communicating to internal and external stakeholders, including the media.

Having a practical, strategic communication plan has to in fact be part of an overall operational crisis communication plan. They are not separate initiatives.

Let me make some comments here about company CEO Ben Hatfield. He was clearly one of the more compassionate and caring corporate executives. You could see the pain and anguish on his face as he spoke to the media about how poorly he and his colleagues handled the situation. If he weren't so compassionate and empathetic to the families of the dead miners regarding the three-hour "delay," the situation could have been even worse. There are countless cases in which corporate executives appear to lack any of these essential human emotions for those who have been hurt by their actions. Ben Hatfield can't be compared to Lawrence Rawl, the Exxon CEO who in 1989 waited nearly three weeks to go to Alaska after one of his company's oil tankers hit a rock and began spewing millions of gallons of crude oil, destroying the ecosystem and the livelihood of countless fishermen in Alaska. Rawl ducked the *Valdez* crisis for as long as he could and tried to put it in the hands of subordinates.

To his credit, Ben Hatfield faced the music head-on. He took responsibility for the failure of his company. He said it was the worst mistake he had ever made in his professional life. He said he wished he could take back what he and his colleagues did by waiting three hours to tell the families that their loved ones were dead. You could sense his remorse. Yet, as the cases in this book demonstrate, good intentions aren't nearly enough in a crisis. These intentions must be tied to sound actions and execution.

Different Case, Different Outcome

The communication mistakes made in response to the mine collapse in West Virginia provided lessons for Robert Murray, CEO and president of Cleveland-based Murray Energy Corp., which owns the Emery County mine in Utah. A year after the Sago Mine collapse, Murray found himself in a similar circumstance. Although mistakes were made, the communication between Murray and the media and the miners' families was far better than it had been in West Virginia. Murray's communication was immediate, consistent, truthful, and highly responsive.

Although Murray was criticized by some for what was perceived as his blunt and extremely direct manner in describing how unlikely it was that any miners actually survived, his approach was preferable to Hatfield's decision to allow rumors of hope to spread and persist for several hours even after he knew the miners were dead. I believe Murray was aware of the heartache the delay caused in West Virginia and made sure to avoid building such false hopes.

It is important to note that even though Robert Murray may have communicated and led in the best way he knew how and with the best intentions, it is the nature of crisis-oriented situations involving life and death and tragedy that it is inevitable that leaders will be criticized because of the human suffering involved. Therefore the objective in a crisis such as this is to minimize the fallout, the public relations damage, and the impact on the company's and its leaders' reputations while being compassionate, empathetic, and responsive to all key stakeholders, particularly family members of those affected.

Unfortunately, Ben Hatfield and his West Virginia company did not strive to meet these objectives. They will forever be identified with this horrific case of "miscommunication." Millions will never forgive them for waiting to tell the families that their family members were not alive. On the anniversary of the Sago Mine disaster, some media organizations will pull out old video of family members crying hysterically and blasting company officials for letting them suffer unnecessarily.

Unfortunately, devastating tragedies like this are inevitable, but how they are dealt with is up to the leaders involved.

Organizations that are involved in such risky activities must incorporate realistic "mock" scenarios and role-plays that help prepare managers and leaders to face the kind of intense media and stakeholder pressure that will surely come if such a situation actually occurs.

The Church's Pedophilia Scandal

SKELETONS IN THE CLOSET

What were they thinking?

The leadership in the Catholic Church was thinking that it could solve its problem with a three-prong, ill-conceived strategy: 1) ignore, 2) deny, and 3) try to pay your way out of trouble.

The Lesson

It is always better to be proactive and deal directly and publicly with an exposed "skeleton in the closet."

The problem of pedophilia in the Catholic Church and the crisis of communication that surrounds it is nothing new. Certain priests, sick and dangerous ones, have been molesting young boys (and to a lesser extent girls) for decades, shrouded and protected by the organization's unwritten, apparent code of silence. As a lifelong Catholic, I am quite familiar with the pedophilia issue. In an opinion piece for *The Times* of Trenton, New Jersey, that I wrote fifteen years ago, I said, "There were stories and rumors about priests 'you should stay away from' as far back as I can remember."

Despite all the gossip and the stories about priests, this potential time bomb was never discussed in public twenty or thirty years ago. Most kids were scared to death to tell their parents (never mind Church leaders) that the priest in the pulpit giving the sermon on Sunday was the same guy who the day before asked the altar boys to do unspeakable things. That was the environment in the 1970s. The Church was infallible. So as a kid, you would never accuse a priest of such a heinous act because you would have been not believed by your parents. This is a big part of why so many of the complaints were not voiced until twenty or even thirty years after the incidents occurred.

When Old Facts Emerge

Even though most of the boys did not make direct accusations at the time of their abuse, I have a hard time believing that those who could have done something about the estimated 5,000 priests known to be pedophiles had no clue that something very sinister was going on. I can't help but think that if my Church, which is so vigilant about the conduct and morals of its parishioners, had tried harder or been more receptive to media inquiries based on the early complaints of parents, a lot of kids could have been spared the physical and emotional pain of this abuse.

But it was only after several highly publicized and sensationalized cases broke and after the initial convictions of some molesting priests that the Catholic Church hierarchy finally began to act. Consider just a few examples of friendly neighborhood priests who eventually got their due justice through the legal system, not through the Church's internal checks system:

- A deposed pastor in New York accused of running a "sex club" involving up to fifty boys.[1]
- Father Raymond Pcolka from Bridgeport, Connecticut, who was convicted of molesting young boys from 1966 to 1982.[2]
- Father James Porter of Minneapolis, who abused more than 100 victims, many of whom were altar boys in then Father Porter's parishes. Porter left the priesthood in 1974.
- Father James Hanley, who molested dozens if not hundreds of boys in the Paterson, New Jersey, diocese between 1972 and 1982, while his boss, Bishop Frank Rodimer, sat back and did nothing except resist the press and parents of Hanley's victims when confronted with the accusations.[3]

- One of the worst cases was in Boston, spanning over three decades between 1962 and 1999, and involved Father John Geoghan. The strategy of Cardinal Bernard Law (like that of many of his peers in the Church hierarchy) was to orchestrate millions of dollars in out-of-court settlements, which included gag orders. This had the effect of perpetuating and exaggerating the pedophilia problem in the Boston Diocese.[4]
- A pattern of abuse of young boys by Father Galden at Good Counsel School in Newark, New Jersey, during the 1960s and 1970s came out many years later during a long and painful court case, ending in a guilty verdict.

While there are countless such cases of pedophile priests and accommodating bishops, the handling of the cases regarding Galden and Hanley has had a particularly strong impact on me. Father Galden supervised the altar boys at my local parish back in the late 1960s. One of my best friends (who served Mass with him) told me at the time of the priest's practice of pulling down the boys' pants and spanking them as punishment for being late. This sure seemed weird to us, but at that time we had no idea of the extent of Galden's perversion.

It turns out that this was only the beginning of a pattern of abuse by a priest who took advantage of being in private quarters with his young charges. One kid in the late 1970s finally told his parents about an incident involving nakedness, and the situation exploded as other kids came forward and told their stories. Charges were filed and with the guilty verdict Father Galden finally got nailed, but not before dozens, if not hundreds, of young boys had suffered.

Then, a few years ago I conducted an interview on a television program I host called *One-on-One with Steve Adubato* on the Comcast Network. My guest was Mark Serrano, a then-thirty-eight-year-old former altar boy from Mendham, New Jersey.

Serrano had been sexually molested for seven years in the 1970s by his pastor, Reverend James Hanley. He sat across from me and graphically detailed how Father Hanley first started fondling him and later put his "big fleshy tongue" in Mark's mouth. Mark told me he wanted to vomit, but Father Hanley kept telling him it was just a way of showing affection ("You kiss your father, right?").

Later, the priest, who was extremely popular at St. Joseph's, performed oral sex on Mark and asked Mark to perform oral sex on him. All this time, pornography was provided by Father Hanley. While Mark was confused and frightened, Hanley kept telling him that they had to keep it a secret, especially from Mark's parents, who would be extremely hurt if they knew. Mark began to feel terrible shame, and he didn't know where to turn. In fact, it wasn't until he was a twenty-year-old at Notre Dame University that he first acknowledged aloud what had happened to him.

As I sat across from Mark listening to his sickening account, I felt tremendous sympathy for him but also great anger at the code of silence that allowed this to happen. I also felt fortunate that it hadn't happened to me—although it easily could have. The worst I got was a punch in the face in the early 1970s delivered by a drunken priest by the name of Heavey in the schoolyard of St. Peter's. The good priest was on his way home from the Red Shingle Inn in Belleville to the rectory. Later, when I went there to tell the other priests and nuns what had happened, they assured me that Father Heavey was sorry and that he was going through some tough times. When I told my parents, they told me not to make a big deal about it. I was only twelve years old, for God's sake, and I couldn't understand why this priest whom I liked would haul off and punch me in the face, and worse yet, why no one would do anything about it. But like I said, I was luckier than Mark Serrano.

While listening to Mark's description of his abuse, I thought of my then nine-year-old son Stephen and couldn't conceive of this happening to him. I grew angrier, particularly when Mark told me what happened when he approached Father Hanley's boss, Paterson Archbishop Frank Rodimer, in 1985. Bishop Rodimer acknowledged to Mark that Hanley admitted the abuse, but promised Mark that "it would not happen again." Father Hanley was never defrocked, never charged, and never disciplined by Bishop Rodimer, despite the fact that it is now known that Hanley had sexually molested numerous young boys at St. Joseph's.

Later, when Mark and his parents confronted the bishop, Mark's mother demanded to know what the bishop was going to do about Hanley. Rodimer responded, "I don't answer to you; my boss is the Pope." That was nearly seventeen years ago. Just a few years ago, Mark Serrano and eleven men, all of whom were molested by priests in Bishop Rodimer's diocese, confronted him on his abominable handling of these issues over the past two decades. Then Mark finally asked the bishop, "Putting all legal constraints aside, do you feel that Father Hanley should be behind bars for the crimes he has committed?" The bishop paused for a very long time and then finally said, "I don't know." The men in the room were stunned. Some booed.

Ignoring the Problem at the Top

Bishop Frank Rodimer didn't get it. He had no idea how to respond to this crisis nor to the tough questions it would naturally bring to his door. And he was not alone in this irresponsible communication and leadership void. Cardinal Egan in New York, Cardinal Law in Boston, and countless other top Catholic leaders not only ignored the problem of priests in their charge who were sexually abusing young boys, but they perpetuated the problem by moving these priests from parish to parish, allowing them, whether by design or not, to prey on other unsuspecting kids—allowing them to take kids on overnight camping trips and be alone with them in the church's rectory.

Reverend Andrew Greeley, one of the few Catholic priests who spoke out publicly on the pedophilia issue when it began to break in the mid-1990s, said in a *New York Times* op-ed piece in 1992: "If Catholic clerics feel that charges of pedophilia have created open season on them, they have only themselves to blame. By their own inaction and indifference, they have created an open season on children for the few sexual predators among them." At the time, Father Greeley's commentary was a scathing indictment of his colleagues in which he said they often "deny" that sexual abuse occurred, protect the priests at whatever costs, and cover up and blame the victim in the media. The worst accusation in Father Greeley's 1992 commentary was never rebutted by Church officials; he concluded that those responsible for handling pedophilia cases "had no reservation in reassigning, after a few months of treatment, priests who had faced such accusations—sometimes to the role of pastor."[5]

Several years earlier Jeffery Anderson, an attorney from St. Paul, Minnesota, who was handling twenty-five child-abuse cases involving Catholic priests, said in a April 4, 1988, *National Journal* article that the Church's "institutional response" had been up to that point to "appease families, keep it from the police, and transfer the priests to another parish where the abuse begins again. Instead of removing the priest, they think of themselves and the priest—and not the parishioners."[6]

Painful Lesson in What Not to Do

One of the most striking lessons we can take from the Catholic Church hierarchy's mishandling of the pedophilia problem is that it is virtually always better to be proactive and deal openly with an internal problem before others—particularly the mainstream media—expose it. I believe that many in the Catholic Church's leadership convinced themselves that they could keep this thing quiet, that they could keep a lid on it and that if they paid enough money to victims they could actually buy their silence over a lifetime. They deluded themselves into thinking that somehow these victims wouldn't go to the press and tell their stories when the gag orders were lifted.

In retrospect, it is hard to imagine that the Catholic Church hierarchy could be so naive and misguided, not to mention insensitive and apparently uncaring about the young victims of their priests. But the other aspect of this debacle is that it was ignorant about how a crisis actually plays out, especially in a modern media age in which information is disseminated quickly amid countless forums, making it virtually impossible to "keep a lid" on anything. Any way you look at it, the Catholic Church was going to take a huge hit on the pedophilia issue. The nature of the crime and the fact that children were the victims ensured that. But the Church could have acted more ethically and responsibly.

If the Church leadership had not been so delusional and insensitive as to think it could hide the problem by moving pedophile priests from parish to parish, things certainly would have turned out differently. But that didn't happen. The lawyers ran the show. The bishops and cardinals stuck their heads in the sand. They stonewalled the media and tried to cast doubt on the victims. They refused to cooperate with the authorities, particularly the police, and tried to manage the scandal themselves with their own set of unwritten, outmoded rules.

This Crisis Could Have Been Avoided

This chapter describes a serious and enduring crisis for the Catholic Church, one in which the initial damage could not have been totally prevented and, after the fact, could not have been undone. But it was one in which, when it was exposed, the Church would have been much better off responding proactively and assuming full responsibility. The Church crisis makes it clear that ignoring, denying, and bribing are not only ineffective and unethical—they're fuel for the fire.

Instead, any business administrator facing the exposure of an employee's past wrongdoings (whether in his/her employ at the time or not), must face the problem. The following offer some strategies:

1. Act quickly (as soon as the first substantiated or legitimate accusation catches your ear) to identify, question, and remove a person known to have personal skeletons of sexual abuse, rape, pedophilia, or the like. If the leaders of the Catholic Church had done this, they it certainly would have cut short the enormity of the scandal and saved many subsequent victims their ordeals.

2. If this circumstance could bring negative publicity to you or your company, publicly acknowledge the problem to other employees and company stakeholders before it gets out to the public—despite the risk of public condemnation or ridicule. If the Church had acknowledged that the problem existed and not tried to sweep it under the rug, it would have taken the first positive step toward saving its reputation. Take full public responsibility for what has transpired.

3. If appropriate and possible, reach out to comfort, counsel, and care for the victim(s). By ignoring or blaming the victims of the pedophilia crisis, Church leaders turned the tide of public opinion against them.

4. When your lawyers recommend that you seek an out-of-court settlement, such a recommendation should be analyzed carefully—there are many factors to consider. The out-of-court settlements reached by the Catholic Church served to exacerbate the Church's public relations problem and caused its reputation to take a devastating hit when it was revealed that they were tied to "gag orders" binding the pedophilia victims to maintain their silence for many years in order to receive payment from the Church. The public's outrage in response to this fact was a product of the Church's taking the so-called moral high ground on a variety of societal issues and therefore raising the bar for expectations for their actions. This expectation did not include convenient out-of-court settlements and the gagging of victims of sexual abuse by Catholic priests. However, in other cases, such a settlement is clearly the smartest and most prudent way to go to minimize the public relations fallout. (See the case of Bill O'Reilly and the sexual harassment charges leveled against him, and the horrific mistake made by Madison Square Garden and the New York Knicks in going to court versus settling the sexual harassment case filed against them by Anucha Browne Sanders.)

5. Call in appropriate law-enforcement authorities. If you try to handle the problem internally, stonewall the media, refuse to cooperate with authorities, or try to cast doubt on the victim, you and your company will become headline news—in a negative spotlight. The Catholic Church did all of these things. Use them as your shining example of why none of these are good strategies.

Without such a definitive plan of communication, the damage done to an organization by this type of scandal is incalculable. Today there is no way to determine how many Catholics have left the Church because of the pedophilia scandal. There is no way to calculate how many people either refused to or are uncomfortable with putting donations in the basket at Sunday Mass for fear that that their money will go to paying out-of-court settlements. It is impossible to calculate how bad a hit the Church has taken with respect to its image and reputation. It will take at least a generation and billions of dollars (not to mention countless apologies) for the Church to have a shot at regaining the place of respect that it once had in American society. A crime like this is always an abomination, but the cover-up makes such a heinous crime that much worse.

Dick Cheney

MISFIRING UNDER PRESSURE

What were they thinking?

Vice President Dick Cheney was thinking that the accidental shooting of his friend while on a hunting trip was a private matter that did not require an immediate and official public disclosure.

The Lesson

Leaders in the public eye who choose to withhold information make matters worse by creating the appearance of a cover-up.

Dick Cheney, vice president to George W. Bush, has never liked or trusted the mainstream media, particularly the Washington press corps. During his tenure in the White House, he didn't court reporters, editors, or key media decision makers, and his press conferences and interviews were few and far between. Cheney's basic approach to dealing with the media has been to treat them as a necessary evil of his office, but still to avoid them whenever possible. He kept them at a distance regarding his early meeting with an energy task force, and butted heads with them regarding the Valerie Plame affair.

Such an attitude toward the media may have contributed heavily to what just might be the dumbest communication decision in recent history, following Cheney's much-publicized "shooting a friend while hunting" accident. This case raises the bar for stupidity in crisis communication. It is a good illustration of how a poor communication plan can turn an innocent accident into a national tempest.

There is no doubt that the accident itself was not the cause of the controversy and ensuing crisis (although such an accident clearly is newsworthy and certainly makes great fodder for comedians and late-night talk-show hosts). Rather it was the absurd and inappropriate fashion in which Dick Cheney handled the communication responsibilities surrounding the event, combined with his history of evasiveness, that caused him and the White House so much grief.

A Hunting Trip Gone Bad

On late Saturday afternoon, February 11, 2006, Dick Cheney was hunting quail with a group of friends in Corpus Christi, Texas, when the vice president—the person who is a heartbeat away from being the president—accidentally shot his seventy-eight-year-old friend and fellow hunter, Texas lawyer Harry Whittington. Whittington was hit with scattered buckshot in the neck and face at relatively close range. He was brought to a local hospital as Cheney and the hunting party did all they could to help Whittington through this trying and difficult time.

The hunting party then retired to the home of Katharine Armstrong, a lobbyist and land owner who was hosting the private hunting group on her Texas property. During this time of concern over the serious condition of a friend, could Dick Cheney be expected immediately to report the incident to the White House communication staff? Apparently he did not think so.

Late that Saturday night, White House press secretary Scott McClellan was informed that there had been a shooting accident in the Cheney hunting party. But he didn't know until the next day that it was Cheney who shot Whittington.[1] In fact, twenty-four hours later, when Cheney called the White House to speak to Chief of Staff Andrew Card, he didn't disclose the full details of how Whittington had been shot. So at that point even those in critical communication positions in the White House were left in the dark by the vice president. You and I can see that this is going to look bad for the entire Bush administration—and the bungling of the communication regarding the accident was just starting.

On the day following the shooting, Armstrong—a private citizen with no official ties to the White House—was given the task of informing a local Texas newspaper, the *Corpus Christi Caller-Times*, about the incident. The newspaper posted the story on its Web site late Sunday. The story was then picked up by media organizations across the country.

The communication that followed from the White House attempted to make the argument that Dick Cheney was on a private hunting expedition (the reason Katharine Armstrong as a private citizen was the one who disclosed it) and that in fact Harry Whittington may have actually contributed to the accident by being in the wrong place as Cheney was shooting (the White House quickly backed off that argument). As one might expect, the mishandling of the Cheney shooting incident was roundly criticized.

According to a *New York Times* editorial entitled "White House Shoots Foot":

Let's see. The vice president of the United States accidentally shot someone while bird-hunting on a Texas ranch. It took the White House nearly 24 hours to share that information with the rest of the nation because Dick Cheney thought it would be better for the ranch's owner to give the story to the local newspaper first. And by the way, it was all the victim's fault. . . . [A]ccording to the White House, Mr. Cheney was so busy attending to Mr. Whittington that he was unable to inform even President Bush about what had happened for a very long time. His retinue—usually bristling with cell phones, pagers, BlackBerries and satellite phones—was also oddly incommunicado.[2]

This is how bad communication turns the innocent into the disastrous and scandalous. As a *New York Times* reporter noted: "The vice president appears to have behaved like a teenager who thinks that if he keeps quiet about the wreck, no one will notice that the family car is missing its right door. The administration's communications department has proved that its skills at actually communicating are so rusty it can't get a minor police-blotter story straight. And the White House, in trying to cover up the cover-up, has once again demonstrated that it would rather look inept than open."[3] Yes, the Bush administration had shot itself in the foot, and at a time when the administration had plenty of other problems and issues on its plate.

Of course the vice president was emotionally upset and shaken from the shooting of his friend. Of course Whittington needed to be immediately attended to, yet Cheney's responsibility as a leader and vice president should have simultaneously been considered with, if not superseded by, any of those feelings.

The Impact on Others

This case study of poor communication also offers us insight into what can happen within an organization when one of its members drops the ball in a crisis. There were published reports that the respective staffs of the president and the vice president were at serious odds over how this incident and its aftermath should have been communicated: "The tension between President Bush's staff and Mr. Cheney's has been palpable, with White House officials whispering to reporters about how they tried to handle the news of the shooting differently."[4] Many on the Bush team felt that the vice president should have personally disclosed the accident immediately—within an hour or two—or that the announcement should have come from an official in the White House, either from the president or the White House office, and not from Katharine Armstrong.

A source close to the administration told CBS News correspondent Gloria Borger that "people within the White House are livid and that signals are being sent to the vice president's office that the issue has been handled poorly." Senate Democratic

Leader Harry Reid of Nevada noted that the furor over the accident and the White House's delay in making it public are "part of the secretive nature of this administration."[5]

Perhaps criticism from Democrats was to be expected, but some of the worst critics of Cheney's crisis communication performance came from Republican loyalists, including Marlin Fitzwater, who was George H. W. Bush's top communication advisor. Saying he was "appalled" by Cheney's bungling of the incident, Fitzwater added: "The responsibility for handling this, of course, was Cheney's." In the online edition of *Editor and Publisher*, Mr. Fitzwater was quoted as saying: "What he should have done was call his press secretary and tell her what happened, and she then would have gotten a hold of the doctor and asked him what happened."[6]

And of course, the entire controversy landed in the lap of then White House press secretary Scott McClellan. When he led a press briefing on February 14, 2006, the pressure on him from reporters was intense. McClellan was being asked to explain several oddities regarding the incident and how and when it was communicated: 1) the disclosure of the accident by a private citizen, Katharine Armstrong, to a local Corpus Christi newspaper Web site, 2) the nearly twenty-four-hour delay of this announcement, 3) the fact that the White House didn't disclose the incident to major media organizations in the nation's capital. In an organization, such delays naturally lead to questions of "What else is there?" and "What's being hidden?"

Vice President Cheney's decision to ignore the press and the White House communication department obviously became a source of great debate in American politics. And, as already stated, it came at a time when the Bush White House was engaged in a whole range of other crises and controversies around a variety of more important issues, many involving disclosures and media issues, and so did not need this divisive distraction.

Cheney Finally Faces the Music

Even after publicity about the shooting accident was being whipped into a frenzy and politicians on both sides of the party line were grabbing the mic and spotlight to add their two cents, Cheney continued to be unnecessarily secretive and less than forthright. He was pictured in numerous newspapers across the country slipping into the side door of the White House in the days following the incident—seemingly attempting to hide from the press and public sight. Did he really believe that not speaking publicly about the shooting would allow the controversy surrounding the circumstances of his hunting accident to somehow go away? Cheney would not be the first bright person to hope for that kind of outcome, but doing so soon backed him into a corner and into a defensive position of response to this now full-blown crisis.

On Wednesday, February 15, 2006, a full four days after the incident, Dick Cheney agreed to an in-depth interview with the FOX News Channel, a cable news station many perceive to be friendly toward the White House and Republicans overall.[7]

In a conversation with Brit Hume, Cheney said, "I am the guy who pulled the trigger and shot my friend. . . . That is something that I will never forget. . . . [Y]ou can talk about all the other conditions that existed at the time, but that is not the bottom line. It's not Harry's fault. You can't blame anyone else."[8] This was a good start. We've seen in other high-profile cases that pointing the finger of blame usually backfires. In his attempt to gain the nation's understanding, Cheney took a small step forward by taking full responsibility for the shooting.

Cheney then could have taken a second step in the right direction by emphasizing the human side of the story to explain why he did not immediately notify the press about the awful incident. Clearly, the vice president was personally affected by the trauma of shooting his friend Whittington, who wound up in intensive care in a Corpus Christi hospital and would later have cardiac issues which were directly connected to his being shot. Cheney had the sympathy factor on his side to explain his lack of judgment in communicating this crisis. But he did not go there.

When asked by Hume about the belated disclosure, which in fact came from Katharine Armstrong and not the vice president himself or any member of the White House staff, Cheney refused to acknowledge that any mistakes had been made. Now that was a big mistake.

Cheney would say that it was important to get accurate information about Whittington's medical condition before releasing information and that it made "good sense" for Armstrong to be the primary disseminator of information as opposed to anyone in his office. His argument was that she was an eyewitness to the shooting accident and an "acknowledged expert in the field." Further, the vice president said that disclosing to a small South Texas newspaper was not an effort to downplay the incident. "There wasn't any way this was going to be minimized," said Cheney.[9]

Because Cheney attempted to defend the indefensible, the FOX interview, despite getting off to a good start, did little to stem the tide of public criticism toward him. The fact that Cheney refused to acknowledge the absurdity of a private citizen, and not a White House official, disclosing the shooting incident only exacerbated his problem.

Further, Dick Cheney's insistence that this was a private incident that occurred on his private time—and hence didn't rise to the level of public, governmental concern—strained his credibility. It didn't pass what I often call the "giggle test," or what a reasonable person might think is reasonable. Simply put, would a reasonable person feel that if our country's vice president shoots someone in the face, the public he serves has a right to know about this even minor incident immediately or at least promptly? Further, it is reasonable to assume that the vice president himself or someone on his official staff should have been the one to publicly announce the occurrence.

While the Bush White House largely disagreed with the vice president's approach, they did little if anything to rescue the botched opportunity for honest communication. Dick Cheney really didn't choose to do the FOX News interview with Brit Hume four days after the accident. In many ways he was forced into it. He was embarrassed into it. By that point, regardless of what Cheney said publicly, for many Americans it was simply too late. His overly secretive communication style— seemingly the product of his intense distrust and disdain for the media—appears to have clouded his judgment in this most embarrassing and memorable moment in the vice president's public life.

Proactively Disclose and
Get the Benefit of the Doubt

According to Chris Lehane, a communication strategist who helps businesses deal with difficult controversies and crises: "The incident would have blown over relatively quickly if they'd addressed it within hours after it occurred: 'Here's what happened. Here's why it happened.' Get some credibility and trust points for putting it out on your own terms. Failing to disclose only reinforced one of the views people have of this administration, which is not being straight and being secretive."[10]

There's a lot we can learn from Dick Cheney's bungling communication style. Let's start with these lessons:

1. Immediate and accurate disclosure is absolutely essential. Monday morning quarterbacking is easy, but Communication 101 teaches us that when an incident or accident occurs, particularly one in which we are not at fault, we cannot delay making a public announcement. The longer a leader waits to disclose, the worse the controversy is going to get, and greater becomes the interest in the details surrounding it.

2. When dealing with the media, understand that it isn't personal. No matter how much you dislike or distrust the media, it should never cloud your judgment in a crisis or controversy as to what the most appropriate and smartest communication approach should be. The more you allow personal feelings to get in the way of your decision making in a time of crisis, the more likely you are to make bad decisions.

3. There can only be one leader or key decision maker when a crisis hits. Dick Cheney worked for President George Bush. It was in fact George Bush who should have dictated how and when information about this shooting incident should have been communicated—and who should do the talking. Instead, the vice president was allowed to determine what approach he would take, even if it directly contradicted Bush's philosophy in a similar situation. When the head of an organization does not step up to direct the flow of communication in a crisis, bad things are bound to happen.

4. You cannot delegate communication responsibility in a crisis to someone outside your organization or company. There is no excuse for dodging responsibility and hiding behind others who agree to speak to the public in your behalf. By allowing Katharine Armstrong to report the shooting to the local press, it appeared to many that Dick Cheney was attempting to avoid having to face the music, which in a crisis is one of the worst things a leader can do. What's particularly striking about this perception of Cheney is that from every indication the vice president didn't do anything wrong. It was an accident. Clearly he didn't intentionally shoot Harry Whittington. Therefore it is perplexing that he was not willing to directly address the nation. Hiding behind

Armstrong only created a new crisis narrative that went well beyond the incident itself.

5. A leader must be open to constructive and candid feedback about his/her crisis communication plan. Dick Cheney stubbornly refused to listen to anyone else about how to best handle his situation. That rigidity did not serve him well. Having convictions and a strong sense of how you should handle things is important, yet being open to other approaches is absolutely critical.

6. Whoever speaks publicly on behalf of an organization must have all the necessary and relevant information at his or her fingertips. If this person does not have all the facts about the crisis, he or she is left vulnerable to questions and public disclosures and can ultimately be blindsided because he or she was left in the dark by those who should have been more forthcoming. Because the vice president did not fully disclose the details of the incident to key colleagues and decision makers, including President Bush and White House Press Secretary Scott McClellan, he put those around him in an untenable and unnecessarily vulnerable position. McClellan looked terrible in his public communication surrounding this crisis, but it wasn't his fault. The vice president put him in that position, which was inexcusable. Leaders who do this to those who speak for an organization should ultimately be held accountable.

This fiasco was about communication and leadership skills rather than actual events. The vice president could have easily minimized the fallout of the shooting incident, but his secretive approach toward the media fanned the flames of distrust and suspicion. The longer he took to speak in public, the less benefit of the doubt and public sympathy he was able to gain. By waiting the four days and then ultimately speaking to a media organization that many considered overly friendly, he missed the opportunity to be pressed and challenged on the questions that many Americans truly wanted answered and hence could regain their trust in America's second in command. Unfortunately, for many, that never occurred.

The Glen Ridge Rape Case

"STAND BY OUR BOYS"

What were they thinking? ───────

School superintendent Rose McCaffery
and the Glen Ridge town officials were
thinking that they could sweep news of
a horrific event under the rug of their
small-town persona and move on like
nothing had happened.

The Lesson ───────

Being woefully unprepared to communicate
in a crisis leaves community leaders with
only one option: hide! And this is a
prescription for disaster.

The story broke on May 23, 1989, but the impact continues to be felt in the small suburban community of Glen Ridge, New Jersey. The details are still shocking: A seventeen-year-old mentally impaired girl named "Leslie Farber" (a pseudonym) was allegedly raped by a group of Glen Ridge High School athletes—many of whom were star baseball and football players—in the basement of one of the player's homes. These were the most popular and charismatic boys in the school.

Actually, the horrifying incident had happened almost three months earlier, on March 1, 1989. Although it's known that as many as two dozen boys were in the basement, it is unclear how many boys were actually involved in the rape—which included oral sex as well as the insertion of a broomstick, a drumstick, and a mini–baseball bat into the young girl's vagina. As some of the boys cheered the athletes on, others stood by and watched.

And then they all went home. According to Bernard Lefkowitz, author of a fascinating book on the Glen Ridge case titled Our Guys: "For almost three months before the arrests [of the four boys ultimately charged] the kids had kept it to themselves. . . . Maybe the silence of Glen Ridge students was a symptom of grief and shame, colored by self interest. Maybe they were thinking: keep quiet for a couple of months and this will blow over and we'll graduate and slip off to college."[1] But when it comes to a crisis or scandal of this proportion, "keeping quiet" is never really a good option. Glen Ridge officials would learn this lesson in a brutally painful fashion.

Wanted: One Credible Communicator and Leader

As soon as the incident became public, national and regional media outlets from dozens of television, radio, and print organizations descended on Glen Ridge. And it wasn't just the media who demanded answers. It was parents, prosecutors, other students, and advocates for the mentally challenged. How could this happen in such an affluent, well-educated community where nearly all of the class of 100 or so seniors at Glen Ridge High would go on to college—many to the Ivy League? What would happen to the boys involved? Why did the other boys in the basement not try to stop the assault? Where were the parents? How would school officials restore order while the "rumor mill" was running rampant?

Who would be the lead spokesperson in the community communicating with the media? Who would lead the students and parents and others in Glen Ridge through this difficult crisis—Glen Ridge's most shocking and dramatic to date? The task would require a superior communicator.

By default, the job was handed to Glen Ridge Schools superintendent Rose McCaffery, a longtime administrator with virtually no experience communicating in a pressure-filled environment. The superintendent's previous communication experience consisted of presiding over school events, making routine announcements at PTA meetings, and dealing with the faculty over administrative and work-related issues. McCaffery, and in turn Glen Ridge, was in big trouble as soon as she opened her mouth. According to Lefkowitz, who interviewed dozens of Glen Ridge seniors, McCaffery said in the first of many sessions with students regarding the incident that "seniors needed to show solidarity." She told students not to "judge" the rape suspects but should in fact "stand by our boys." She said absolutely nothing about the girl who was raped and traumatized in the Glen Ridge basement.

Rose McCaffery set the tone and Glen Ridge High School principal Michael Buonono jumped on board when he told the students that they needed to get past the incident, by saying, "Let's just go on." McCaffery and her team were clearly trying to sweep the scandal under the rug and keep things quiet. Such a communication strategy is a prescription for disaster, especially when the national media is banging down your door.

At a school forum, McCaffery was challenged by a few students, who yelled at her for urging them to support the alleged rapists. But she had no idea how to shift gears and communicate a clear, credible message and be disciplined and focused in her dealings with the media. It got worse—a lot worse. The superintendent was winging it, being inexperienced with impromptu communication in public forums. She had no one to turn to for advice on how to handle such a communication and leadership crisis. She didn't identify in advance any tough questions she might be asked, much less try to practice answering them. She had no overwhelming credible or concise message that would serve as her anchor when things got dicey. She was simply hoping for the best, which is no strategy at all.

McCaffery also didn't seem to understand the need to be seen as fair and evenhanded when communicating about the rape allegations and those involved, which included the accused and the victim—as well as a student who offered to come forward and speak up about what had happened in the basement of Kyle and Kevin Scherzer's home. (The two were co-captains of the Glen Ridge football team and among the most popular athletes in town.)

In a Crisis, Appearance Matters—a Lot!

Charlie Figueroa was a football player at Glen Ridge High School. He was also a really big kid and one of only three black students in the senior class. Charlie was outside the Scherzer's basement on the afternoon of March 1 when the sexual assault took place. He would later be the only student-athlete to come forward and report to school and police officials (including Detective Richard Corcoran, whose son Richard Jr. would later be charged in the case) that he overheard some of his teammates boasting about what they had done to "Leslie" in the basement. Charlie reported that "the complainant was repeatedly penetrated . . . by baseball bats, broomsticks, and a musical drumstick." He also reported that "oral sex" had occurred during the incident.[2]

Charlie Figueroa immediately became a target at school and among his fellow jocks. He had broken the code of silence. He had not shown "solidarity," as Superintendent McCaffery had urged. When Charlie's accusations became public, his name started coming up in media accounts. Word got out that Charlie had told school and police officials that some of his fellow athletes had asked him to videotape a followup sexual encounter with Leslie.

When asked about Charlie by reporters who had descended on Glen Ridge, Rose McCaffery said that Charlie liked to "fantasize" and that he was often "seen in the school's resource room" where he was receiving counseling. McCaffery, apparently realizing that she was on very thin ice in speaking about the one Glen Ridge student who had the courage to speak up about the brutal attack on this seventeen-year-old retarded girl, added: "I'm not saying this is not true at all. Because of the statements he made, we immediately notified the police."[3]

Others in her position might have praised such a brave young man or at least understood the need to communicate neutrality. But instead, McCaffery was offering opinions about Charlie Figueroa and making disparaging public statements about his character on national TV and on the front page of the New York Times. She was taking sides. She was talking about things that should have been confidential regarding one of her seventeen-year-old seniors. She was minimizing his accusations, all the while saying nothing about the four student athletes who would later be charged and the eighteen kids who apparently stood and watched the brutal rape take place. She was fanning the flames of a community in turmoil by putting more heat on an individual student—further making him a target for the media horde that had taken over the town.

Later, a $25 million defamation of character suit would be brought by Charlie Figueroa and his family against Rose McCaffery and other township officials. Yet, McCaffery would say with confidence at the time that she and everyone else in the Glen Ridge School System as well as all town officials had handled the crisis well.

Communicating without Words

Reading Rose McCaffery's statements in print certainly demonstrated the scope of her ineptness in communicating in such a pressure-filled situation, but seeing her communicate was worse. A few days after the scandal broke, McCaffery agreed to do a live interview for the evening news on New Jersey Public Television. Wearing a housecoat, no makeup, and with disheveled hair, McCaffery was interviewed at a baseball game that was taking place at Glen Ridge High School, while her eyes darted everywhere except into the camera.

The scene behind her was loud and boisterous, with lots of yelling, cheering, and laughter, and, yes, the crack of baseball bats. The symbolism was lost on McCaffery but not on those who watched her performance. Yelling at the top of her lungs to be heard over the game, McCaffery said: "All four students received a ten-day suspension." Rocking back and forth, looking at nothing in particular, distracted by the game, she added: "We have three snow days built into our calendar. We are fortunate to not have used any . . . the . . . ah . . . we tacked one of these days onto the Memorial Day weekend . . . ah . . . uh . . . and this determination was made before this issue surfaced."

It isn't so much Rose McCaffery's words in this public television interview that are so disturbing; it is how utterly clueless she was about doing the interview in such an absurd and inappropriate setting. It was the Memorial Day weekend. The town was in turmoil. Decorum and dignity were called for. The last place she should have allowed for such an interview was at a loud and boisterous Glen Ridge High School baseball game.

I've shown the McCaffery interview to literally hundreds of my media and communication students at Rutgers University, Montclair State University, and Seton Hall University. I've also shown it in dozens of media and crisis communication seminars, and the reaction is universal. Viewers say things like: "She's really not the superintendent, is she?" "She's wearing a house dress. Doesn't she know how terrible she looks?" "How could she possibly do the interview with a baseball game going on behind her? Why didn't she just do the interview in her office?"

"This woman is a mess. Didn't she look in a mirror before doing the interview?" And finally, "How can she not understand the symbolism of the baseball game and the baseball bat, given the details of the incident?"

The Art of Damage Control

Where do you start with Rose McCaffery? There are so many communication gaffes in this case that exacerbated an already serious situation. Let's look at five simple lessons that might help us all better face a potentially volatile situation.

These lessons are particularly relevant for school administrators who increasingly face crises and potential scandals surrounding such incidents as school shootings, weapons confiscation, gang violence, assaults on teachers, sexual or physical assaults by teachers, or embarrassing and in some cases illegal relationships between students and teachers. With all the training and in-service professional development programs, few if any school districts plan for any of these crises or potential disasters as part of their curriculum. This is a serious omission.

1. The best leader to communicate in a crisis very often is not the highest-ranking person in the organizational chart. Rose McCaffery was the wrong messenger to speak on behalf of Glen Ridge given the severity of the situation. Given the time pressure the officials in Glen Ridge were under, creating a mock media scenario and posing tough press questions would have been a useful approach. However, it appears that no media training could have gotten McCaffery where she needed to be when the national media converged on town officials.

To be fair to Rose McCaffery, there is little if any reason to have expected that she could have handled this situation with confidence and clarity. Town officials should have found a more appropriate representative who was more empathetic and presentable to communicate on behalf of the town and the school system.

If you should face a potentially explosive situation, stop and carefully choose the best possible spokesperson. Do not let someone step up to the microphone or take the call from a reporter just because that person is "in charge." Ideally, you will have someone in your organization who is trained in crisis communication long before a crisis arises. But if a crisis hits and you haven't a trained communicator on board, at the very least, call an emergency meeting of all potential communicators. Explain the criteria required of a spokesperson in this situation. Then choose the person who all believe can be a solid communicator—someone who

- is evenhanded
- is a strong leader
- is compassionate
- is clear and concise
- can balance the vested interests of a variety of people
- can deal with extremely difficult and challenging questions and accusations
- is visually presentable
- is calm under the "hot lights" of the media glare

2. Identify tough questions that might be asked and practice answering them. When a few students questioned why McCaffery didn't support the rape victim, she had no idea how to respond. She should have seen that one coming. When the reporter asked her to describe Charlie Figueroa, she spoke off the cuff, revealing confidential information and making defamatory comments about his character. How could she not have prepared a better response?

In a crisis, you have to be prepared for the tough questions. There is no substitute, long before a crisis hits, for getting into a room with colleagues who will pose the most difficult, challenging, and uncomfortable questions to the person speaking on behalf of the organization. Preferably, these sessions should be videotaped and analyzed by an outside, media communications expert who can offer tangible advice and feedback. This exercise must be repeated until the organizational representative is ready to face the media onslaught for real.

3. Be unbiased, fair, and evenhanded. McCaffery and other Glen Ridge officials planted themselves firmly on the side of the athletes. As soon as McCaffery advised the student body to "stand by our boys," she lost objectivity and credibility. She fueled the media focus on the Glen Ridge athletes and seemed clueless and insensitive as to the horror of what had happened to this young, vulnerable teenage girl.

In situations where someone in your organization or community is being blamed for a wrongdoing, it is vital to come out of the gate with a statement of concern and compassion for the victim—and then with an unbiased, credible, and concise message that will serve as that anchor in a storm to keep you in place regardless of how the winds blow for or against that victim.

This kind of statement takes time and effort to create. Without planning, it will not be there on the tip of your tongue when you need it most.

4. Be aware that in this age of instant access, your problem will not go unnoticed.

As in the Glen Ridge case, some communities and organizations convince themselves that they are isolated from such a communication crisis because they are outside the big-city media spotlight. When school principal Michael Buonono told the students that they needed to get past the incident, saying, "Let's just go on," he was thinking the whole incident could be kept quiet. A very foolish, if not dangerous, belief. The truth is that in this day of Internet information dissemination, no one is isolated from the media. Rose McCaffery didn't understand that. Glen Ridge town leaders didn't understand that. But worst of all, it appears that the majority of citizens in Glen Ridge didn't understand that and so they resented the media's coverage of this scandal. They wanted the media to go away, to leave them and their town alone. Closing ranks has its place, and being unified is important, but it will not keep a scandal hidden.

No matter how small, how innocuous, how remote your organization, business, or community, you must always prepare to face national attention. Do not let anyone convince you that a scandalous situation is "no big deal" or that "nobody will know about this." If the Glen Ridge scandal broke today, the outcome would be even worse for the community given the current, 24/7 media and the Internet-dominated world we live in.

5. You say as much with your body as you do with your words. McCaffery dug herself further into the hole that would bury her reputation as soon as she stepped in front of the TV news camera in a disheveled state. This wasn't a surprise interview, a rogue reporter showing up unexpectedly. McCaffery agreed to the interview in advance and chose the location herself. Perhaps by this point in the crisis, she was worn out and overwhelmed. No excuse. Anyone who takes on the role of spokesperson must pull him/herself together in any public forum.

What you wear in a media situation like this should not distract or detract from you or your message. It isn't a question of there being a perfect or optimal dress or suit or hair style or makeup or jewelry. The most important thing is that nothing in your appearance takes away from what you have to say.

The scar of this brutal 1989 rape by four star athletes in a basement while eighteen young men watched and many in the town closed their eyes will forever be a blemish on the reputation of Glen Ridge, New Jersey. As bad as the incident itself is, the exceptionally weak communication skills of "leaders" like Superintendent Rose McCaffery made things a lot worse than they should have been. Sometimes you can't stop what happens—but by choosing your words wisely, you can control the damage.

The Death of Pat Tillman

THE COVER-UP IS ALWAYS WORSE

What were they thinking?
Officials in the U.S. Army, the Pentagon, and the Bush White House thought that they could cover up tragic news by lying to the public with a "positive" version of events that seemed more palatable but was an outright lie.

The Lesson
No matter how bad the embarrassing incident may be, an attempted cover-up is going to be perceived as being worse than the "crime."

One would think after more than thirty years since Richard "I am not a crook" Nixon left office in disgrace in the wake of Watergate that professionals, particularly those serving in high-level positions, would do all they could to avoid obvious "Nixonian" communication mistakes, especially relating to attempted cover-ups. In fact, after Watergate it became a common adage in the world of crisis communication that "the cover-up is always worse than the crime."

Yet, because government officials often ignore the lessons that should be learned from cover-up fiascos, the long and often embarrassing history of "truth manipulation" continues. We have recently seen the irresponsible attempts to suppress the truth in high-profile cases like the Abu Ghraib prison scandal, the NSA wire tapping case, the Walter Reed military hospital debacle, and the Jessica Lynch prisoner of war rescue "story." But one of the most egregious and outrageous schemes to mislead the American public came in the immediate aftermath of the April 22, 2004, death of Army Ranger Pat Tillman in Afghanistan.

Officials in the U.S. Army and the Pentagon as well as in the Bush White House engaged in one of the most insensitive, bumbling, and worst of all, unnecessary cover-ups in American history. The Pat Tillman affair demonstrates a self-induced crisis created out of efforts to lie, distort, and avoid responsibility for a tragic accident.

Pat Tillman—A True American Hero

Pat Tillman was a twenty-seven-year-old athlete playing in the National Football League who had signed a multimillion-dollar contract with the Arizona Cardinals. He was smart, articulate, and telegenic. He volunteered to be an Army Ranger and go to Afghanistan in response to the 9/11 attacks on our country. Despite his football celebrity and the big-money deal he had signed, Tillman, along with his brother Kevin, felt it was more important to fight Osama bin Laden and al-Qaeda on their home turf. Pat Tillman's actions were patriotic and brave on many levels, especially since he never sought publicity or praise for his unconventional and courageous decision to leave a lucrative NFL career behind and opt for a dangerous, unpredictable future fighting the enemy in a foreign land.

While there was a modest amount of media attention given to Tillman at the time of his brave decision, he suddenly became a household name and symbol of sacrifice and heroism within hours of his tragic death on April 22, 2004, in Afghanistan. The shooting took place at 7:30 P.M. local time in the small Afghanistan village of Sterah. The first official accounts of his shooting that came from the U.S. Central Command said that Tillman was likely killed by "devastating enemy fire." More specifically, the official military statement read: "The enemy action was immediately responded to by the coalition patrol with direct fire and a fire fight ensued. During the engagement, one coalition soldier (Pat Tillman) was killed and two wounded." The statement went on to say that "an Afghan military force soldier was also killed but that the enemy broke contact during the engagement." The Pentagon's official story was that Tillman was killed by enemy fire as he exited his vehicle and later died in an Army field hospital.[1] The response to Pat Tillman's death at the hands of the enemy in Afghanistan was swift and emotional. He was called heroic by many and the Bush White House offered its condolences to the family, calling Tillman "an inspiration both on and off the football field."[2]

Arizona Cardinals vice president Michael Bidwell, son of team owner Bill Bidwell, spoke for many in the NFL and beyond when he said, "In sports we have a tendency to overuse terms like courage and bravery and heroes . . . and then someone like Pat Tillman comes along and reminds us what those terms really mean."[3]

U.S. Senator John McCain, a prisoner of war during Vietnam and recognized as a bona fide war hero, said after hearing of Tillman's death: "I am heartbroken today by the news of Pat Tillman's death. The tragic loss of this extraordinary young man will seem a heavy blow to our nation's morale as it is surely a grievous injury to his loved ones."[4]

On May 3, 2004, there was a much-publicized nationally televised memorial honoring Pat Tillman. All the major cable news networks carried the service live while more praise was heaped on the former NFL star. Again and again he was called a war hero who died "in the face of devastating enemy fire." He was eulogized by many of his colleagues who stuck to the narrative that Tillman was gunned down by "the enemy."

This nationally televised memorial galvanized public opinion and brought great sympathy not only to the Tillman family but to all soldiers fighting this courageous battle in the treacherous hills of Afghanistan against the terrorists whose goal was to kill us all. It was a powerful narrative that resonated on a deeply emotional and visceral level.

During this time neither the Pentagon, the army, or the Bush White House did or said anything that would question the publicly disclosed account of how Pat Tillman was killed.

The Cover-Up Begins

Yet, it is clear that shortly after Pat Tillman's death numerous top military officers and Pentagon officials knew that he was not killed by "devastating enemy fire" but rather more likely by someone in his own platoon. They call it "friendly fire." The technical term used by the army is "fratricide."

According to published reports, Lieutenant General Stanley McChrystal attempted to warn top Pentagon officials as well as President George Bush in a detailed memo dated April 29, 2004, that they should not continue to use the story about Pat Tillman being killed by "devastating enemy fire," because he may in fact have died by fratricide. Later, McChrystal said he was concerned that President Bush and top Pentagon officials would continue to use the Tillman death narrative and that doing so "might cause public embarrassment if the media and the public came to know that Tillman was actually killed by a member of his own platoon."[5]

But here's the twist: McChrystal sent the memo acknowledging the possible false nature of the official military account of Tillman's death, even though one day earlier the same McChrystal approved the awarding of the prestigious Silver Star citation to Tillman. According to a report in the *Washington Post*: "Army Commanders hurriedly awarded Pat Tillman a posthumous Silver Star medal for valor and released a nine-paragraph account of his heroism that made no mention of fratricide."[6]

One wonders what the major players were thinking. Did they honestly believe that if they kept quiet about their friendly fire suspicions, no one would ever know? Did they rationalize their silence by convincing themselves that it was better for everyone involved if the truth never came out? Did they trust that the army code of silence was strong enough to keep this dirty little secret forever? Did they believe that the risk of damaging their reputations by dealing with the truth was greater than the risk of being quiet? These are all issues that we can assume were on the minds of those who chose to manipulate the facts in this case. Anyone in a similar situation would also go through this process of weighing the pros and cons of coming forward with the truth. That's understandable.

In the end, representatives of the U.S. Army, the Pentagon, and the Bush White House all decided to continue the charade and hope for the best—a communication plan destined for disaster. This is beyond understanding.

The Cover-Up Continues

For a full five weeks after his death, top military officials along with the Bush administration continued to publicly say that Pat Tillman was killed by the Afghanistan "enemy." Then, finally, on May 29 the head of the Army's Special Operations Command, General Philip Kensinger, called a news conference to disclose in a brief statement that Tillman probably died by friendly fire. Kensinger refused at the time to answer any questions.[7]

Amazingly, this meant that Tillman's family was not told this painful truth from April 22 to May 29, even though those closest to the Tillman affair had their suspicions immediately following his death. As the tragic facts from the battlefield became public, the crisis for the White House and the military intensified.

According to eyewitness accounts, the painful truth is that Pat Tillman definitely was killed by members of his own platoon. Further, Tillman did not die in a military hospital as the army first reported, but rather, according to SPC Bryan O'Neal in testimony on December 4, 2004, he "lay dying behind a boulder . . . with him shouting, 'Cease fire! Friendlies! . . . I am Pat [expletive] Tillman damn it. . . . ' He said this over and over again until he stopped."[8]

O'Neal was the last one to see Pat Tillman alive. He testified in 2007 before Congress about how he desperately wanted to tell the Tillman family, especially brother Kevin, exactly how Pat died. "I wanted right off the bat to let the family know what had happened, especially Kevin, because I worked with him in a platoon and I knew he and the family all needed to know what had happened. . . . I was quite appalled when I was actually able to speak with Kevin, I was ordered not to tell him."[9]

When asked by congressional investigators who in the military gave him the order not to tell the truth to Kevin Tillman, O'Neal identified then Lieutenant Colonel Jeff Bailey, saying, "He basically just said . . . do not let Kevin know, that he's probably in a bad place knowing his brother is dead and he made it known I would get in trouble, sir, if I spoke with Kevin about it being fratricide."[10]

With this information becoming public, the crisis worsened for the three major players in the deception: Defense Secretary Donald Rumsfeld; General Richard Meyers, chairman of the Joint Chiefs of Staff; and General John Abizaid, head of the U.S. Central Command. Here a leader has to make important decisions. Explain? Come clean? Admit fault? Apologize? Take responsibility? Facing the public only when their backs are to the wall is a common communication mistake for many great leaders. What they say can mark their tenure forever. So what did these leaders decide? They decided to stick by the lie: They each insisted that there was in fact no cover-up or any intentional effort to keep the truth as to how Pat Tillman was killed from his family or the American public.

- Abizaid sat before Congress and the national media, with Pat Tillman's closest relatives sitting in the room, saying he had no responsibility or accountability to disclose the truth about Pat Tillman's death.[11]
- Rumsfeld insisted that he couldn't recall ever discussing the Tillman incident with the White House until after May 29, when the friendly fire conclusion was officially reached by the military.[12]
- General Meyers told the House Committee that he in no way was responsible for disclosing the truth about Tillman's death. He went so far as to say that doing such a thing would have violated the standard operating procedures and a breach of protocol outlined by the U.S. Army. Said Meyers, "I think it would have been absolutely irresponsible of me to interfere with the army procedures frankly."[13]

When pressed at a White House briefing about the testimony of Rumsfeld, Meyers, and Abizaid, then White House Press Secretary Tony Snow stood behind them: "I'm certainly not going to contradict Rumsfeld . . . it is deeply regrettable that this sort of thing happened and you try to make sure that it doesn't happen at any time."[14]

A Flawed Communication Plan

So what was the problem with the communication plan here? Its weakness was not in problems we've seen in other cases in this book: It wasn't without careful preparation; it wasn't naïve; it wasn't a rush to judgment; it wasn't based in wishful thinking, nor did it deny the facts that ultimately became public.

No, the communication plan in the Tillman case was carefully prepared, and therein lies one of its black marks. It was a constructed line of defense that took no responsibility and offered no apology. The officials in the U.S. Army, the Pentagon, and the Bush White House defended the decision to lie to the Tillman family and the American public by referring to "policy." Their "see no evil, hear no evil" testimony denying any responsibility for the now-evident cover-up attempted to show that their actions were based in communication and systems-driven procedures that couldn't be altered regardless of the circumstances. Telling the truth, they claimed, would have violated official army procedures.

Not everyone in the government was buying this defense. Before the House Oversight and Government Reform Committee, chairman Henry Waxman (D-California) consistently rejected the explanations of how the Pat Tillman affair transpired and didn't hold back his criticism, particularly at the August 1, 2007, congressional hearing featuring Rumsfeld, Meyers, and Abizaid. Waxman summed up the weakness in the way information had been communicated by saying: "You've all admitted that the system failed. The public should have known, the family should have known earlier. None of you feel you are personally responsible, but the system itself didn't work . . . the system didn't work, errors were made—that's too passive, somebody should be responsible."[15]

Waxman is right. In any government, corporate, or organizational crisis, someone must step forward and take responsibility. Donald Rumsfeld, General Richard Meyers, and John Abizaid refused to acknowledge that a cover-up took place. In January 2005 the Pentagon concluded that there was "no cover-up" in the Tillman affair.[16] The crisis and the response to this crisis by key government and military personnel were bungled from the beginning. There were lies of omission. Memos with accurate truths were passed around, and the facts were ignored or were conveniently forgotten. There was virtually no leadership or accountability in this case. Such a pattern of deception and deceit would create a crisis in any organization.

The Tillman Family Theory

One has to wonder why, in an "organization" as large as the U.S. government and military, communication lessons from past cover-up fiascos were not learned and implemented in the Tillman case. Lying, denying responsibility, and passing the buck has never worked for these institutions before. Why try it now?

Pat Tillman's brother Kevin has a theory that sounds plausible. Kevin Tillman told the House Committee that after the embarrassment of Iraqi detainee abuse in Abu Ghraib, he believed that the military needed a narrative to divert attention away from those scandals and toward more positive stories. Tillman concluded that the military saw an "opportunity" in the death of his brother to peddle what he called the "utter fiction" of how his brother died. Said Tillman: "Revealing that Pat's death was a fratricide would have been yet another political disaster during a month already swollen with disasters . . . the facts needed to be suppressed. An alternative narrative had to be constructed, crucial evidence destroyed . . . these are deliberate and calculated lies."[17]

Pat Tillman's father agreed, saying: "The administration clearly was using this case for its own political reasons. The cover-up started within minutes of Pat's death and it started at high levels. This is not something that lower-ranking people in the field do."[18]

Ironically, it is Donald Rumsfeld who conveyed the problem at the root of this fiasco. Speaking before the House Oversight and Government Reform Committee, Rep. Dennis Kucinich (D-Ohio) demanded to know whether there was a White House and Defense Department strategy to manage press portrayals of the war and other events. "Well," said Rumsfeld, "if there was, it wasn't very good."[19] Exactly. Rumsfeld and friends could not change the initial facts, but they could have communicated those facts truthfully to the Tillman family and the public. Choosing not to do that was indeed not "very good."

Minimizing the Damage

So in reconstructing this debacle, it appears that the crisis communication plan in the Tillman case was a step-by-step effort to: 1) lie, 2) hide behind army protocol, and 3) deny any responsibility. This "plan" communicates a clear lack of leadership and accountability on the part of those who were supposed to be in charge and offers us graphic evidence of how leaders should not respond to a crisis.

Let's say a crisis—some sort of scandal or tragically bad news that could negatively affect your bottom line—hits your company or organization. At first it's possible that you might panic and look for ways to cover it up. How can you deny? Lie? Hide? Divert blame?

It is understandable that most of us go through this mental process in a desperate but understandable attempt at self-preservation when initially faced with a potential disaster. But then reason, objectivity, ethics, and common sense should take over. We can learn from the many cover-up attempts of the U.S. government that although bad news can hurt, attempting to cover it up guarantees that the final outcome is going to be worse.

Rather than follow the example of the U.S. government in the Pat Tillman case, when a crisis strikes that engenders public criticism or even condemnation, immediately:

1. Choose a high-level spokesperson who can present a consistently calm and respectful response.

2. Proactively disclose "bad news" to reputable media sources and the general public.

3. Resist the temptation to lie or deny.

4. Show immediate and genuine empathy with anyone (customers, clients, and especially family) who has suffered as a result of your actions.

5. Reach out for the support of potential advocates—those who are likely to understand the situation from your point of view.

6. Be ready to take criticism without expressing anger or irritation.

7. Stick to your position that takes responsibility, offers empathy, promises swift action, and follow up.

Case after case shows us the positive power of this type of sensible communication plan. Sure, you may have to take a hit in the form of initial public outrage, but a straightforward and honest approach is the only way to control the degree and duration of damage and to maintain a sense of credibility. One has to wonder what it will take for some people in Washington, D.C., to finally understand and accept the adage that "the cover-up is always worse than the crime."

Rudy Giuliani

A TALE OF TWO LEADERS

What were they thinking?

Responding to the crisis on September 11, 2001, New York City Mayor Rudy Giuliani was thinking with his heart as a human being involved with the American people and he came across as a strong and compassionate leader and communicator. Yet in other instances, Giuliani often came across as combative and defensive.

The Lesson

In times of crisis or when under intense pressure, a leader must remain calm and be able to speak from the heart to gain the support and trust of others who rely on him or her for information, direction, and inspiration.

I write this chapter as we approach another anniversary of 9/11, and like all Americans I have my own vivid and hard-to-forget recollections of the events of that horrific day. Also like most Americans, it was 9/11 and the following chaotic and unforgettable days that cemented for me the reputation of then New York City Mayor Rudy Giuliani as an extraordinary and powerful leader, facing the daunting, and in many ways unimaginable, challenges surrounding September 11, 2001.

On that morning, Giuliani raced to the scene from his breakfast meeting to find something that no mayor or chief executive could ever have prepared for. But prepared or not, it was Giuliani—not President George Bush nor New York governor George Pataki—who was the public figure that most American citizens looked to for elusive hope, direction, and a sense of proportion. This cataclysmic event offers us a crisis communication example par excellence.

Oddly enough, this example of powerful communication comes from a man who, in many other circumstances, was, and still is to some extent, defensive and quirky—proving that crisis communication skills are not something owned by some leaders but not others. In fact, they can fluctuate from exceptional to inexplicable even within one person—depending on the circumstance.

The Confident, Calm, and In-Control Rudy

In his book *Rudy Giuliani: Emperor of the City: The Story of America's Mayor*, Andrew Kirtzman paints a vivid image of that morning:

The scene the mayor encountered down town was right out of the apocalypse. Hundreds of people were running out of the towers, gasping for air. Windows were shattering 100 stories above, raining glass down on the streets and striking people on the ground. Plane parts were falling from the sky. So were body parts. The streets were greased with blood. Standing in the shadow of the burning buildings near the fire department's makeshift command post on West Street, Giuliani squinted up at the skyscrapers. A man jumped out of the top floor and the mayor's eyes fixed on him as he hurdled through the air to his death on the pavement below.[1]

There was Rudy Giuliani, on the scene, fully engaged. Hands-on. Talking to first responders. Walking just a few blocks from the flame-engulfed Twin Towers with a small group of advisors, trying to make sense of an increasingly chaotic situation. Giuliani was trying to calm all New Yorkers as well as all Americans while realizing that the terrorist attack that was unfolding before our eyes on live television was bound to have a devastating and lifelong impact on countless victims and their loved ones—as well as on New York City itself.

In their book *Grand Illusion: The Untold Story of Rudy Giuliani and 9/11*, authors Wayne Barret and Dan Collins (Barret had been one of Rudy Giuliani's harshest critics) had nothing but praise for Giuliani in the immediate aftermath of the terrorist attack on 9/11, saying: "While George Bush was making America wonder who was watching the store, Giuliani lead a television news conference at the police academy at 2:50 P.M. It was a masterful performance that left no one in doubt that New York City, at least, was in strong hands." They add, "The mayor's day had become a blur of grief and horror punctuated by dozens of decisions that needed to be made and a series of public pronouncements. Yet, he invariably struck the right tone."[2]

The tone that Rudy Giuliani needed to strike in his communication had to be a balance between hopefulness and candor. He didn't want to sugarcoat the horrific and grim reality and ultimate challenges and hurdles to be faced, yet he wanted to give people a sense of direction. And, remarkably, he did it.

Giuliani's first detailed comments to the media came in a live telephone interview with NY1, New York City's twenty-four-hour cable news channel, at 10:54 A.M., a little over two hours after Flight 11 smashed into the North Tower. Sitting in a makeshift office in Greenwich Village, Giuliani spoke with NY1's Pat Kiernan and Sharon Dizenhuz. Giuliani's comments were riveting:

The first thing I'd like to do is take this opportunity to tell everyone to remain calm and to the extent they can, to evacuate lower Manhattan . . . we've been in contact with the White House and asked them to secure the space around the city. They've been doing that for at least the last hour, hour and a half. I've spoken to the governor several times and the governor and I agree that the election today [the New York City mayoral run-off election] should be canceled.[3]

At 2:35 P.M. Giuliani held his first official press conference before a hoard of reporters. He was in control. He was the chief spokesperson flanked by his top aides, who were able to provide him with specific information. No detail was too small. No question was off limits. Giuliani was calm, confident, clearly focused, and, most of all, in control. In that press conference he stated:

Today is obviously one of the most difficult days in the history of the city and the country . . . the tragedy that we are all undergoing right now is something that we've had nightmares about—probably thought wouldn't happen. My heart goes out to all the innocent victims of this horrible and vicious act of terrorism. . . . Our focus now has to be on saving as many lives as possible . . . we have hundreds of police officers and firefighters who are engaging in rescue efforts in lower Manhattan. We will strive now very hard to save as many people as possible. And to send a message that the city of New York and the United States of America is much stronger than any group of barbaric terrorists. That is our democracy. That is our rule of law, that our strength and our willingness to defend ourselves will ultimately prevail. . . . I ask the people of New York to do everything they can to cooperate, not to be frightened, to go about their lives as normal. Everything is safe right now in the city.[4]

As Giuliani started taking questions from the media after his opening statements, Governor George Pataki was standing in the background. It was clear that even though politically Pataki outranked Giuliani, the mayor was the man in charge. He was the strong leader, capable of providing comfort and emotional and psychological support to millions through his unscripted and clearly heartfelt words. It was these words that put the extraordinary nature of 9/11 into perspective and that would be remembered by so many: "The numbers of casualties will be more than any of us can bear ultimately."[5]

There is little question that Rudy Giuliani's public performance in the hours and days after the 9/11 attacks on New York were extraordinary by any standards. When *Time Magazine* selected him as "Person of the Year," the editors said of Giuliani:

In the hours that followed, he had to lock parts of the city down and break others open, create a makeshift command center and a temporary morgue, find a million pairs of gloves and dust masks and respirators, throw up protections against another attack, tame the mobs that might go looking for vengeance and somehow persuade the rest of the city that it had not just been fatally shot through the heart.[6]

A tall order for any man.

Giuliani also attended countless funerals and public memorials in which he always seemed to find the right words—the right tone—for grieving families as well as for confused and fearful citizens. He did the same at the very public memorial event at Yankee Stadium, which was nationally televised and in many ways brought the nation together.

No One Is Perfect in a Crisis

Accolades aside, understandingly, Giuliani made many mistakes surrounding the crisis of 9/11. It would be impossible for any leader not to stumble given the scope and unprecedented nature of this tragedy.

For example, Giuliani was legitimately criticized for not making sure fire department administrators put fully functional two-way radios into the hands of firefighters. This radio communication failure had a devastating and deadly impact on 9/11, as firefighters in the Twin Towers were unable to clearly communicate with each other. In the ensuing confusion, hundreds of firefighters continued to move upward in the World Trade Center buildings when every effort should have been made to get out.

Further, many have criticized Giuliani's decision to house New York's emergency command center at World Trade Center Building 7. Building 7 would ultimately collapse on September 11, and critics argued that it was a tactical mistake to put the city's emergency command center near a location that previously had been a terrorist target—the World Trade Center was bombed in 1993 and was consistently considered a potential target.

Additionally, there are serious questions as to whether Giuliani did all he could to encourage if not demand that rescue workers at Ground Zero wear protective masks. (In this book's chapter examining Christie Whitman's role regarding the federal government's handling of the air quality issue at Ground Zero, we'll see that Whitman claims she tried to get Giuliani and his health department to enforce stricter safety standards for rescue workers.)

Despite these and other areas where he apparently fell short, Giuliani gained unprecedented public support and was crowned a hero by many. Why? Because of his extraordinary communication skills in the worst crisis on American soil. Many of his mistakes were tactical and operational, but few had to do with his strategies of communication that made him an inspirational leader of not just the city, but the country as well. This case gives us a unique view of the power of well-executed crisis communication: it is the strongest weapon we have—sometimes stronger even than our actions—when we need to move, inspire, and give hope to others. *New York Times* columnist Bob Herbert talked about Giuliani in a way few political figures were ever described. Herbert, who had never particularly liked Giuliani and made that clear in his commentary, said: "Giuliani moves about the stricken city like a God . . . people want to be in his presence. They want to touch him. They want to praise him."[7]

Consider the following additional praise heaped on Giuliani from a variety of sources, including some who were never big fans of "America's Mayor," and note how often the accolades focus on his leadership communication skills:

- According to Herman Badillo in the book *Giuliani: Flawed or Flawless: The Oral Biography*, by Deborah Hart Strober and Gerald S. Strober, "Giuliani reacted strongly to take direct and forceful action to reassure the people of the city and the country and to say that we are going to fight back against this type of thing and we should hold steady and meet the crisis."[8]

- Mark Green, the perennial New York City mayoral candidate who never was a fan of Giuliani's, said: "I can see some public officials overplaying the tough card, but I saw him close up during the weeks after 9/11 and he struck just the right chord of toughness and compassion."[9]

- Interestingly, rarely does anyone question Rudy Giuliani's toughness or his ability to take charge, but it was again the emotional and empathetic piece of Giuliani's crisis leadership equations that was particularly impressive to many. According to Fran Reiter, " the way he effectively brought hope to the people of the city and kept their spirits up . . . anyone who ever watched Giuliani at cops' funerals knows that he is very emotionally invested in this part of the job."[10]

- Even David Letterman paid tribute to Rudy Giuliani in his first program after the 9/11 tragedy. Letterman said of Giuliani: "Watch how this guy conducted himself." Letterman began to cry in front of the studio audience and millions of viewers: "Rudy Giuliani is the personification of courage." A week later, when Giuliani was Letterman's guest on the show, he received a loud and sustained standing ovation.[11]

- In a *New York Post* editorial entitled "A Mayor for a Crisis," these words of praise were offered: "Rudy Giuliani is a rock. From the earliest moments of Lower Manhattan's agony, the mayor of New York City was—and continues to be—simply magnificent. He is telling it as it is, his FDNY ball cap pulled low across his brow, his EMS windbreaker zipped to his neck. America and the rest of the world saw a visible symbol that New York had not been defeated by this horrific attack . . . this has been his finest hour."[12]

- Jonathan Alter of *Newsweek* said: "No matter what happens now, Rudy Giuliani's legend is in place. He's our Winston Churchill, walking the rubble, calming and inspiring his heartbroken but defiant people. His performance in the weeks after Tuesday is setting a new global standard for crisis leadership: strong, sensitive, straightforward and seriously well informed about every detail of the calamity."[13]
- Interestingly, Tom Roeser, a columnist for the *Chicago Sun-Times*, wrote about Giuliani as he watched the federal government's failure to deal effectively with the Hurricane Katrina crisis in New Orleans. Roeser wrote: "All I could think of was what Giuliani would do. Threats to our country demand a Prince of the City: a prince fearless enough to write his own rules to establish order."[14]

Although the criticism of Giuliani's mistakes and missteps during the 9/11 disaster has some degree of merit and legitimacy, when it came to his role as chief communicator in a crisis, particularly one of such epic proportions, Rudy Giuliani was masterful, setting a standard for crisis leadership that remains unmatched by any public or private sector leader profiled in this book or in any other serious examination of crisis communication.

And Now . . . the "Other" Rudy

A comprehensive analysis of Rudy Giuliani as a communicator is especially interesting because in other circumstances before and, to a lesser extent, after 9/11 he has been an inconsistent, insensitive, and sometimes overly aggressive communicator. In the months leading up to 9/11, he was a lame duck mayor whose popularity was at an all-time low—for a number of reasons.

RUDY AND THE AMADOU DIALLO CASE. At this point in his term, Giuliani had alienated blocs of constituents—particularly the African American community. Many black leaders felt that Giuliani was insensitive and unsympathetic to the perception that some members of the mostly white NYPD were engaged in targeting, profiling, and in certain instances abusing black males. The Amadou Diallo case in 1999, in which New York City police officers fired forty-one shots at Diallo—an unarmed twenty-two-year-old West African immigrant who reached for his wallet in the doorway of his Bronx apartment building—brought these tensions into the spotlight. Nineteen of those shots struck Diallo, making this shooting a seminal event in the ongoing tension between New York City's cops and the black community.

RUDY THE BULLY. Rudy Giuliani had turned off many citizens, including former supporters, with what was seen as an overly aggressive, in-your-face, style of leadership. He was a mayor who had a tendency to pick fights and had little desire or ability to listen to points of view that differed from his own. He battled with former New York City Police commissioner Bill Bratton when Bratton received national publicity and attention for a decrease in the city's crime rate. Many saw this as proof that Rudy Giuliani had little patience for anyone on his team receiving more public credit than himself.

To compound his problems, Giuliani had an antagonistic relationship with the media in New York. He didn't trust them and didn't think he needed them to run the city the way he saw fit. On his weekly call-in radio program on 77-WABC, Giuliani would often chastise and scold callers who dared challenge or disagree with him.

RUDY AND HIS FAMILY AFFAIR. The same Rudy Giuliani who would demonstrate an amazing sense of compassion and sensitivity to the families of 9/11 victims demonstrated an amazing lack of concern or apparent compassion for his own family when he announced in a public press briefing that he and his wife, Donna Hanover, were getting divorced. His wife and two children, Andrew and Caroline, first heard that their husband and father had decided to end the marriage on the evening news. As someone who has experienced divorce, I am reluctant to analyze anyone's family issues. Yet, certainly Giuliani's approach was mean-spirited and wrong, and poorly communicated. It would ultimately have a powerful impact on the Giuliani family structure.

Further, it was revealed that Giuliani was romantically involved at the time with Judith Nathan, who would later become his third wife. Apparently, ex-wife Hanover and her now-grown son and daughter have never forgiven Giuliani for the way he bungled this personal situation. In fact, after declaring himself a Republican candidate for the 2008 presidential nomination, Giuliani was often pushed by the media to explain the negative and embarrassing public statements made by son Andrew about their "estrangement" and the fact that daughter Caroline barely acknowledged her father (except, in one rather passive-aggressive way, when she joined an Internet-based group supporting Democratic presidential candidate Barack Obama).

RUDY'S EMBELLISHMENTS ON HIS 9/11 RECORD. Even after reclaiming his reputation through his calm, compassionate, and clear communication and decision making in the hours and days after 9/11, he later got into hot water for boasting (some say inaccurately) about his role at Ground Zero. Giuliani angered first responders and rescue workers who had labored on "the pile" by embellishing the physical risks and dangers he said he had faced. In a series of public speeches and in response to questions in press briefings regarding his role in protecting rescue workers at Ground Zero from dangerous and potentially deadly asbestos, dust, and metal-filled air, Giuliani communicated in a clumsy and cavalier fashion. He said he had been "at Ground Zero as often, if not more, than most of the workers" and that "I was there often enough so that every health consequence that people have suffered, I could also be suffering." These remarks pulled Giuliani into an ugly and ongoing battle with New York City firefighters over their perception that Giuliani was exploiting 9/11 for political gain and not showing enough concern for their plight.

Giuliani's reputation as a masterly communicator certainly took a hit as his words in these situations alienate him from key constituents, emergency responders, the media, and his own family. This is how easily and quickly poor communication skills can tarnish the image of an exceptional crisis communication leader.

Learning from the Good and the Bad

There are so many important lessons to be learned from Rudy Giuliani's public performance—both at his best and worst. Here are the ones we can most directly and immediately apply to our own communication challenges.

LEARNING FROM GIULIANI'S MISTAKES

Let's first take a look at the communication challenges in which Giuliani fell short.

Avoid praising yourself in public. First, it looks tacky. Even if you are accurate about your performance, it is not for you to say but rather for others to praise you. In Giuliani's case, he was not only Time Magazine's person of the year in 2001, but he was recognized by millions for his exceptional leadership and communication after 9/11. He didn't need to blow his own horn and embellish his own record.

Some might say that Rudy Giuliani was only trying to defend himself from criticism that he didn't do enough at Ground Zero to protect rescue workers from dangerous air quality. However, public self-praise never deflects attention from criticism. Instead, it is seen as an effort to avoid responsibility for mistakes that may have been made. When a leader is seen as not being accountable for his actions, the potential fallout is huge..

If you have performed well under pressure and are tempted to blow your own horn—don't do it. Allow others to recognize your performance. If that doesn't happen, be patient, because no matter what your motives may be or how accurate you may be in your self-assessment, praising yourself in a public way sends the wrong signals to key colleagues and stakeholders. It says to them that, instead of being confident and secure in who you are, as a leader you need to remind yourself and everyone else of what you've done.

I am not saying that aggressive public relations and promotion is wrong (my name and face are not on the cover of this book by accident). However, third-party testimonials about you and your organization in connection with a high-profile crisis or controversy are always more significant and credible than your own public assessment of your efforts.

1. When a crisis hits . . . listen. Responding to the crisis of 9/11, Giuliani was a sponge, absorbing everything around him, getting feedback and advice from top aides. Yet, in other instances (particularly the tragic Amadou Diallo case, and the Patrick Dorismond case), Giuliani was not a great listener. In fact, he ignored and refused the advice of many around him who said he should meet with African American leaders who were growing impatient and upset with what they perceived as Giuliani's strident and unconditional support of the New York City Police Department and all of their dealings. Giuliani was seen as stubborn, if not dangerously loyal, to New York cops, at the expense of young black men who in some cases felt victimized by the police.

2. Empathize with all sides. In the Diallo case, Giuliani's support of the police—who have a virtually impossible job—was admirable, but at the same time he needed to show more compassion and empathy to not just the Diallo family, who lost a son and loved one, but to many in the black community who felt his death was symbolic of a much larger and serious problem of bad blood between the black community and the NYPD. Remaining level-headed is important, but being compassionate to those in need is just as important.

3. Don't use the media to make personal announcements. To date, it appears that Giuliani is still feeling the effects of his very public and messy divorce announcement and awkward courtship of Judith Nathan. Giuliani seemed to instinctively understand what the victims of 9/11 needed from him, yet with his own family and in his personal life he often badly missed the mark. The lesson for all of us, but particularly those in very public positions: If you are going to do or say something that has a direct impact on those closest to you, make sure you tell them first before you inform the much larger community. If you don't, it is a mistake from which you may never recover. Rudy Giuliani may have become "America's Mayor," but his own two children, Andrew and Caroline, had little positive to say about their own father when he was seeking the presidency.

LEARNING FROM RUDY'S STRENGTHS

In many circumstances, Rudy got it right and offers us constructive lessons.

Great leaders remain calm in the face of the worst crisis—even when they themselves are experiencing fear or overwhelming emotion. That's what Rudy Giuliani did in spades after 9/11 and it rubbed off. It helped others be just a bit calmer than they otherwise would have been. His tone and demeanor was reassuring on many levels. Other leaders and managers need to keep this in mind when dealing with any crisis, but maybe especially the smaller ones that tend to get blown out of proportion.

1. Being tough and aggressive as a leader doesn't mean you also can't be compassionate and empathetic. Giuliani struck that delicate and hard-to-achieve balance as the crisis leader of New York and the country in the aftermath of 9/11. It is not enough to simply say you are one type of leader or another. Truly great leaders are flexible and can rely on a variety of styles that come together in a moment of truth.

2. A crisis leader must be fully engaged. Giuliani did not send other officials to the scene of the Twin Towers attack. He himself arrived immediately afterward and used his body language to deliver messages of both grief and calm. A strong leader cannot communicate important messages from a distance (witness President George Bush immediately following the 9/11 attacks). Giuliani had a group of trusted advisors, but he was clearly the quarterback, in charge, giving directions. While Giuliani consistently communicated in a clear and calm manner, his ability to speak extemporaneously and quickly was a huge asset during this horrific crisis.

3. Use the media to your advantage. Despite Giuliani's frosty relationship with the media leading up to 9/11, he was smart enough to understand that in the moments after the attacks, he needed the media to get his message to the public. He worked the press corps in a masterly fashion. He made it clear to them that they were needed as a conduit to communicate to the fearful masses. He was totally accessible to them and in turn they were accessible to him. In a crisis, no leader or manager can be effective without utilizing a variety of communication vehicles, including the media.

Christie Whitman and the EPA

COMING CLEAN ON GROUND ZERO

What were they thinking? ─────────────

When forced to testify before Congress, EPA administrator Christie Whitman was thinking that, even in this age of electronic recording and easy retrieval via the Internet, she could rewrite her words, blame others, and hide behind her lawyers rather than acknowledge a mistake.

The Lesson ─────────────

Once you leave behind a record of your words, you cannot change that reality—so don't try.

Once the World Trade Center collapsed on September 11, 2001, countless brave men and women willingly jumped in to save as many people as possible. Soon it became clear that few would survive the collapse of the Twin Towers.

Still, rescue workers continued day and night to recover as many bodies as possible and clear thousands of tons of iron, concrete, and other debris. All of this was done with little, if any, concern for the potential health hazards that first responders and volunteer workers might face. Emotions were running high. There was a tremendous commitment to help in any way possible at Ground Zero—without thinking of one's own health.

Nothing like September 11 had ever happened in our nation's history. It was a crisis of epic and unprecedented proportions. Government officials at every level were overwhelmed by the need to cooperate and coordinate their efforts as well as their communication. Who really was in charge of what? Who had the final say? The jurisdictional lines were blurred and confusing. Much of the chaotic response to the 9/11 crisis was understandable given the overwhelming nature of the havoc and devastation it wreaked. Yet, the performance of one federal agency—the Environmental Protection Agency (EPA) and its then administrator, Christie Whitman—graphically demonstrates how not to communicate in a crisis and its aftermath.

What Was Said

The EPA was responsible for monitoring the air quality in and around Ground Zero. It was no secret that after the attack and the World Trade Center collapse, a toxic cloud along with a horrific odor emanated from Ground Zero. Of course the public was concerned about the danger of breathing such air and turned to the EPA for information. The first public statements from Christie Whitman and the EPA regarding the air quality at Ground Zero were reassuring to many.

On September 13, only two days after the terrorist attacks, Whitman made the following claim: "The EPA is greatly relieved to have learned that there appears to be no significant levels of asbestos dust in the air in New York City."[1] Then on September 14, Whitman and the EPA added: "The good news continues to be that air samples we have taken have all been at levels that cause no concern."[2] On September 16, Whitman reiterated: "There is no reason for concern."[3]

Continuing to bear good news, on September 18 Whitman put an exclamation point on her analysis of the air quality at Ground Zero by saying: "Given the scope of the tragedy from last week I am glad to reassure the people of New York and Washington, D.C., that their air is safe to breathe and their water is safe to drink."[4] Even fourteen months after the 9/11 attack, in December 2002, the EPA would say that people who returned to Ground Zero were "unlikely to suffer short-term or adverse health effects" from contaminated air.[5]

It's understandable that Whitman might misspeak in the midst of confusion and chaos, yet it is unclear why she would offer such persistent reassurances without any credible evidence to support her claims. What she said just wasn't true.

What Was True

In a crisis, it is essential to communicate a clear and unequivocal message, and that is exactly what EPA administrator Christie Whitman did regarding the air quality at Ground Zero. But her confident authority came into question as the facts revealed that Whitman's public claims in the immediate aftermath of the 9/11 attacks were not accurate.

Over the past six years, hundreds of those heroic and brave rescue workers have become seriously ill because of the toxic and deadly air that they breathed in at Ground Zero. Some have died and others suffer serious and debilitating respiratory ailments that medical and health experts say are the direct result of breathing in contaminated air at Ground Zero—the same air that the EPA and Christie Whitman said was "safe."

According to an interview on September 10, 2003, in the *San Francisco Chronicle*, University of California at Davis scientist Thomas Cahill, an expert in physics and atmospheric science who led a team of scientists that studied the aerosols around Ground Zero, said: "The site [Ground Zero] was hot for months. The metals burned into fine particles. They rose in a plume and moved over people's heads on most days. There were at least eight days where the plume was pushed down into the city. Then people tasted it, smelled it, and saw it. But people who worked in the pile were getting it every day. The workers are the ones I worry about most."[6]

Cahill and his scientific team concluded that these "very fine metals" would interfere with lung chemistry. Further, that "sulfuric acid would attack lung cells and carcinogenic organic matter" would travel to the lungs and through the bloodstream to the heart.[7]

Over the years, as the federal government's response to 9/11 was examined more closely, Christie Whitman and the EPA were criticized for falsely reassuring safety workers at Ground Zero. A massive public relations and credibility crisis was growing and it had Whitman in its crosshairs. This was a crisis Whitman would not handle well. In fact, her public comments and, later, her lack thereof, would make this crisis worse.

One Misstep after Another

Fast forward. When the reports regarding the unsafe air quality levels at Ground Zero became public, Christie Whitman found herself in need of a crisis communication strategy. Her words and actions at this point, however, make it quite clear that she did not have one. As you read through the following series of events, see if you can spot the missteps.

When pushed in May 2003 to explain her assurances immediately following the 9/11 attack, Whitman shocked us all by saying: "We said from the very beginning that people should wear respirators . . . we kept telling them again and again. I don't think we could have been any stronger than we were about the danger of people working on the site. Now you have the problem of potential long-time health concerns because of exposure to asbestos and everything else in the air. If they [the rescue workers] had worn the devices [masks] we'd see a lot less problems. Everybody would have been a lot better off."[8]

On September 10, 2006, Christie Whitman spoke out publicly in an interview with Katie Couric on CBS's 60 *Minutes* and once again tried to rewrite history and put a positive and confounding spin on her public pronouncements in the immediate aftermath of September 11. "We always said consistently you've got to wear protective gear. . . . [W]e didn't have the authority to do that enforcement, but we communicated the need to wear respirators to the people who did." Whitman went on to say that the EPA communicated "in no uncertain terms" to New York City Mayor Rudy Giuliani that the "pile at Ground Zero" was dangerous and that rescue workers faced serious risks.[9]

The communication tactic used by Whitman is a common one: when cornered, pass the buck. In her effort to rewrite history, Whitman put the blame on Giuliani and his top health officials. She was saying that she and the EPA could do nothing to force rescue workers to wear protective masks because it was New York City's responsibility. The problem with Whitman's argument is that even if New York City could have done a better enforcement job (and there is evidence to support such an argument), at no point is there any public record of her holding a press conference or saying anything in any media interview to the effect that it was absolutely essential for Ground Zero rescue workers to wear protective masks. It may have been an item on the EPA's Web site or in some obscure EPA directive, but it was clearly not a top priority. Whitman never took a leadership role in shouting from the rooftops how important it was for rescue workers to wear protective masks. And the media, along with the American public, were not going to let her off the hook for that.

Apparently still feeling unfairly criticized, Whitman then attempted to play the communication game of "what the definition of *is* is" by trying to differentiate between her public pronouncements regarding the air quality at Ground Zero versus air quality in Lower Manhattan. She explained: "The readings [in lower Manhattan] were showing us that there was nothing that gave us any concerns. That was different from the Pile itself, at Ground Zero. . . . [W]e did everything we could to protect people from that environment and we did it in the best way we could, which was to communicate with those people who had the responsibility for enforcing . . . the city of New York was the primary responder."[10]

This effort to clarify that her comments on September 13, 14, 16, and 18, 2001, reassuring rescue workers that there was "no reason for concern" referred only to Lower Manhattan and not Ground Zero is absurd and disingenuous at best. Whitman had to know that virtually everyone interpreted her initial comments about the air quality as being related directly to Ground Zero. Once she suspected that there might be some confusion, she had a responsibility to publicly communicate and clarify that she was talking about Lower Manhattan's air quality, and not Ground Zero's. But she didn't do that—perhaps for a very good reason.

To be fair to Christie Whitman (whose tenure as New Jersey governor from 1994 to 2001 I reported on and analyzed as both television commentator and newspaper columnist), she had to answer to President George Bush and top White House officials while at the same time being accountable to the American public—particularly rescue workers at Ground Zero and nearby residents. Clearly, as it relates to 9/11, much of the public communication from cabinet members and the Bush administration was being handled by political and media operatives in the White House.

In fact, a report in August 2003 by the EPA inspector general acknowledged that the agency had been under heavy pressure from the White House to put out misleading information regarding the air around Ground Zero. Other reports confirmed that the White House convinced Whitman and other EPA officials to publicly downplay the health risks at Ground Zero. Ultimately, the White House put the National Security Counsel in charge of all EPA communications, according to the inspector general's report.[11]

Consider the ramifications of this. While the EPA and its scientists were the ones who knew best regarding the air quality problems at Ground Zero, it was the White House and their key political operatives who would ultimately be in control of the public messages put out regarding this crisis. To be clear, this is not simply a question of using politics in an effort to gain some cheap public relations points in a matter of no great concern. We're talking about a matter of life and death—literally. Christie Whitman knew that, but did not lead as if this were a matter of highest priority.

Instead, years later, when called to testify before the House Judiciary Sub-Committee in June 2007, Christie Whitman would initially choose silence to uphold the party line. Her lawyer, Joel Korbet, wrote a letter to House Judiciary Sub-Committee chairman Jerrold Nadler (D-NY), explaining: "It would be inappropriate for Governor Whitman to testify about a subject involving litigation that is pending against her and other government officials."[12]

Korbet's reference was to a federal lawsuit by numerous New York City residents against Whitman and the EPA contending that the federal agency didn't protect their health. Whitman did everything she could not to testify before Congress, even though many of her colleagues who were serving at the EPA and other federal agencies would voluntarily give public testimony before the judicially committee. In fact, in February 2006, a federal judge who allowed the suit against Whitman and the EPA wrote, "Christie Whitman's deliberate and misleading statements . . . shocked the conscience."[13]

Further, Congressman Nadler challenged Korbet's assertion about her inability to testify because of pending litigation. Said Nadler: "If it were a criminal case, she could refuse to answer questions . . . but not in a civil case. Our committee must have her testimony at some point, so the American people can hear her direct response to many lingering questions."[14]

By the summer of 2007 Whitman was under heavy pressure to clarify her statement in the aftermath of 9/11 regarding the air quality at Ground Zero. The headlines in the New York tabloids were brutal. On May 16, 2007, the headline read, "Christie

Won't Clear Air on Mess at Ground Zero." It was followed up by an editorial on May 19 in the *Daily News* blasting Whitman.

On May 17 the *Daily News* ran an editorial with a big picture of Christie Whitman under the following headline: "Cluck, Cluck, Cluck, Cluck." The article began: "Christie Whitman is a coward. No other word will suffice. Rather than clearing the air (pun intended) over her post 9/11 performance as EPA Administrator, she is hiding behind her lawyer's briefs instead of answering a call to testify before Congress."[15]

Apparently Whitman got the message, because within twenty-four hours of the *Daily News* onslaught, which was matched by tremendous criticism of Whitman in the *New York Post*, she decided to ultimately testify before Congress, saying in a letter to Chairman Nadler: "If you insist that I appear before the Sub-Committee while that litigation is pending, I am prepared to honor your request and make myself available. . . . I am extremely proud of the EPA's work in response to the terrorist attacks on our nation on September 11, 2001."[16]

When Whitman finally appeared before the congressional committee, the tone of her testimony further alienated her from a concerned public and strained her credibility. It was problematic that she acted indignant when challenged with legitimate and pressing questions that seemed reasonable to most people based on the evidence and facts available. She had clearly decided to communicate in an assertive, and some might say aggressive, fashion toward anyone who questioned or challenged her. This decision certainly influenced media coverage and public perception of her. The Shakespearean expression "the lady doth protest too much" is appropriate here. Whitman seemed intent on arguing virtually every point, including her confusing and seemingly contradictory statements regarding air quality at Ground Zero immediately after September 11.

No doubt, handling a massive public health crisis as the head of the EPA in the midst of chaos and confusion is extremely difficult. When emotions and fear and adrenaline are running so high, the challenge is even greater. Being a leader during a crisis, with the president and his White House operatives breathing down your neck, only makes things more difficult. But all of these complex factors only make it more imperative to have a well-prepared crisis communication strategy that is straightforward and honest. In reviewing Whitman's various tactics and strategies, it is especially troubling that six years after September 11, 2001, she still refused to acknowledge her mistakes or make any apologies for her misinformed words.

The Lessons: Let Me Count the Ways

Where to begin? There are so many things we can learn about crisis communication from this one incident. Let's see how Whitman's most obvious mistakes can save us the same type of disgrace and embarrassment.

1. Be honest and straightforward. This lesson has been discussed in many cases in this book. Yet, one must be vigilantly aware that in the age of instant communication and the Internet, the public comments of a leader are instantly archived and easily accessible over time. Any attempt to argue or quibble with this permanent public record is dangerous and quite honestly dumb. Whitman was attempting to argue with her own words regarding her comments after 9/11, which were part of a permanent public record—and she paid a hefty price.

Remember that history and the facts will reveal the truth—in this age of electronic archiving you cannot rewrite history by claiming, "I never said that."

2. Say what you mean. Playing with the meaning of words is a Clintonesque communication strategy ("It depends on what the meaning of is is.") that is explored in several cases in this book (most notably in the case of Alberto Gonzales). Although this parsing of language is a common and acceptable practice for lawyers in the court of law, in the court of public opinion and public relations it is extremely risky. It gives the appearance that you are trying to avoid responsibility by manipulating words and the obvious facts.

3. Take responsibility. One of the communication challenges for a leader in a crisis is avoiding the temptation to redirect the focus onto the actions of someone else. Even if you are in the right, simply put, it is not your place to do that, and no matter what your intentions, the perception will be that you are not taking responsibility for your own actions.

Passing the buck and blaming Rudy Giuliani and the New York City Health Department may, on some level, have been technically legitimate, but it just simply looked bad for Christie Whitman, especially after she had assumed a leadership and communication role. Own your part and let others judge the performance of other parties. Over time it would become clear that even though then Mayor Giuliani did an exceptional job communicating under pressure in the immediate aftermath of 9/11, the performance of New York City's Health Department with respect to protecting workers at Ground Zero was anything but stellar.

However, it was inappropriate for Whitman when, under pressure to explain her own actions and words regarding the air quality at Ground Zero, to point the finger at New York City.

4. Don't hide behind your lawyer. Christie Whitman had every right to say that she couldn't or wouldn't testify before a congressional committee because her lawyer had advised her accordingly. Yet, in the court of public opinion and perception, it looks bad to "lawyer up." Ultimately, Whitman should have realized that the public pressure from the media as well as from congressional leaders and first responders and their families would be so intense that she would be forced to testify eventually.

Instead, she resisted for as long as she could, so that, when she did ultimately testify, she started out on the defensive. Once again, this lesson points out the dramatic difference between the rules in a legal or court-driven proceeding as opposed to those involving public relations. Use your lawyer, but don't hide behind him or her in an effort to avoid being held accountable. It looks bad.

5. Communicate proactively. Don't wait until your back is against the wall and you are forced to testify and answer tough questions. The sooner you speak up voluntarily, the more likely you are to gain the benefit of the doubt.

Sometimes in a crisis you can be stuck in the middle, serving too many masters. At times, we are expected to communicate certain messages in a crisis that may not be consistent with our own sense of right and wrong or what we believe to be true. It is a reality of organizational life that is clearly not unique here in the case of Christie Whitman.

Whitman was in an especially tough spot. She was accountable to the president and the White House as well as to millions of Americans, particularly to the brave rescue workers at Ground Zero and residents of the area. If being accountable and responsible to those two masters was difficult, it simply goes with the territory. But if answering to a boss causes one to potentially put the health and lives of innocent citizens at risk, a leader must ultimately ask: Can I live with my words and actions?

Of course it is easier said than done, but Christie Whitman needed to ask in the days after 9/11 if she felt a reasonable person would assume that she was declaring that the air quality at Ground Zero safe. Instead, when testifying before Congress years later, her goal seemed to be to paint herself as a victim of those who might have some political or personal agenda against her. Simply put, as the head of the EPA, Christie Whitman had a huge conflict of interest between what she knew in her heart and what she was being told to say. One can imagine that she might have considered actually resigning in protest because of the pressures she was getting from the Bush White House to say and do things that she perceived to be less than ethical as they related to first responders putting their lives on the line on "the pile" at Ground Zero. Since she opted not to resign at the time, we have to assume that she was willing to stand by everything she said and did at the time, which means she is ultimately accountable and responsible. No one else. That is the price of being a leader in a crisis. It may not seem fair or easy, but no one said it would be.

6. Manage your emotions. The lesson here is similar to the one offered in the Michael Brown/FEMA case study. Both Brown and Whitman when under pressure before Congress opted to take an adversarial stance in response to questions regarding their performance in highly publicized national crises. Over time, our public perception of these figures would be influenced by this argumentative and defensive tone. The ultimate lesson is that, when problems have been encountered, being conciliatory and even contrite—willing to admit errors in judgment or actions— offers more hope of a better outcome than remaining obstinate and stubborn in defending a wrong.

In many ways Christie Whitman's contradictory and less-than-candid public comments surrounding the air quality at Ground Zero after September 11 cast her in the worst possible light in a case that will forever taint her public reputation. She turned a bad situation into a professional and personal disaster. By not having a well-practiced crisis communication strategy, she herself brought on the negative and embarrassing headlines in the New York tabloids as well as tremendous criticism from the mainstream press and from the rescue workers who continue to suffer serious and debilitating respiratory ailments.

Prudential's Terror Threat

THE "ROCK" GETS IT RIGHT

What were they thinking? _____

Prudential CEO Art Ryan, Vice President of Global Security Hank DeGeneste, and Chief Communications Officer Bob DeFillippo were thinking that they needed to handle a pressure-filled "under fire" situation with great care, or the company might easily and quickly take a serious hit to its reputation and image.

The Lesson _____

A thoughtful and unified communication plan can help a company or organization not only maintain, but actually enhance its standing in even the most dire of circumstances.

The threat of a terrorist attack is a constant worry in our daily lives—for good reason. Many terrorism experts believe that another attack is coming; we just don't know when or where. Given this fact, it's reasonable to assume that most organizations have a disaster plan that includes a comprehensive crisis communication strategy. But they don't. It is estimated that the majority of American workers don't have any idea what such a plan would be in their individual workplace.

So what would you do if you were informed by credible government sources that your organization was a target of a terrorist threat? How would you make this information public? How would you keep your employees calm? How would you keep your stockholders from jumping ship? How would you protect both life and assets? No easy tasks for sure, but these are the kinds of questions we all have to be able to answer before disaster strikes.

Consider the case of Prudential Financial, which was specifically identified as a prime terrorist target of al-Qaeda. The call came from federal government officials to Prudential CEO Arthur Ryan on Sunday, August 1, 2004. Immediately Prudential executives, lead by Ryan, put a communication plan in place that serves for all of us as an example of getting it right.

Step-by-Step

Ryan's first step in handling this crisis was to identify his key communication people. He turned first to Bob DeFillippo, the company's chief communications officer, who would coordinate all communication efforts. It was DeFillippo's role to determine how and when the insurance giant would share sensitive information with employees, the media, and other key stakeholders. The job of sharing this information would be reserved for Ryan himself. DeFillippo also called in Hank DeGeneste, vice president of global security at Prudential, to help him communicate directly with Prudential employees.

In August 2004 I spoke with DeFillippo at length about Prudential's handling of the situation,[1] and he made it clear that one of the most significant aspects of the success of the company's communication efforts was the immediate and direct involvement of Art Ryan.

Ultimately, key stakeholders determine how an organization is evaluated in a crisis. In the case of Prudential, evaluators would certainly include Wall Street and the media, but most directly it was Prudential's employees who would be most affected by the frightening news and would have the greatest impact on how the company handled the crisis. Many employees were rightfully reluctant to take what they saw as a risk in entering the twenty-four-story Prudential office complex in downtown Newark, New Jersey, which was the specific location of the terrorist target. If they expected to calm those fears,

Prudential execs needed a communication plan to give accurate and up-to-date information.

According to Eric Battenberg, writing in the fall 2004 edition of *The Public Relations Strategist*: "The company immediately began communicating [information and safety] measures to employees and explaining the strategies behind them. It did this through an emergency telephone hotline that employees could dial into and through e-mail from CEO Art Ryan."[2]

In addition to the electronic communication via e-mail and telephone hotlines, creating opportunities to communicate face-to-face was also critical to the corporation's crisis communication efforts. DeGeneste lead employee town hall meetings immediately after Ryan was informed about the threat to the company.

Providing immediate, real-time, and honest communication helped jittery Prudential employees feel much more secure. These actions assured them that Prudential's top management was actively engaged and concerned and was making it a priority to inform them regarding any and all key aspects of the situation. According to Barbara Elder, a top public relations executive at Hill and Knowlton: "It all comes back to the fact that smart employers show employees that they matter."[3]

Beyond the communication lines established between Prudential's top executives, the crisis team also established a line of communication that became extremely important in keeping Prudential employees informed and involved. Top-level executives kept managers and supervisors informed not only about the relevant facts, but also about the key organizational messages that needed to be communicated to employees seeking updates and direct answers. Rumors can't be totally controlled in problem situations, but they can be minimized and managed by offering consistent, relevant facts from credible sources.

At the same time, Prudential took immediate steps to ensure the safety of its corporate headquarters and its employees in

Newark. Two rows of concrete barriers were erected all around the Prudential headquarters and other buildings. In addition, local and state law enforcement officers with automatic weapons were dispatched around the Prudential complex at strategic locations. This was the result of a crisis team that was not worried about hiding their problems from the public. Their first concern was for the safety of their people—and it showed.

But public perception of this major national company could not be ignored. Ryan needed to go public with the threat to Prudential. So on the same day he was notified by federal authorities that Prudential was in fact listed as a potential terrorist target, Ryan appeared on television with top government officials standing in front of the Prudential building in Newark. He also appeared as a guest on numerous national and regional media television outlets including an August 3, 2004, appearance on CBS's *Early Show* on which Ryan spoke not only to Prudential employees, but to millions of television viewers.

Although Ryan didn't sugarcoat the potential seriousness and credibility of the terrorist threat, he understood the importance of keeping perspective and taking a positive but realistic attitude about the situation. For example, he assured viewers, "While they [potential terrorists] spent a lot of time walking around the building and doing surveillance, they never gained entry to our building." Ryan was candid while still making it clear that the situation was under control. His presence had a calming effect.

According to a CBSNews.com online report on August 3, 2004, Art Ryan announced that customers were not fleeing the company and that the "overwhelming majority" of employees reported to work. "Everything we've heard so far has been reinforcing. 'We're with you.' That's basically what we've heard from most of them," Ryan said.[4] That's what can happen when the communication plan is credible and responsive.

Of course, Ryan and his team wrestled with the issue of how

much information to divulge. Full disclosure has its drawbacks. Some argue there is a danger in communicating or sharing too much information in a sensitive situation or crisis in which fear and panic are always real possibilities and where too much information could potentially jeopardize the effectiveness of security measures. Says Elder, "If they [employees] see that there is a mindset of keeping employees safe, then they will understand that there could be some measures you can't talk about."[5] Everything in moderation.

Bob DeFillippo disagrees, saying: "Don't be paralyzed by fear, share vital information even if it makes some people nervous. I don't know if you could ever have too much information in a situation like this." DeFillippo acknowledges that in some situations it may be possible for people to be inundated and overloaded with too much information to the point of not being able to decipher what information is most important or relevant to them. Yet, Prudential apparently didn't hold back sensitive or difficult to hear information from their employees, and it made a difference.

In Retrospect

In the summer of 2007, on the three-year anniversary of the Prudential terrorist scare, I again spoke to Bob DeFillippo. He offers us the following valuable perspective.

What was in place at Prudential before the call came?

There was a crisis committee in place that included all of the critical functions—operations, law, communications, human resources, and security. In instances where there is an emergency, the committee convenes to see whether employees should come to the building, whether they should work at home, or if we have alternate worksites in the event we can't convene in the building. Some of what we did came from lessons we learned after 9/11.

After I had met with the crisis committee, I called together my senior managers—it was Sunday night—and we were on the phone along with our media-relations people determining what the tough questions would be. I don't think you can do this job unless you anticipate what you are likely to be asked by your various audiences, especially your employees and the media. It is not a complex exercise to sit around with a set of trained communicators and then run through every possible scenario to come up with the kinds of questions that would be asked and then seek out the people who have the answers to those questions.

What were your first steps in handling this crisis?

We reached out to *The Star-Ledger.* We didn't wait for them to call us. They knew us, and we knew them. We invited a *Ledger* reporter to join us in the building—to witness first-hand how we were addressing the crisis. Building relationships with key people in the media is invaluable. You also need to facilitate what they need. You have to be open about what you can and can't say. Trying to prevent them from reporting something is never a good idea. The media-relations staff was out in front of the building with coolers of water because it was hot outside that day.

And we didn't try to stop employees from talking to the media. We told our employees that if they wanted to talk to the media, do so, but if not, don't feel like you have to. The media focused on our employees—they became the focus of the coverage. There was no line separating internal and external communications. We made sure that all our employees knew what our messages were and they helped us communicate them.

Were you worried about sharing too much information with employees?

We believed that the more our employees knew, the better they would feel about coming to work. You need to put yourself in the employee's place at that moment. They have been told that their building is a target of terror. Why would they come to work on Monday unless they got completely unbiased information from us? They needed to know that we were talking to the authorities. They needed to know what steps we were taking to make the building safe and whether there was an ongoing threat or not. There's a fine line between too little and too much information. I suppose you can step over the line and give them information they don't need. But once we told them what we knew, it made it that much easier for them to deal with it. The downside was that if our employees found out through some other source something that we hadn't told them, our credibility would have been put into question. We couldn't have that.

What are the most important lessons you have taken away from this that you would want to share with other organizations?

As I think back, we were faced with a situation that came upon us with little or no advance warning. In the communications world, it is natural for your first thoughts to be about how big a public relations problem you are facing. But, it didn't take us long to realize this was an exercise in communicating with our employees worldwide. That became the single most important thing we had to focus on. Not the line of reporters or television cameras, or the media coverage. The way to address the problem was to address our employees. For a short time [before work on Monday], the employees weren't allowed in the building. When we did turn to the media, we were telling the media things our employees needed to hear. They [the media] became both willing and unwilling partners to what we were doing. The audience we were trying to reach most in the beginning was our employees. We wanted them to hear that we had taken steps to make the building safe.

By assuring our employees, we were also talking to our shareholders, saying that we were doing the things necessary to keep business running. When we said to our employees [that] we were doing things to keep the building safe, we were telling our shareholders that we were doing things to get business back up.

What the Prudential Case Teaches Us

There are so many lessons to be learned from the way the execs at Prudential handled this crisis. At the very least, we can all apply the following seven points to our own crisis communication plans:

1. The CEO must be actively involved right from the beginning. Prudential CEO Art Ryan got the call from the feds on Sunday, August 1. Within hours he was meeting with communications experts and his top security and operations people to make critical decisions and gather more information. Further, Ryan was accessible to the media and used various platforms to communicate with employees and key stakeholders. CEO Ryan's direct and early involvement was key to Prudential's success in this case.

2. There must be a designated and skilled communications officer. The fact that DeFillippo was a competent and credible communication point person was also critical to Prudential's handling of this crisis. Too often the person in this position is well-polished and able in practiced, standard scenarios, but lacks the appropriate skills and tools—as well as the presence—to handle a pressure-filled "under fire" situation.

3. Everyone has to be communicating from the same page. One of the biggest dangers in these types of situations is the sending of mixed messages by company officials. This wasn't the case with Prudential, since virtually all of the communication was being handled through a key point person, specifically Bob DeFillippo. Such a system made sure that consistent messages were communicated at critical times. It also allowed the media and other key stakeholders to know where they could turn to get timely and accurate information.

4. Of all your audiences, employees are number one. Bob DeFillippo says, "Employees are a critical audience and need to be well informed. One of the things we called right early on was letting our employees know what was going on and that we were making Prudential a safe place to work. That helped our employees to have the confidence to come to work and to keep the company going."

5. Use all available technology to communicate directly with employees. Ryan and DeFillippo utilized e-mail and PruTV, the internal communication system to keep their employees in the loop with real-time, detailed information. They also had in place a toll-free telephone number employees could call at any time to get the most up-to-date information on the situation.

6. Face-to-face communication is also critical. While technology can help quickly facilitate information sharing, there is no substitute for the personal, human connection. Town hall meetings led by Hank DeGeneste, vice president of global security, were critical to successfully communicating to groups of Prudential employees. It created a communal environment. According to DeFillippo, all questions were fair game and each session was well attended by employees. These meetings were also tied to the use of technology—the sessions were videotaped and aired on PruTV, reaching employees who were unable to attend.

7. Make sure your actions match your words. It's one thing to say security is going to be "beefed up" (anyone can say that), yet it is essential to back up those words in very visible ways. Within hours, additional security including police and the FBI were called on to the scene. They were stationed in front of the building where cement barricades were also installed. Further, everyone entering the building went through "airport level" security checks. Simply put, pleasant-sounding rhetoric alone won't get the job done.

In this book we explore the ways high-level leaders respond when a lie is uncovered, an unethical act is exposed, a personal scandal imposes on the credibility of the company, an off-hand remark that smacks of bigotry is broadcast, causing national condemnation, an illegal practice is revealed, false rumors threaten a company's viability, and many other such situations. Despite the diversity of circumstances, the outcome in each of our cases was largely dependent on the level of skillful communication strategies employed. When Prudential faced the crisis to beat all crises, the company's response became an excellent example for all of us, regardless of our business or organizational affiliation. The fact that Prudential did not lose employees, customers, or stockholders when the crisis period passed is a testament to the power of good communication to reduce damage in even the most dire of circumstances.

I encourage you to model your communication plan on this example, so that if in the future you should find yourself facing a crisis under the media spotlight you will be prepared and will stand as one more example of good crisis communication.

Virginia Tech

A DEADLY DELAY?

> **What were they thinking?** _____
>
> After the report of a double homicide on campus, Virginia Tech University president Charles Steger and his security staff were thinking that the worst was over and hence there was no need to disrupt or worry the entire campus with this terrible news.

> **The Lesson** _____
>
> Consider the worst and over-respond, if necessary, regardless of what you hope to be the case.

On April 16, 2007, Cho Seung-Hui, a twenty-three-year-old South Korean native who was an English major at Virginia Tech, gunned down thirty-two innocent people on the campus and ultimately turned the gun on himself. There are many, including me, who believe that some of those deaths could have been prevented if the school had had a better crisis communication plan. That's how important this issue can be.

At 7:15 A.M. campus police got a call about a shooting in the West Ambler Johnston Hall dormitory. A man and a woman were left dead. Virginia Tech president Charles Steger outlined for the press the next day the steps that were taken at that point: Johnston Hall dorm was locked down immediately. Resident advisors in the dorm knocked on virtually every door to inform nearly 900 students of what had occurred and security guards took control of the dormitory. It was surrounded by security guards and the nearby streets were cordoned off.[1] This sounds like it might be a reasonable crisis plan—but it was flawed.

After the initial shootings, certain assumptions were made by Virginia Tech officials that would later prove both incorrect and deadly. With no apparent confirmation, Steger and his top campus security team believed that the man and woman killed in the dormitory were somehow involved in a "domestic dispute." They also believed that the suspected shooter had left the Virginia Tech campus and had heard that off-campus police had quickly detained what was described as a "person of interest." They assumed this was an isolated incident and that the danger had passed. This is where their crisis plan fell apart.

Based on these assumptions, Virginia Tech officials decided not to publicly announce the dormitory killings. They decided not to lock down the sprawling 2,600-acre campus. They also decided not to cancel classes or use the public address system to announce what had occurred just after 7 A.M. on that fateful day. According to Steger, "We had no reason to suspect any other incident was going to occur."[2] But soon after 9 A.M. Steger would find that such a simplistic assumption cannot dictate crisis response.

At 9:26 A.M.—two hours and eleven minutes after the first 911 call regarding the Johnston Hall shooting—Virginia Tech officials finally sent out the first official e-mail. "Subject: Shooting on campus. A shooting incident occurred at West Ambler Johnston earlier this morning. Police are on the scene and are investigating. The university community is urged to be cautious and are asked to contact Virginia Tech Police if you observe anything suspicious or with information on the case. Contact Virginia Tech Police at 231–6411. Stay attuned to the www.vt.edu. We will post as soon as we have more information."[3]

Then, within minutes, a second horrific shooting occurred on the Virginia Tech campus; this time at 9:40 A.M. at the Norris Hall classroom complex. Thirty-three people—including the gunman—were dead. The killer clearly had planned this murderous attack for a considerable amount of time. He had ample ammunition and moved methodically from classroom to classroom, shooting fellow students as well as faculty members.

We would later witness a video that would come to be called a "manifesto" from Seung-Hui that was ultimately released by

NBC News in which he attempted to explain and justify his deadly and cowardly attack on so many innocent victims. Equally interesting, from a communication point of view, is an analysis of the explanations and justifications university officials would present in the weeks and months following the attacks for their woefully inadequate crisis plan. The series of e-mails sent on the day of the shootings give us a glimpse of the university's growing awareness of the severity of its problem:

> After the thirty-two additional members of the Virginia Tech community were killed, school officials sent out a second e-mail at 9:50 A.M.: "Subject: Please stay put; A gunman is loose on campus. Stay in buildings until further notice. Stay away from all windows."

> Then a third e-mail was sent at 10:16: "Subject: All Classes Canceled; Stay where you are. Virginia Tech has canceled all classes. Those on campus are asked to remain where they are, lock their doors and stay away from windows. Persons off campus are asked not to come to campus."

> Then finally at 10:53 A.M.: "Subject: Second Shooting Reported; Police have one gunman in custody. In addition to an earlier shooting today in West Ambler Johnston, there has been a multiple shooting with multiple victims in Norris Hall. Police and EMS are on the scene. Police have one shooter in custody and as part of routine police procedure, they continue to search for a second shooter. All people in university buildings are required to stay inside until further notice. All entrances to campus are closed."[4]

In our post-9/11 world, leaders cannot assume that a second attack or assault is not possible in an unfolding crisis. Who would have thought that after the first plane hit the Twin Towers on 9/11 that a second plane would hit the second tower minutes later? But now, post 9/11, assuming the worst and communicating accordingly is a critical part of any crisis communication strategy.

Failing to Spread the Word

Although not trained in crisis communication, many Virginia Tech students were quick to recognize following the event the weakness in the university's security plan. Many students were angry at the decision not to communicate immediately about the first shooting in Johnston Hall. Virginia Tech student Tina Harrison told CNN: "I feel like there should have been an e-mail sent out or some sort of notice that there was a shooting in the West Ambler Johnston earlier that morning. Regardless if they thought it was an isolated incident, the students should have known and classes should have been canceled."[5] Brant Martel, a twenty-three-year-old Virginia Tech junior, agreed, saying, "I was troubled with the fact that two hours elapsed from the first shooting."[6]

Many in the media and in the security field agreed, too. Security experts, including Bruce Blythe, who heads the firm Crisis Management International, have been especially critical with how Virginia Tech officials came to the decision not to notify students and others on the campus immediately after the initial shootings. In an article entitled "Virginia Tech Shootings: Crisis Magnifies the Significance of Small Weaknesses,"[7] Blythe identified what he called a series of miscalculations by Virginia Tech officials.

The most significant miscalculation, according to Blythe, was the decision not to immediately notify everyone on campus. "The president of the University rationalized that people were in transit and couldn't be reached. The administration assumed that it was an isolated 'domestic' situation and the gunman had left the campus. With a double homicide on campus, uncertain motive and a gunman on the loose, it would certainly pass the 'reasonable person test' to immediately notify everyone to stay out of harm's way and to be on the lookout for anyone fitting any known description of the shooter."[8]

President Steger argued that the administration could not immediately notify all students nor lock down the entire campus because thousands of students were in transit. He pointed out that many nonresident students were arriving for 8 A.M. classes and others were in and around Virginia Tech parking lots. Steger asked rhetorically, "Where do you lock them down? . . . We obviously can't have an armed guard in front of every classroom every day of the year. . . . You can only make a decision based on the information you know at that moment in time. You don't have hours to reflect on it."[9]

Blythe doesn't agree, saying:

The excuse that people couldn't be notified is not plausible. Crisis-prepared organizations are equipping themselves with immediate notification tools that could have notified everyone in the entire school via phone and e-mail simultaneously within a matter or seconds. This points to a lack of crisis preparedness, before the crisis occurred. In the absence of a technological solution an emergency notification phone tree could have been enlisted. Paul Revere was able to warn people that the "British were coming" even without phones. The excuse that people were in transit was an inadequate rationale not to notify students and faculty who were potentially in harm's way. The university needed to show a best faith effort to notify everyone immediately. An e-mail blitz two hours after the first shooting was clearly an anemic and untimely attempt at emergency notification.[10]

Lock Down!

The second major miscalculation identified by Blyth was the decision by Tech officials not to lock down the entire campus. Imagine that you are the leader in charge at the time of an unexpected and violent incident. You have a double homicide and the perpetrator at large. Would it make sense to lock down the school? A risk-reward analysis would clearly move a thoughtful leader to err on the side of caution. Lock the school down . . . now!! The likely downside would be a disrupted class schedule for the morning. The reward could be protecting the lives of students and faculty. And, as in the Prudential case study, would demonstrate a sense of caring and concern for constituents.

In analyzing the entire situation, clearly Blythe has an advantage as a "Monday morning quarterback" over Steger and his administrators, who made their decisions on the spot. Appropriate and thorough communication in a real-time crisis is challenging and in some cases nearly impossible. Yet, Virginia Tech laid itself open to criticism for not assuming the worst and therefore not even trying to immediately notify students and lock down the campus. They did not understand that the most important thing that they could do under such a violent set of circumstances was to consider worst case scenarios and communicate accordingly. Although President Steger said at the time that there was "no reason to suspect a second incident," some perplexing questions remain: Why assume that the shooter had left the campus? Why assume that there was no chance for additional shootings? Why assume the incident was isolated to a "domestic situation" when none of these assumptions were backed by any evidence?

We are talking about a double homicide in an age of crazed gunmen—especially recently on school campuses—engaging in shooting sprees that leave dozens of innocent and unsuspecting victims wounded or dead. The Virginia Tech shooting was only the latest in a series of tragic campus shootings. Vincent Bove, a nationally recognized security expert, wrote a compelling analysis of the Virginia Tech tragedy entitled "Virginia Tech Tragedy: A Crisis of Leadership." In this piece, he is critical of how little campus leaders and administrators at Virginia Tech seem to have learned given so many previous violent campus incidents. He refers back to Early Warning, Timely Response, which is a document jointly developed by the U.S. Department of Education and the U.S. Department of Justice in response to the May 1998 school shootings at Thurston High School in Springfield, Oregon, in which two students were killed and twenty-five others were injured. It is a guide its creators believe "should be seen as part of an overall effort to make sure that every school in this nation has a comprehensive violence prevention plan in place."[11]

With this in mind, it is significant to note that Seung-Hui had a history of threatening violence on the Virginia Tech campus. Reports were filed and claims were made by several female students of his actions. Seung-Hui was put in a mental facility because of his actions and his writings, but was ultimately let out of that institution and back on to the Virginia Tech campus. There was no way of knowing for sure what Seung-Hui would do on that fateful morning, but clearly there was reason for concern.

Yet, Bove argues, nearly a decade after the Early Warning, Timely Response report was released, campus and school security officials have done little to identify potential warning signs. He argues that the Virginia Tech tragedy was the manifestation of that lack of preparedness.[12]

Lessons in Hindsight

In the months and possibly years following these campus shootings, Virginia Tech's state of preparedness will be thoroughly analyzed in an attempt to assign or diminish culpability. From this examination leaders and managers of all schools, companies, and organizations will hopefully learn valuable lessons about the importance of a well-practiced crisis communication plan. Surely the most significant lessons will include the following:

1. A practical crisis communication and/or emergency plan must be written down and in place *before* an incident like this occurs. During a crisis, no one should have to "wing" a response..The plan must be distributed among all personnel and then it must also be thoroughly discussed, practiced, and periodically reviewed.

2. It is critical to test security and communication technology before an incident occurs with a "crisis communication fire drill." A dry run or dress rehearsal of a crisis plan at Virginia Tech would have alerted officials to the fact that the campus security cameras were not working properly and perhaps that an outdoor PA system was needed for quick, wide-area communication.

3. Make sure the top person in the company or organization is skillfully prepared to address those involved and the media. Virginia Tech president Steger gets points for staying out front and visible during the media frenzy following the tragedy, but too many of his early statements were uninformed, defensive, and subject to criticism.

4. Designate a spokesperson who is trained in crisis communication. Campus spokesperson Larry Hincker was clearly nervous and unprepared for the pressure. He fumbled, mumbled, and made it clear that he wanted to get away from the microphone as quickly as possible while the media and other concerned parties were peppering him with legitimate questions. He obviously was not prepared to handle a crisis of this magnitude—no one is unless they receive adequate training.

5. When a crisis hits, communicate immediately. Waiting more than two hours to notify those likely to be most directly affected by the first shootings is hard to justify on any level.

6. Don't rely too much on e-mail as the exclusive means of communicating with large numbers of people in a crisis. Varied modes of communication should be employed. At Virginia Tech, the faculty and student body could have been notified in real time about the unfolding crisis by e-mail as well as by a campus-wide PA and television system that could be seen in all public places, including cafeterias, dorms, lobbies, etc. A university representative speaking on camera directly to anyone who could see or hear exactly what was happening and what needed to be done would then be fairly easy to accomplish.

7. Assume the worst and over-respond, if necessary, regardless of what you hope to be the case. Split-second decisions are easy to second guess; however, the primary goal in any violent incident like the one at Virginia Tech must be to minimize the potential danger and harm to those in and around your location.

8. Always put safety first. Although all leaders must strive to protect the reputation of their company or organization, this consideration cannot be a priority when making tough decisions in the midst of a crisis. Instead, acting immediately to prevent a worst-case scenario is imperative, regardless of how the preventative and defensive actions may be perceived by the public. As the news of the shooting at Virginia Tech got out, top administrators were focused too much on how this was going to affect the school's image, reduce the number of future applicants, and overshadow the many positive accomplishments of its students. However, when the reputation of an organization comes before the safety of key stakeholders, the PR fallout is generally far worse than the scandal the executive leaders were trying to avoid in the first place. In the case of Virginia Tech, these stakeholders were the students and faculty on campus as Seung-Hui began his murderous spree. If a reasonable person comes to the conclusion that Virginia Tech officials did not act to the degree that they could to protect the faculty and students on campus, thereby putting their lives at greater risk, then ultimately the reputation of the institution will suffer more from this perception than from the shootings.

Time will tell how the reputation of Virginia Tech will be affected by the Cho Seung-Hui shootings. At this point, the focus of criticism is not on the fact that a student killed other students, but rather it is directed at the weaknesses in the school's crisis communication plan. On August 29, 2007, a Virginia state panel convened by the governor's office sharply criticized decisions made by Virginia Tech, saying, "University officials could have saved lives by notifying students and faculty members earlier about the killings on campus."[13]

The official 147-page state report was extremely critical of Virginia state administrators for downplaying the initial shootings. According to the report: "If University had issued an alert earlier or canceled classes after Mr. Cho shot his first two victims, before moving on to shoot the rest in a classroom building, the death toll might have been lower." It found that even after university officials had learned the full scope of the massacre, their messages to students played down the unfolding emergency as a "routine police procedure." According to the report itself, "The events were highly disturbing and there was no way to sugar coat them . . . straight facts were needed."

Further, the report was critical of campus police who prematurely came to the conclusion that the double homicide was an isolated domestic incident and further identified a suspect who had left campus and Virginia Tech police were convinced was their man. According to the report the Virginia Tech police "did not take sufficient action with what might happen if the initial lead proved erroneous." Simply put, the Virginia Tech crisis communication team had no plan B. No backup. Planning for the worst—and then some—is critical in ensuring an effective response to a potentially devastating and deadly incident.

Don Imus

"I CAN'T GET ANYWHERE WITH YOU PEOPLE"

What were they thinking?

Radio talk show host Don Imus was thinking that, with powerful friends in the media, he could give a late, lame, and awkward apology regarding an insulting and totally inappropriate racial comment about the nationally acclaimed Rutgers University women's basketball team without suffering any long-term consequences.

The Lesson

An apology has to be delivered immediately through an appropriate medium and in words that express genuine regret while offering no caveats or qualifications in the process.

Sometimes even veteran, accomplished broadcasters create their own crises and then make it worse by not immediately recognizing the severity of the situation. Consider Don Imus and his now infamous April 4, 2007, "nappy-headed hos" comments directed toward the Rutgers University women's basketball team, which was playing for the NCAA national championship in the spring of 2007.

This despicable and deplorable racist comment was part of a larger Imus riff that morning making a convoluted comparison between the darker-skinned black women from Rutgers (whom he and his producers saw as tough, unattractive, and thug-like) and the lighter-skinned, more attractive, and, apparently Imus believed, more "likeable" Tennessee team. The terms "jiggaboos" and "wannabes" were used by the all-white, all-male Imus broadcast crew. This went over the line even for a crew known to lack sensitivity to any race, color, or creed.

It was like so many other unscripted, unprompted, and in this case unfunny riffs that Imus had conducted, except this time, he picked the wrong target and used the wrong words to ignite a controversy that captured the attention of the nation for several weeks, until the Virginia Tech tragedy turned the media spotlight in a new direction.

When Imus made that stupid comment, it is a safe bet to assume that he thought nothing of it—neither did any of the on-air team he was working with. His sidekicks, producers, and the people behind the scenes didn't even blink. In fact, the next morning, Imus went on the air and made light of the "nappy-headed hos" bit. Basically, he said that people should learn to take a joke and not take themselves so seriously. But others were taking Imus's comments very seriously.

The Flames of Controversy Ignite

Media Matters, the liberal media watchdog that keeps track of television, radio, and Internet commentary, blasted Imus. They made his "nappy-headed hos" comments available on the Web for those who had missed the original radio cast or the simulcast on MSNBC.

Still, most mainstream media outlets didn't pay much attention to the incident until the National Association of Black Journalists (NABJ) jumped into the fray and blasted Imus for his comments. This raised the ante significantly. The issue of race and how it could and couldn't be talked about on the public airwaves was now front and center.

NABJ president Byron Monroe saw and heard Imus's on-air rant against the women's basketball team on the Media Matters Web site and immediately sent out an e-mail to his board of directors with the following subject line: "FYI—Do we need to address." Mr. Monroe, who is also a top-level editorial director at both *Jet* and *Ebony* magazines, then wrote: "I heard the words come out of his mouth and thought, 'Has he lost his mind?' "[1]

Once the NABJ blasted Imus on their Web site and sent out an e-mail with their position, things began to happen quickly. The NABJ said they were "outraged and disgusted." They demanded an "immediate and sincere apology" from Imus. That statement and the challenge by the NABJ were posted at 5:30 A.M. on Friday, April 6. Don Imus went on the air at 6:06 A.M. and attempted what would be his first apology, which went like this: "I want to take a moment to apologize for an insensitive and ill-conceived remark. Our characterization was thoughtless and stupid, and we're sorry."[2]

Instead of squelching the problem, this apology made the story even bigger. It was now forty-eight hours past the insensitive racial rant, and Imus was feeling big pressure from CBS and NBC, his radio and television employers, respectively, to say something apologetic—this pressure made his on-air mea culpa come across as insincere, as well as too little too late. More and more people were calling for Imus to be fired or at least severely reprimanded.

After the perfunctory "I'm sorry," Imus didn't help his cause when he tried to defend himself. He began to talk about his New Mexico ranch where children recuperate from life-threatening diseases, making a point of mentioning how many children at his ranch are black. He talked about how he had black friends and associates. But Imus's "some of my best friends are black" approach was making things worse. The fact that he waited forty-eight hours to even begin to acknowledge his mistake could not be wiped away because he had black friends.

Losing Support

Other mainstream media organizations like the *New York Times* were jumping into the Imus fray. *Times* media writer David Carr went after Imus on Monday, April 9, saying this of his "nappy-headed hos" comments: "Mr. Imus's slur was the kind of unalloyed racial insult that might not have passed muster on a low-watt AM station in the Jim Crow south."[3]

The public attacks directed at Imus were now in full swing. WFAN, the radio station that carried Imus's CBS radio program in the New York market, offered no support of their biggest on-air talent and money-maker, saying, "We are disappointed by Imus's actions earlier this week, which we find completely inappropriate." WFAN also committed to "monitoring" the program's content going forward.[4]

MSNBC, which had been carrying Imus's radio program in a television simulcast from its studios in Secaucus, New Jersey, for over a decade, offered similar comments, "calling Imus' comments 'racist' and 'abhorrent.'"[5]

At about the same time, as a way of expressing disapproval, several key sponsors, including Procter and Gamble, decided to pull the plug on their advertising on all of MSNBC's daytime programming, which included Imus's program. Later other major advertisers would also jump ship, including General Motors, American Express, Sprint, and Glaxo Smith Kline.

Predictably, Al Sharpton jumped into the Imus controversy, along with Jessie Jackson. Sharpton and Jackson have a long and largely undistinguished history of fanning racially volatile situations. Sharpton called for Imus to be fired and led a protest/rally in front of the CBS building in New York on April 9, 2007. He was insistent that Don Imus be held accountable for his comments directed toward the Rutgers team. The mainstream media swarmed all over Sharpton, who can always be counted on to deliver highly quotable sound bites. Sharpton's attack on Imus, as well as the CBS and MSNBC rebukes of Imus, were major media events. Sharpton was baiting Imus and Imus took the bait.

You Have No Friends in the Media

An off-hand comment had now turned into a major communication crisis that Don Imus could not ignore. So what to do? According to a *Wall Street Journal* article, Imus and his long-time friend and associate New York City detective Bo Dietal were discussing how to handle the raging controversy when Imus suggested that he might appear on Sharpton's syndicated radio program. Dietal says he advised Imus against it, saying that Sharpton would "use Imus to advance his own agenda."[6] Still, Imus insisted, relying on his own counsel and instincts to handle a complicated media and public relations situation. This would prove to be a critical mistake.

Imus apparently convinced himself that because he had had Sharpton on his program on many occasions, Sharpton would offer a safe environment as well as a credible presence in the minority community that would help the shock jock make amends with blacks and others who were offended by his comments. No such luck. Sharpton continued to call for Imus's firing right up until the broadcast and repeated the same message during a live radio program that was heavily covered by many media organizations that Sharpton gladly invited into the studio. A long-time media veteran, Al Sharpton saw the opportunity to make the most of Imus's weakened position.

Further, Sharpton's radio audience, mostly black and urban, participated in the broadcast through numerous live telephone calls blasting Don Imus, who was clearly unprepared for the onslaught. During the program's commercial breaks, Imus and Sharpton barely spoke and according to various firsthand press accounts, the tension in the studio was palpable.

Imus continually said during the program that he was "a good man who had done a bad thing." He should have stuck to that message. But he then responded to an angry black caller by saying: "I bet you I've slept in a house with more black children who were not related to me than you have." Even though his intent may not have been malicious, what followed would be his final undoing. When black Congresswoman Carolyn Cheeks Kilpatrick called into the show saying that she was appalled at his remarks, Imus responded by saying: "It's like the old country song, 'God may forgive you, but I won't. Jesus loves you but I don't.' So I can't get any place with you people, but I can get someplace with Jesus."

Sharpton had hooked his prey. "Who is 'you people,' Mr. Imus?" he asked. Imus responded, "You and this woman I'm talking to. Don't try to hang that on me. That's jive." Imus was burying himself with his own words.

In that very moment, you could sense that it was falling apart for Don Imus. In the course of apologizing for his initial comments, he compounded the problem by using the expression "you people" in front of the largely black audience of Al Sharpton's radio program. Regardless of his intent, for many this reinforced the belief that Don Imus was hopelessly out of touch on the issue of race and may in fact harbor racist feelings. The next day, April 11, the tabloids, cable news programs, as well as the Internet had a field day with the "you people" comment.

Imus was extremely frustrated with the treatment he got on Sharpton's radio show as well as the peppering he got from *Today Show's* Matt Lauer on April 9, 2007. Imus told Lauer that he was not willing to be "slapped around." Well, Mr. Imus, in a PR/media crisis like this, you don't get to set the parameters or boundaries as to what you will or won't take in terms of criticism. Imus's perception that he was somehow being abused or victimized in his apology tour made him a less sympathetic figure than he could have been. This is true especially because of who he is—a person who has dished out an odd brand of radio humor for thirty-five years—calling people names, cutting off their microphones, making derogatory references to people's race, gender, stature, and sexual orientation. It was time for Imus to take his medicine and he wasn't prepared (or willing) to do it.

Dissecting the Mess

Clearly, Imus did not realize the scope of his problem. Did he really think that no one would care about his racist remarks directed at a local amateur women's sports team? Did he think it would blow over? If he did, he miscalculated on many levels.

The most significant miscalculation was his timing. The incident occurred on April 4 and he didn't apologize on the air until April 6. What was going on in those forty-eight hours in Imus's head? How could he miss the opportunity to say he was wrong on April 5—or sooner? Yes, Imus did ultimately apologize several times, but for many it was too late.

According to Clem Price, director of the Institute on Ethnicity, Culture, and the Modern Experience at Rutgers University, Imus could have avoided much of this crisis if he had responded right away. "I think he would have fared better had he immediately apologized. Apology, within the context of race, gender, and sexuality, should be immediate and it should be sincere, and earnest." Further, when asked about Imus not apologizing directly to the Rutgers student athletes, but rather doing it via the Al Sharpton syndicated radio program, Dr. Price responded: "In retrospect it was a bad move. What might be at work here is the overindulgence in celebrity culture. The injured parties were those athletes and their coach and maybe the larger Rutgers community. Going on another guy's show to offer a 'hot-button apology' I think worked against Imus. It may have also worked against Al Sharpton."[7]

Imus also miscalculated the seriousness of the problem. As a powerful and successful media figure, he had been getting away with his brand of "humor" for so long that he probably believed that his comments about the basketball players were no big deal. When he called Gwen Ifill (a first-rate journalist who happens to be a black woman) a "cleaning lady," nothing terrible happened to him, although at the time he promised to never again engage in racial comedy. So much for promises. When he called NBC-4 sportscaster Lou Berman "Lenny the Jew," nothing happened, even though Berman, a respected New York broadcast veteran, refused to appear with Imus on the air. And again nothing happened to Imus when he told 60 *Minutes* producers that he had hired Bernard McGuirk to make "nigger jokes."

But this time, things would be different. CBS and MSNBC initially suspended Imus for two weeks. But after the Sharpton radio program and the continued onslaught of criticism from all circles, it was clear—with advertisers fleeing in droves—that Imus could not survive. Ultimately, he was fired on April 12, 2007. While more blacks than whites agreed with the dismissal, there was significant support in all communities for this action. According to the Pew Research Association, 54 percent of Americans approved of Imus's firing. (Imus would be back on the radio late in 2007 when WABC hired him and nationally syndicated his program.)

After his firing Don Imus sued CBS for $40 million, which he said was the amount they owed him on his contract. His position was that he was doing what he was paid to do—be edgy, controversial, and say provocative things. But if Imus was doing only what he was paid to do then why would he apologize for his "nappy-headed hos" comments in the first place?

Was Imus on some level treated unfairly by his employers who for years reaped the profits of his shock jock persona? Obviously. Imus will say that he was a victim and was wronged, but even Imus should know that race is still a volatile topic in the media. He had been around this media game long enough to know that if you live by the ratings and advertising sword, you can die by it as well.

Other Lame Apologies

Imus's "apology" was reminiscent of the on-air apology offered by comedian Michael Richards. His on-stage rant directed at two African American audience members was caught on a cell phone camera and played on the Internet and in turn countless media outlets for all to see and hear. The rant, according to an MSNBC account, proceeded thusly:

> As he was heckled by one or both of the black audience members, Richards screamed "Shut up! Fifty years ago we'd have you upside down with a [expletive] fork up your a—." He then paced across the stage taunting the men for interrupting his show, peppering his speech with racial slurs and profanities. "You can talk, you can talk, you're brave now [expletive]. Throw his a— out. He's a n———!" Richards shouts before repeating the racial epithet over and over again.[8]

Richards's friend and former *Seinfeld* castmate Jerry Seinfeld suggested that Richards go on the David Letterman *Late Night* show to apologize. It was a disaster. Richards, appearing on a monitor from Los Angeles, came off as nervous and uncomfortable. The people in the studio audience, as well as millions of viewers watching at home, weren't sure if the segment was meant to be serious or some sort of *Late Night* bit. With Seinfeld on the set, it caused many to recollect Richards as the goofball Kramer character that he played on the hit NBC series. Letterman also seemed uncomfortable as he tried to set the appropriate tone. As Richards apologized, the audience continued to laugh, and Seinfeld scolded them. Richards got more and more frustrated, and it showed. This was another apology gone bad.

One had to wonder why Michael Richards was apologizing to the viewing audience of a late-night talk show and not to the two African American audience members he insulted with his verbal tirade. His explanation that he didn't know who or where they were didn't ring true. His appearance on Letterman's show felt contrived and uncomfortable. When the audience didn't respond the way he had hoped, Richards became irritable and overreacted. This appearance and the media coverage of Richards's apology made the situation worse—similar to what happened when Don Imus appeared on Al Sharpton's radio program.

The celebrity ranks are littered with high-profile people such as Imus, Michael Richards, Mel Gibson, and Isaiah Washington of Grey's Anatomy whose careers are put in jeopardy by "getting caught" using off-the-cuff comments that are racially insensitive or, in the case of Washington, seen as "homophobic." In every one of these cases, the follow-up apology/response exacerbated the crisis and fanned the media flames. Obviously, there is a right and a wrong way to say "I'm sorry."

A Pound of Prevention

While these cases involve high-profile media and/or Hollywood celebrities, their experiences offer business leaders and other professionals several lessons in crisis communication. The first would be: Avoid the problem to begin with.

1. Assume anything you say (or write in an e-mail) has the potential to become public. In today's media/technology-dominated environment, you can't defend an insensitive or offending comment by claiming it was not intended for public consumption. Making that excuse is like saying that you're sorrier for getting caught than for what was actually said or for the person who was offended or hurt.

2. Refrain from using "humor" that is racially or sexually oriented. In our current social and cultural environment, this kind of humor is bound to offend someone within earshot of the "joke." The follow-up explanation or "apology" typically creates more problems and gives legs to the particular crisis.

3. If you are the leader of an organization, offer and promote useful and relevant cultural diversity training for all employees. While diversity is certainly a desired goal in any company or organization, it is important to acknowledge that diversity has the potential to produce internal—and in some cases very public—controversies. Having diversity training is not simply a question of being "politically correct" but rather being proactive in helping employees understand how something said—even in the spirit of humor or jest—can be perceived by some as hurtful and/or insensitive.

4. Have a written policy that bans the use of language offensive to any race, culture, or gender. While each case must be judged individually due to the subjective nature of an "offensive" remark, having a written policy in place is essential to protect you and your company or organization.

The Skill of Contrition

A crisis communication plan must include the specific action steps to be taken if such a racially, culturally, or sexually oriented controversy occurs. Such a plan must:

- include an immediate response and apology to those who may have been offended
- be genuine and be offered in person to the offended party
- come from the person or persons who engaged in such actions (regardless of their original motives or intent) as well as the organization itself
- be communicated to key audiences or parties who may have a particular interest or concern. This may include the media, but once you include them, the stakes become much higher.

If your apology, offered immediately and directed to the offended parties, is not accepted or received as you had hoped, resist the urge to qualify the apology, or to take back or fight back ("I can't get anywhere with you people!"). After you have made your effort to be sincere and direct, all you can do is to allow the court of public opinion and perception to run its course. In most cases, people will be willing to understand—if not totally forgive—and you will not be thrown out of a job as Don Imus was after his botched "apology" following the "nappy-headed hos" crisis.

Jon Corzine

GETTING IT RIGHT . . .

AND GETTING IT WRONG

> ### What were they thinking? ———
>
> **New Jersey Governor Jon Corzine was thinking that in one case involving his private life, he owed the public a direct and honest response, while in another, similar case he could claim "executive privilege" and refuse to respond to legitimate questions and inquiries.**

> ### The Lesson ———
>
> **Leaders need to address all crisis situations using a carefully prepared and practical communication plan that addresses not only the legal aspect of the case, but also the vital PR aspect that greatly influences public opinion.**

Sometimes a leader can handle a crisis in an extremely effective and strategic fashion yet struggle mightily to get a different—yet no less challenging—crisis right. Consider the case of New Jersey Governor Jon Corzine, a multimillionaire who spent well over $100 million of his own money getting elected first to the U.S. Senate in 2000 and then winning the governorship of New Jersey in the aftermath of the Jim McGreevey scandal in 2005.

Corzine had considerable experience in the corporate world dealing with high-pressure situations as co-chair of the investment firm Goldman Sachs. Yet, leading in the public arena is a very different game, played by a more convoluted and complex set of rules. In 2007 alone, Corzine faced two public-relations crises rooted in his personal life. In one, he gives us an example of a communication model we can admire and take as our own; in the other, he shows how easy it is to lose public support with a poor communication plan—even when you're in the right.

The Good

Following the April 12, 2007, car accident that nearly killed him, Corzine was smart, candid, and genuine. He owned his mistakes and his contribution to the accident. He said directly and without equivocation that he was distracted and not paying attention to the fact that the state trooper who was driving him was going more than thirty miles an hour above the speed limit. He also immediately made it clear that he was not wearing a seat belt. He never blamed others, not even the state trooper driving at the time of the accident.

Corzine screwed up big time, yet he handled it with class. He took a bad situation and made something positive come from it. He did a powerful public service announcement only a few weeks after the accident. Standing on crutches and appearing pale and frail, he looked directly into the camera and said, "I'm New Jersey Governor Jon Corzine and I should be dead." The PSA was produced by the National Highway Traffic Safety Administration and was taped on May 15 in the governor's mansion in Princeton. Corzine didn't have to do the PSA so soon after the accident. And he didn't have to be so candid about his own mistakes that caused him serious medical problems, putting him in intensive care on a ventilator for eights days with a broken leg, eleven broken ribs, a broken collarbone and sternum, a gash in his head, and the loss of more than half his blood.

In the PSA, Corzine said, "It took a remarkable team of doctors and a series of miracles to save my life when all I needed was a seat belt . . . I have to live with my mistake, you don't . . . buckle up." In the last few seconds of the ad, Corzine walked off on crutches. American Automobile Association spokesperson

David Weinstein called the spot "extraordinarily powerful . . . it will save lives."[1]

Unlike so many chief executives profiled in this book, Jon Corzine never pointed the finger at anyone else in connection with his April 12, 2007, accident. He alone took responsibility. He spoke for himself and ultimately paid his own considerable hospital bill, which totaled in the hundreds of thousands of dollars. He appeared on television in not the best physical condition. He took a dumb, life-endangering mistake and did something positive with it, and he succeeded. There is little doubt that thousands of drivers, including me, have become much more vigilant when it comes to buckling up and slowing down. Corzine's handling of his own personal health crisis surrounding his much publicized car accident was a classic case of how a leader should handle a crisis.

The Not So Good

The fact that Jon Corzine could give us such a fine example of quality public communication makes the mishandling of the controversy surrounding his relationship with Carla Katz even more perplexing.

This story begins back in 2005 when Corzine was running for governor. He was hit with a potential public relations nightmare when it was revealed that he had "loaned" Carla Katz nearly $500,000 to purchase a home in Hunterdon County. Katz and Corzine had had a romantic relationship from 2002 to 2004 and, as a private citizen with very deep pockets, Corzine had every right to later forgive the loan to Katz, who he felt had little ability to pay it back.

But when Corzine became governor, this private affair grabbed the public eye when it was revealed that Katz was a high-powered New Jersey public employee union leader who represented over 10,000 state workers in the Communication

Workers of America (CWA) Local 1034—a union that would be negotiating a multiyear contract with the state of New Jersey through the new governor. The media sensed a scandal.

Along with numerous political commentators and journalists, I asked then candidate Corzine in a public television interview about his financial relationship with Carla Katz. He politely but directly told me that it was a private matter and that he felt no compelling responsibility to discuss it. Later, it would be revealed that in addition to the $500,000 "gift" to Katz, Corzine allegedly gave his former girlfriend over $6 million in total, including a significant cash payment as well as allegedly financing her two children's private school education. That amazingly large number was supposedly reached in an agreement hammered out by lawyers for both Corzine and Katz. People began to wonder what Katz had on Corzine.

Corzine was able to hold his own during the controversy and was elected governor—and negotiated the union contract. In the eyes of many, including this writer, this new state contract with the CWA was a victory for the state of New Jersey. It offered a 13 percent increase over four years for state employees, but they would be required to pay for a portion of their own health benefits, otherwise known as "give backs." So it was fair to the union members, and frugal by any reasonable standard to the taxpayers of New Jersey. In fact, some in the CWA, including Katz, publicly criticized the deal and lobbied members to vote against it. That effort failed. Nothing about the final contract suggested that Corzine was in any way influenced by his previous relationship with Katz.

Still, despite this and despite the fact that Corzine began a new relationship with another woman, media interest and speculation regarding the nature and extent of the Corzine/Katz romantic and financial involvement was becoming intense. Publicly, Corzine said only positive things about Katz, but the controversy surrounding their private communication was about to make big news. In May 2007 rumors swirled around the state-house that Katz and Corzine had e-mailed each other while the CWA employee contract was being negotiated.

Then Republican State Chairman Tom Wilson, along with several news organizations, saw an opportunity to put Corzine and the Democrats on the defensive by calling for the Corzine/Katz e-mails to be made public based on the Open Public Records Act. Wilson's argument was that the public had a right to know if Carla Katz exerted any undue influence on New Jersey's governor during the contract negotiations. The irony was that many, including several Republican leaders and legislators, praised the final contract. This wouldn't deter the opportunistic and media-savvy Tom Wilson, who smelled a huge political and PR opportunity.

Corzine was being pushed to respond. He needed crisis communication strategy to help him present his side of the story and to gain public support for his refusal to make the e-mails public. He took a stand saying that he would not release the e-mails because at no time did the e-mails between him and Carla Katz address the negotiations going on between his representatives and those of the CWA. Corzine insisted that all serious negotiations regarding a state worker contract were done at the bargaining table, not in personal e-mails.

This approach may have worked if he were not blindsided by a legal brief filed by Katz that gave a different account of the story. Although Katz too argued against the release of private e-mails, according to news reports, this document "appeared to refute Corzine's claim that they did not hold serious discussions about the contract . . . Katz acknowledged that she had e-mailed Corzine directly with her concerns about the contract negotiations in what Corzine's ethics advisors called an 'end run' around the state's team of negotiators."[2]

In preparing his communication strategy, Governor Corzine had not considered this worst-case scenario. Numerous New Jersey media outlets, as well as the New York Times and tabloids such as the New York Daily News, the New York Post, and the Trentonian, had a field day with the implication that New Jersey's governor was lying. It was great media fodder. What was in those e-mails that Jon Corzine didn't want made public? Were Corzine and Katz still secretly romantically involved? Why exactly did the governor's lawyers allegedly negotiate a whopping $6 million settlement with a woman he was never married to or, as far as anyone knew, even engaged to? What did Carla Katz have on Jon Corzine?

Still, Corzine refused to release the e-mails, insisting that his private life and correspondence were not open to public scrutiny. There are cases in which a public figure has every legal right to protect his privacy and stand up against media intrusion. However, in that often unfair court of public opinion, his decision catapulted Corzine into a public relations battle that was impossible for him to win. By publicly fighting the e-mail issue, the governor made it a much bigger media story than it should have been, as well as a potential embarrassment that could have been avoided. Public opinion polls showed that while most voters cared little about the private and romantic history between Corzine and Katz, they were somewhat more curious and concerned about those e-mails.

That curiosity was further fueled on June 6, 2007, when a front-page New York Post story screamed out with the headline, "Katz Out of the Bag: Corzine's Ex Spilled the Beans." It was an explosive exclusive story written by gossip columnist Cindy Adams (arguably the most aggressive and obtrusive gossip columnists in the country) that included a large photo of Carla Katz on the front page along with a head shot of Governor Corzine. Under the caption, the story began with these words: "Carla Katz—the ravishing, raven-haired former lover of Governor Jon Corzine—dishes to The Post on the uber-power pair's passion, his marriage proposal, and what finally drove them apart."[3]

In the article, Carla Katz talked in intimate detail about her relationship with New Jersey's governor. Under a sub-headline entitled "Jon's ex tells all," Katz told Adams about a ring Jon Corzine had given her, adding: "I mean this man proposed to me." Katz also gave Cindy Adams a copy of a very private and personal handwritten note Jon Corzine had given to her on U.S. Senate stationary. In the letter, he called her a strong and remarkable woman.[4]

Now here's another twist that Corzine didn't see coming: This *New York Post* exclusive ran in the midst of an intense and protracted legal and PR battle in which both Corzine and Katz were arguing against the release of the e-mails. So . . . although Katz was contradicting Corzine's public statements regarding the content of those e-mails, she too was claiming in a court of law that the e-mails were private. Then she went to Cindy Adams of the *Post* with a "tell all" exclusive interview and released private letters from Corzine in an effort to prove how close they really were—while both of them were arguing in public and through the courts that their private life should be kept private. Perplexing is an understatement throughout.

The *New York Post* story fueled more media attention. It was clear that Corzine and Katz were not on the same page regarding this developing PR nightmare. To his credit, Corzine remained dignified and understated.

Although a state ethics panel ruled in favor of Governor Corzine on the e-mails, it came as little surprise when on August 3, 2007, Superior Judge Paul Innes declared that the ethics committee was not infallible. Judge Innes determined that Katz and Corzine had to produce the e-mails and related documents within thirty days, saying that New Jersey citizens had as much right to see those e-mails as the state ethics panel, who had read them and determined that they should be left private.

Republican State Chairman Tom Wilson embraced the Innes decision, saying, "We got everything we wanted at this proceeding." Wilson called the judges' ruling a victory for the people of New Jersey. "It's a victory for openness, transparency and accountability in government and its leaders."[5]

On the day of Judge Innes's ruling, the media confronted Corzine at a public event. Corzine stuck to his message and repeated that there had been no substantive discussion regarding the new state worker contract away from the bargaining table. When pressed about Carla Katz's legal brief stating that some e-mails she sent to the governor complained about the pace of negotiations and other issues, Corzine would say only: "There can be communication with no discussion."[6]

While I have great respect for Jon Corzine and have said that New Jersey is fortunate to have him as our chief executive, his stubbornly deaf response to the public on this issue is inexplicable.

On one level I genuinely appreciate and understand Corzine's position. His private life should be just that, private. I have written numerous columns and said many times on the air that his romantic life is no business of mine, nor of the people of New Jersey. However, sometimes things can and do get a bit fuzzy when talking about a private relationship that has the potential to impact directly on the public's business—and he should know that.

The Katz e-mail controversy and the pair's financial arrangements should never have received as much publicity as they did. What could Corzine have done? He could have volunteered the nature of the e-mails. In a May 2, 2007, column that I wrote entitled "Corzine Must Face the 'Katz Issue,'"[7] I wrote the following:

> To date, the governor has argued that his previous romantic relationship with Carla Katz is a personal matter. . . . During the 2005 campaign it was disclosed that Corzine had forgiven a loan of $470,000 to Katz, the value of a mortgage that enabled her to buy out her ex-husband of a Hunterdon County home.

Corzine won the election easily in spite of that controversy, but the issue has never gone away and Corzine has continued to be pretty tight-lipped about the Carla Katz issue. But now *The New York Times* has gotten involved and has blown the lid off this story, even though the U.S. Attorney's Office and a state ethics panel has said there were no ethical violations on the part of Governor Corzine or Carla Katz.

The *Times*' story is a powerful one. I am not convinced it would have ever gotten to this point if the governor had opted to proactively and voluntarily disclose all the relevant details himself including a series of e-mails between himself and Katz that apparently addressed contract talks between the state and the CWA.

The New Rules

I empathize with the governor's situation and his point of view, and I have no desire to have the details of any of his romantic relationships made public. I wouldn't want my own personal information, including any details about my first marriage, to be a matter of public discussion. Yet, the rules regarding what is now fair game for high-level elected officials have changed dramatically in this intensive media environment. Being right is not always a good enough reason to refuse to communicate.

From the experience of Jon Corzine, there is a set of lessons for all of us, not just governors of states, but any leader who struggles with finding the ever-shifting line between private life and public responsibilities.

1. Don't fight the disclosure of information if there is any possibility that you will ultimately have to disclose in the end. The longer you fight, the more it appears that you have something to hide, even if you don't.

2. When faced with potential scandal, it is important to seek the advice of an attorney. But never forget that pursuing a legal strategy is very different than pursuing a successful public relations strategy.

3. In a crisis, it is essential to anticipate that other key players in the case (for example, Carla Katz) may not share your stance, and choose to disclose information. This little detail has been the downfall of many public figures besides Corzine, including Ken Lay, Jayson Blair, Martha Stewart, and Alberto Gonzales. Do not assume those involved in the situation will cover for you—or even that they will stick to the truth.

4. Few of us will be in the governor's position of evoking "executive privilege" to avoid answering probing questions. However, those in positions of leadership do often feel that being a "higher-up" gives them privileges not accorded to the average person. That's a big mistake in any potentially scandalous situation. Doing this can come across as "Nixonesque" regardless of one's motives. Public opinion is generated from the person on the street, who is apt to mistrust anyone who thinks he or she is better than everyone else.

In summary: Don't assume you are a master crisis communicator just because you have masterfully handled problems in the past. Each new crisis demands a unique approach that carefully considers all new circumstances. Even the most thoughtful and strategic leaders, including people like Governor Jon Corzine, have shown that crisis communication is a skill that must be constantly honed and practiced.

Jet Blue Airways

A LATE-NIGHT DISASTER

> **What were they thinking?** —————
> CEO David Neeleman and his communication team were thinking that admitting responsibility in a forthright fashion for a major communication problem, and not taking further action, would be enough to gain forgiveness from their customers and the general public.

> **The Lesson** —————
> Taking responsibility is just the beginning.

Jet Blue CEO David Neeleman gets big points for stepping up and taking the heat when his airline made national headlines on February 14, 2007, for canceling 1,100 flights and stranding thousands of passengers in airports and on tarmacs across the country.

Yes, it was a blizzard. Runways were very icy and the skies above many cities possessed very tough flying conditions, but Jet Blue had operational and communication problems that went beyond that of their competitors. This is ironic because up until that point Jet Blue had been recognized for their superior customer service. But, image means so much. That's why the image of Jet Blue will be tarnished for a long time by intense and embarrassing media coverage of passengers stranded for up to eleven hours in planes stuck (for apparently no good reason) on the tarmac at JFK airport in New York.

"Trapped on the Tarmac" was the headline in *People* magazine, which featured powerful photos of passengers camped out on the floor at JFK. The article quoted passenger Chris Deloge; "Toward the seventh hour, people were yelling at the flight attendant, 'Why can't we get off this plane?'"[1] The attendant had no answer.

"Long Delays Hurt Image of Jet Blue" announced a headline in the *New York Times*. The story recounted once again how Jet Blue delays and its treatment of passengers was significantly worse than that of its competitors.[2]

A week after this Valentine's Day fiasco, media coverage was still negative. A New Jersey *Star-Ledger* headline on February 21 was the lead story on the front page: "Humbled Jet Blue Picks Itself Up Off the Tarmac: A Week after Its Meltdown in Ice Storm, It Initiates a Program of Guarantees." The article talked not only about a new "full refund policy" that Jet Blue would offer if a flight was canceled within twelve hours of a scheduled takeoff and a $25 voucher for a plane waiting more than five hours, but it also featured a recounting of David Neeleman's apologies.[3]

Many of Neeleman's apologetic words also appeared in full-page ads in publications across the country. "We are sorry and embarrassed, but most of all we are deeply sorry." Neeleman would also say: "We love our customers and we are horrified by this. There are going to be a lot of apologies." He also called Jet Blue's performance "unforgivable."[4]

Neeleman seemed to genuinely care about how poorly his airline performed in the bad weather. He showed empathy and compassion for the passengers who suffered—particularly those who sat on Jet Blue planes for between seven and eleven hours. He gets points for this. That is why within days Jet Blue took corrective steps to prevent such a disaster in the future. They developed a so-called Passengers Bill of Rights regarding refunds, vouchers, and guarantees—a good idea, but in crisis management that's a lot like the old saying about closing the barn door after the horses are stolen. It does nothing to help the problem at hand. Jet Blue's performance during this crisis and CEO Neeleman's subsequent appearance on *Late Night with David Letterman* was embarrassing and awkward at best. Clearly, the airline's inability to communicate with their passengers in the midst of the delays and then Neeleman's poor performance with Letterman demonstrates that having good intentions and a caring attitude takes you only so far when a true crisis hits.

Planning Ahead for the Worst

One of the biggest problems with the leadership at Jet Blue involved how poorly they communicated as the crisis was building. They seemed totally unprepared to communicate to passengers in a candid, direct, and timely fashion about how serious things had become. Further, it took Jet Blue representatives too long to communicate directly with the Port Authority, which runs JFK Airport, to let them know there was a serious problem. Increasingly frustrated, passengers could actually see the terminal a few hundred yards away as the hours dragged on without a reasonable explanation as to why they weren't moving. It appeared that Jet Blue was playing the odds. They seemed to be saying: "We've never had a delay of much more than an hour, so what are the odds we will have planes sitting on the tarmac for two, three, or even ten hours? Why develop a communication plan to deal with it?"

While we can appreciate Neeleman's candid comments after the fact about how poorly his airline performed, the truly great organizations go beyond apologetic words and actually plan for worst-case scenarios before they happen. Jet Blue didn't come close to doing that. As in so many other cases in this book, again we see that the "hoping for the best" strategy is potentially disastrous for both an organization and those it attempts to serve. Having a positive "we can handle anything" attitude is admirable, yet refusing or being unable to communicate in a direct, no-nonsense—and timely—fashion is unacceptable. Jet Blue learned the hard way that keeping their passengers in the dark about the nature of the delays and offering no information about the likely extent of the delays was simply wrong. Not allowing anxious Jet Blue passengers to make other arrangements to fly was selfish and short-sighted.

But that is the problem with the "wishful thinking" approach to dealing with a quickly expanding crisis. Rose-colored glasses are not what is needed in these situations; rather, you have to have clear 20–20 vision. You also have to be prepared for the tough questions that are likely to come after a crisis, and that's where David Neeleman was at his worst.

Here's What "Unprepared" Looks Like

The PR and communications people at Jet Blue decided it would be a smart move for Neeleman to appear on a recognized and popular national television program. But instead of going on a tough, hard-nosed news program like *60 Minutes*, Jet Blue opted to have Neeleman appear on *Late Night with David Letterman*. I'm sure they were hoping for the best—that David Letterman would give them a break because he was a comedian and late-night talk show host as opposed to being news talkers like Mike Wallace, Tim Russert, or Lou Dobbs. Well, they were wrong.

Neeleman was awkward and uncomfortable throughout. The audience was giggling in some parts and falling in the aisles bursting out laughing at others (and not necessarily at the right times or for the right reasons) as Neeleman tried to extricate himself from this mess, but he clearly lacked the skills and tools to do so. Letterman was having fun at Neeleman's expense.

Try to imagine this scene as you read these excerpts from the Neeleman interview, including Letterman's several attempts to allow Neeleman to explain the situation:[5]

Letterman: What went haywire here?

Neeleman: Well, it was an ice storm in New York, and you know, it wasn't forecasted. It was supposed to be, turn over to rain, and it never turned over to rain, and we were determined to get people where they were going, and it just didn't work out that way. And so we canceled 250 flights all at once, and we had a bunch of people that were scrambling to try and get the right people with the right planes. We had good systems, we had great people that were well-trained, but it just, we were overwhelmed by that, and it just had a cascading effect.

Letterman: And how was it, it seemed that Jet Blue suffered more greatly than did other airlines under the same circumstances. [Attempt #1]

Neeleman: Well, you know, they were . . . and I was in the command center, and I was there and I watched this thing unfold, and didn't sleep for three days, and it was the most frustrating and most unbelievably difficult time of my life, because it was just a few things went wrong, and if it, it's like, the pieces all break, and then it's very complex to put it back together again. . . .

Letterman: But other airlines must also have canceled flights during that period, right? [Attempt #2]

Neeleman: Yeah, they did, and they were, they canceled on two, it was a two-day event for them for the most part, and ours went on for many days after that.

Letterman: And why was it that your airline suffered, where these other ones suffered, but not as much? [Attempt #3]

Neeleman: You know, there's a lot of reasons, but I think when you get the crews and planes out of position, and you know, it's really hard to rebuild it when you get past a certain point. And, you know, the good news is that we have great people at Jet Blue, we have a brand, people love flying us, and we know when it went wrong, and it's a relatively easy fix, and we've implemented things even today and tomorrow, that if this happened again, we'd be much better off. We've learned a huge lesson from this, and you know, maybe, we went through it, we didn't have to go through it, but we've learned some really important lessons.

Letterman: Let me try to ask you this one more time. [Letterman's fourth attempt as the audience laughs.] With all of the negative publicity and press about the storm and the traffic snarls and delays, it seems like Jet Blue suffered more than did [audience laughs] like any other carrier coming in and out of Kennedy. Were they handling, these other airlines handling the situation better? Was there something specific to your organization that made you more vulnerable? What was the deal there?

Neeleman: Yeah, it was, we had 250 flights, we had 1,100 crew members that had to be rematched up with those flights, and we didn't have, it just took us longer to do it. And it's something that's solvable, it wasn't that difficult, it was something that went wrong, and we know what the problem was, and we're fixing it. And I know it seems inconceivable but these are, in the airline business you have duty day, and you have crews and they're in fifty different cities, and there's fifty different planes, and you know, there's a huge communication challenge, and you know, it was, it's really, really difficult, because you can only work so many hours in the day and just putting it back together again, it proved a challenge and, we got it pretty well back together again on day two.

Letterman: They say . . .

Neeleman: We did, we did get it back together again, but we were overwhelmed at that point in time, so . . .

Letterman: They say that other airlines may have had partner relationships with other airlines. Would that have been an advantage for you?

Neeleman: Not necessarily, because other airlines canceled for two days. I mean I read somewhere, for example, Southwest had a thousand cancellations, and we had eleven, so they don't interline with other airlines. It was a holiday weekend, everyone was full, just a really bad time . . .

Letterman: But your airline must have been through bad weather before at Kennedy, right?

Neeleman: Yes, absolutely. And it absolutely has, and it will continue to be so, because you know, the shame of this event wasn't that, you know, we have weather, [the audience is going wild at this point] because we always have weather, it was the fact that it went on for, for more than one day.

So again, we know what the exact problem was, and we know what it was, and there's a solution . . .

Then, later in the interview . . .

Letterman: When those people are out there [on the tarmac], who's responsible for them? Is it still your responsibility, or is it the Port Authority's responsibility, the FAA's responsibility?

Neeleman: No, it's our responsibility, and you know . . .

Letterman: Were you getting reports from the various stranded aircrafts, we're doing fine, we're not doing fine, you better come get us, what was that communication?

Neeleman: I was actually getting e-mails from people, and we were sending people out and you know, we messed up and we made a mistake.

That's right. Jet Blue is responsible, and again, it is nice that David Neeleman acknowledges that. The problem is that his rambling, scattered, and frankly confounding explanations; ("because we always have weather . . .") just don't help his airline's situation or reputation. If you are going to take responsibility for what went wrong, just do it. But don't stop there. After the "we're sorry" response, you have to be prepared for what's bound to come next.

There Are No Do-Overs, So Be Ready in Advance

So what should David Neeleman have done? He took responsibility without trying to pass the buck. He apologized profusely through various media outlets. He appeared genuinely contrite and humbled. He took steps to prevent the problem in the future by supporting the implementation of the Passenger Bill of Rights. And he appeared on national television to put a face on the apology. Enough? No.

Neeleman should have gathered his top communication and PR advisors in a room and said, "Okay, what are the three or four most difficult and challenging questions the public and Letterman are likely to ask?" Then his communications team should have brainstormed responses to these questions while transitioning or bridging back to Jet Blue's main message.

The biggest lesson here is that you should never go before any form of media (and I'm not talking only about shows such as 60 Minutes) without being prepared for the most challenging questions that you may be asked.

Certainly, the communications and PR people could have predicted that Neeleman would be asked questions such as: "Why did Jet Blue have problems that other airlines didn't? Why did it take you so long to respond? How can you ensure it isn't going to happen again?" So why wasn't he prepared to answer them?

Clearly, Neeleman and his team didn't fully prepare for the interview. Neeleman appeared to be answering the questions for the first time on national television with a smart, funny, and sometimes cynical David Letterman, whose audience was in the mood for laughs and Jet Blue and David Neeleman provided the material without realizing that he was the butt of the joke.

So what was Jet Blue thinking when they decided Neeleman should appear in front of a live audience with a sarcastic and brutally funny David Letterman with no ammunition, no message, no direction, no focus? They were probably thinking: "David Letterman is a fun guy. He is not a serious journalist. He is not going to ask any tough questions. Our boss will go on and have a few laughs with Dave. Neeleman will come across as a really likeable guy who's very sorry and we'll all be able to get past this whole thing." Wrong. Wishful thinking is no strategy at all—it's just wishful thinking. Neeleman and Jet Blue paid the price for counting on it.

The fact that Neeleman seemed like a nice guy and felt bad for what happened to passengers wasn't nearly enough to get through this situation. He needed credible and concise answers.

I'm sure Neeleman realized within a few minutes with Letterman that he was playing in Yankee Stadium on opening day without ever having gone to spring training or ever playing in the minor leagues.

Prepare Yourself

My long-time colleague and friend Dr. Patricia Kuchon is professor of communications at Seton Hall University who has coached many clients through a variety of crises. When we talked about this particular case, she had some insights that you might find helpful. Talking about the TV interview, she said: "When Letterman asked Neeleman directly 'What happened?' rather than following the same rules of crisis management that he had used earlier with the press, the CEO used generalities and focused on the weather as the culprit. . . . Neeleman never did use the opportunity to be direct and honest . . . rather, he made the mistake of using 'spin' to address the crisis. Spin doesn't work in a crisis. People see right through it."

Dr. Kuchon continued, saying, "Neeleman was the right man in the right place with the wrong message." To avoid a similar media meltdown, Kuchon offers the following advice for other CEOs. When a crisis occurs, a CEO must:

- Know all the facts
- Have a plan of action to address the crisis or emergency
- Take responsibility
- Act quickly
- Tell the truth
- Rehearse answers to tough questions

Let's keep our focus on that last point. It's important to rehearse answers to tough questions. Communications consultant Don Teff recommends the $Q = a + 1$ approach. This simply means that a tough question (Q) should be responded to with a brief answer (a) of twenty seconds or less, then bridge (+) to your main message (1). This proactive approach increases the odds that a leader under fire controls and limits his communication to the most effective and concise responses.

This strategy would have assured that the Jet Blue message would have been communicated regardless of what David Letterman or any media interviewer asked. In response to the obvious question (Q), "Why did Jet Blue have problems that other airlines didn't?" Neeleman might have said: (a) "We made mistakes that the other airlines didn't. (1) I take full responsibility. On behalf of everyone at Jet Blue I apologize for the long delays experienced by our customers. It won't happen again, I promise."

This is the kind of proactive and smart communication approach that is essential in a crisis or in any challenging situation. Yet, this will happen only if the CEO or spokesperson practices with a communication team, answering the tough questions (preferably on videotape). Then, he or she needs direct and candid feedback on what worked and what didn't. This question/answer/evaluate process should be repeated as often as necessary. Responding in a concise fashion in twenty seconds or less doesn't just happen—it takes practice and a commitment to improve where you are weak.

David Neeleman was no Lawrence Rawl of Exxon, in Valdez, Alaska, who continues to be the poster child for CEOs who run scared and duck for cover when the proverbial crap hits the fan. But Rawls and Exxon are not the low standard that organizations and CEOs should measure themselves against. They were simply the worst, and doing better than Rawls and Exxon isn't nearly enough. Jet Blue and Neeleman should have known that. What were they thinking?

The O'Reilly "Factor"

KNOWING WHEN TO SHUT UP

What were they thinking?

Bill O'Reilly and the lawyers for FOX News were thinking that "winning" in a court of law would not be worth it if their reputation took a sustained and embarrassing hit and if future earning power was diminished in the court of public opinion.

The Lesson

They were absolutely right. Winning the battle in court is sometimes not worth losing the war in the public arena.

When FOX News producer Andrea Mackris accused the network's superstar Bill O'Reilly of sexual harassment and demanded $60 million from O'Reilly and FOX, all hell broke loose. O'Reilly, a tenacious brawler on the air, went on the offense; he said he would fight the charges to protect his reputation, credibility, FOX, and his family. In fact, within just a few hours of the story's breaking on October 13, 2004, O'Reilly (who had a long history of bloviating on issues of morality and what he perceived to be appropriate and inappropriate conduct of others) filed a countersuit against Mackris and her attorney saying that she was intentionally and falsely trying to destroy his career and hurt FOX News, the most popular cable news operation on television.[1]

It wasn't long before he changed his mind.

O'Reilly on the Offensive

Bill O'Reilly is no fool. He knew that fighting Mackris's charges would put a public spotlight on these very sensitive and embarrassing accusations, and that he could be irrevocably hurt in the court of public opinion. Originally he said that he didn't care. In his own words: "I knew I was going to get vilified and vile stuff was going to be put out there. . . . It's very embarrassing to have this stuff out there. Any human being would be depressed to see this. . . . This is the worst day of my life. . . . I have to protect the people closest to me. If I have to suffer, that's the way it has to be."[2]

So, while fully aware that this was going to get dirty, and with his reputation and his considerable ego on the line, O'Reilly came out of the gate in full stride, using his top-rated prime-time cable news program as a powerful platform to deny all charges against him. On the night of October 13, 2004, he opened *The O'Reilly Factor* program on FOX News this way:

Hi, I'm Bill O'Reilly . . . thanks for watching us tonight . . . we are living in treacherous times. That's the subject of this evening's "Talking Points Memo." Just about every famous person I know has been threatened and worked over by somebody. Fame makes you a target. It is something that has to be taken seriously. As I've mentioned before, I have received many threats over the years . . . everything from death letters to some guy running around the country offering people $25,000 to sign affidavits accusing me of whatever. The lawyers here at FOX News have been dealing with these situations . . . but there comes a time when enough is enough . . . and so this morning I had to file a lawsuit against some people who are demanding $60 million or they will "punish" me and FOX News . . . $60 million. I really can't say anything else. I don't want to waste your time with this. The justice system has the case. We'll see what happens. But in the end, this is all about hurting me and the FOX News Channel. And that's the memo.[3]

So there it was. O'Reilly's initial reaction was to paint himself as a victim of someone who just wanted to hurt him and to say that he would fight back with his lawyers through the judicial system. As always, he was combative and seemed more than ready to go to war and take on what he claimed were false charges.

A few days later there was a change in his "victim" status, but the forward offense was still a go. On *The Radio Factor with Bill O'Reilly*, O'Reilly's popular radio program with millions of listeners, the controversial commentator attempted to explain why he filed the countersuit against Mackris and her lawyer Benedict Morelli: "This is my fault. I was stupid, and I'm not a victim, but I can't allow certain things to happen. . . . I am stupid, I am a stupid guy, and every guy listening knows how that is—that we are very stupid at times, but there comes a time in life where you got to stand and fight and I knew these people were going to do this, I knew they were going to do everything they could to try to destroy me and the channel and I just made a decision that I'm just going to ride it out, and I'm going to fight them."[4]

O'Reilly and his lawyers called the suit against him and his bosses at FOX News a multimillion-dollar shakedown. In the countersuit, the complaint stated: "Defendants have not acted in good faith. Instead, they have sought to extort 'blood money' by threatening to destroy O'Reilly, his family and his career, and to embarrass and severely injure Fox's reputation and financial interests."[5]

The battle lines were clearly drawn for what looked like an ugly, nasty, and personal battle. In some cases, a battle is justified—and necessary. But according to Mark Fabiani, a crisis management consultant who worked in the Clinton White House (where crisis management problems kept him quite busy): "When you draw that first line, it better be a line that's going to hold. If it doesn't, you're often in a worse position than you would be if you said nothing. . . . It happened in the Monica Lewinsky situation, when President Clinton denied having 'sexual relations with that woman,' which is the statement that everyone remembers to this day."[6]

O'Reilly drew a line that he would later find was not worth what he would lose in defending it.

Mackris Fights Back

Andrea Mackris and her attorney Ben Morelli were just as aggressive in using the public airwaves to attack Bill O'Reilly and FOX News. Within a couple of days of the story's becoming public, Mackris appeared in live as well as taped interviews on the *Today Show, Good Morning, America,* and countless other network and cable programs.

The story was picking up steam in the media as well as the larger public arena, including in the blogosphere. The popular Web site, TheSmokingGun.com, along with various Internet-based sites, took the most embarrassing and salacious excerpts and tidbits from the twenty-two-page legal brief that was filed in the case, noting: "While we suggest reading the entire document, TSG [The Smoking Gun] will point you to interesting sections on his [O'Reilly's] Caribbean shower fantasies with a loofah, a Thailand sex show, Al Franken, and the climax of one August 2004 phone conversation."[7]

The case document itself did provide titillating reading and appeared to paint O'Reilly as the sexual oddball Mackris claimed he was. In her suit against O'Reilly and FOX, Mackris said that she had numerous phone conversations with her boss. She recounted that he spoke often, and explicitly, to her about phone sex, vibrators, threesomes, masturbation, the loss of his virginity, and sexual fantasies.[8] She also claimed that after interviewing two porn stars on *The O'Reilly Factor,* O'Reilly went into a "vile and degrading monologue" in front of her.[9]

Mackris also alleged in the suit that after she told O'Reilly during a phone conversation that she knew he had these kinds of conversations with other staffers as well and that he should be careful, he replied:

If any woman ever breathed a word I'll make her pay so dearly that she'll wish she'd never been born. I'll rake her through the mud, bring up things in her life and make her so miserable that she'll be destroyed. And besides, she wouldn't be able to afford the lawyers I can or endure it financially as long as I can. And nobody would believe her, it'd be her word against mine and who are they going to believe? Me or some unstable woman making outrageous accusations? They'd see her as some psycho, someone unstable. Besides, I'd never make the mistake of picking unstable crazy girls like that.[10]

"The details of Ms. Mackris's complaints are grisly," said the *New York Observer*, "and involve late-night dinners, dirty conversations and an electronic apparatus that no boss should ever recommend to an employee as office equipment." In addition, Mackris complained in her suit that beginning in 2002 O'Reilly had bothered her both in person and on the phone with graphic sex talk, and continued to do so until she left the FOX News Network in September 2004. She also alleged in the brief that O'Reilly forced her to have phone sex with him on three occasions and that he made repeated sexual advances.[11]

And the Media Gets a Gift

With Mackris and her aggressive, media-savvy attorney Benedict Morelli throwing down the gauntlet and O'Reilly and his legal team answering in kind, the mainstream media as well as the tabloids and the Internet jumped on the story in a big way.

"We're all over this story," said Bonnie Fuller, editorial director of American Media, which publishes tabloids including *Star* and *The National Enquirer*. "This is not going to go away."[12] According to Peter Johnson of *USA Today*, "For many media outlets, the scandal involving Fox News star Bill O'Reilly is a story that has an endless number of angles to pursue: unknown single woman, famous married man, money, sex, power and morality."[13]

Johnson was right. The O'Reilly/Mackris story had it all. It was the perfect storm for a scandal involving one of the media's most outspoken, conservative talk show hosts who always seemed to have something to say about other people's behavior—including former President Bill Clinton, whom O'Reilly blasted during the Monica Lewinksy scandal. It was within this firestorm of attention that it soon became clear to O'Reilly that his initial plan to take a very vocal stand and fight to defend himself through the judicial process was a strategy wrought with countless pitfalls and serious danger.

When blindsided by a legal suit based on allegations of misconduct that is sexual, racial, or ethical in nature, and that is likely to grab headlines for its sensational interest, anyone in a notable position should think twice, three times, and then once more about taking such a personal crisis into a court of law, where virtually all evidence becomes part of the public arena.

Bill Backs Down

I'm sure on some level O'Reilly really wanted to continue the fight. I've appeared on O'Reilly's program on several occasions and I can attest to his love of hand-to-hand, no-holds-barred verbal combat. But we can assume that it didn't take long for him and his lawyers to suspect that Mackris was smart, savvy, and shrewd enough to have taped the alleged phone conversations. If Mackris had tapes supposedly of O'Reilly talking about vibrators and loofahs and God knows what else, what would happen if those tapes became public? How would O'Reilly explain them? Would he say it wasn't him? Would he say it was someone else's voice made out to sound like him? Would he say that he was taken out of context (a common defense)? And would he continue to try to paint himself as a victim of an angry former producer looking to extort money from him and FOX News just because of who he was and how deep their pockets were?

No matter what he said, and no matter how much O'Reilly saw himself as a fighter, this was no longer a fight he could win in the public arena. The media was not going to let go of the scandalous and embarrassingly lewd and inappropriate comments attributed to O'Reilly. He was indeed a prominent American media icon fighting for his public life in an arena known for character assassination.

In addition to his TV and radio persona as a "culture warrior," O'Reilly had also just published a children's book—much of which focused on when it was and was not appropriate to engage in sexual activities. O'Reilly had way too much to lose.

And he was not the only one whose life would be microscopically analyzed if he continued to fight. Not only was Mackris suing O'Reilly, she was also going after FOX News, the massive cable news operation owned by Rupert Murdoch, which she said allowed O'Reilly to treat her in a degrading and hostile fashion.

No one knows for sure, but it is a safe bet that O'Reilly's lawyers as well as his bosses at FOX News sat him down and said enough is enough. I'm sure they didn't care what O'Reilly did on his personal time or in his personal life, but now his alleged behavior was having a negative impact on their bottom line. Clearly they must have told O'Reilly that it was important to get this behind him and FOX News as quickly as possible and that the only way to do this was to settle this case out of court—to pay Andrea Mackris many millions of dollars to ensure her silence and hold back the tide of this media tsunami building against Bill O'Reilly.

No matter what O'Reilly would say later about this incident, he and his bosses at FOX News did the smart and pragmatic thing. They paid up. Some estimate that they probably paid as much as $10 million to Mackris. If that's the case, it is fair to say they got a bargain, because soon after the settlement was reached, somehow, miraculously, all the degrading, disgusting, and clearly inappropriate comments that Bill O'Reilly was alleged to have made to his young producer lost their power to hurt him. Once the out-of-court agreement was settled, O'Reilly acknowledged it on the air saying: "I will never speak of it again,"[14] and he didn't. And amazingly, few others did either.

Even though O'Reilly had then and still now has enemies who would do anything to take him down, this scandal fell out of the spotlight and it seemed the public lost interest. But that's the way scandals work. If you can get it behind you quickly, before the negative and embarrassing picture is burned into people's psyche, you have a chance of surviving and moving on. You see, in the media-dominated, Internet-driven, 24/7 environment of "infotainment" there is always a new scandal to capture our attention. There is always a Britney Spears, or Paris Hilton, or Lindsay Lohan, or Michael Richards, or Mel Gibson—and the list goes on—who will jump in to redirect the public's attention. O'Reilly's lawyers and the media-savvy bosses at FOX must have known that if they could settle this case and shut up O'Reilly, this crisis would peter out on its own, leaving only a dim memory of "something about harassment" in O'Reilly's past.

So at the end of 2007, as this book goes to print, it's fair to say that as crisis communication goes, Bill O'Reilly and the people who run FOX News handled this one pretty well. They got it right. Not because they handled it perfectly, but because it could have been so much worse. If O'Reilly had resisted efforts to settle this case out of court and instead became embroiled in a court case like the one surrounding the MSG/New York Knicks/Isiah Thomas sexual harassment case—one in which friends, colleagues, and family are called to publicly testify regarding a gazillion details of the defendant's sexual history, practices, attitudes, and behavior, and then those details are used to satiate the feeding frenzy of the national media—I'm convinced that there is little chance he'd be on the air today. If he had chosen to take Andrea Mackris's sexual harassment case to court, the impact would have been devastating, and Bill O'Reilly would probably never have recovered.

But he didn't make that fatal mistake. And so today, not only is he still on the air, but his program is number one in the ratings, and he is still a dominant figure in the media landscape who has the ability to influence millions on a nightly basis. Like him or not, in this crisis, Bill O'Reilly won by shutting up.

Taco Bell's *E. Coli* Scare

WHEN GOOD INTENTIONS
AREN'T ENOUGH

> ### What were they thinking? _____
> Understandably, Taco Bell executives were thinking that when a crisis strikes that shakes consumer confidence, it is more important to be fast than to be 100 percent accurate.

> ### The Lesson _____
> When a crisis hits, respond immediately and as accurately as possible with a prepared statement that acknowledges your concern along with the honest admission that you do not yet have enough facts to fully respond, but will disclose all relevant information as quickly as possible.

When your crisis becomes a punch-line for late-night talk show monologues, you know you have a serious public relations problem on your hands. Consider the case of Taco Bell and the E. coli outbreak that caused seventy-one people to get sick in five states in late 2006. In December, David Letterman delivered these jokes on his show: "You folks been to Taco Bell lately? They have a wonderful new menu item; it's the 'Taco Apocalypto.' But you know, Taco Bell's slogan for a long, long time was 'Think outside the bun.' They have changed the slogan now, [it's]: 'Look outside for the ambulance.'"[1]

Not to be outdone, Jay Leno's Taco Bell material took on a similar tone: "Taco Bell has had to close several restaurants," Leno quipped, "because an outbreak of E. coli has made customers sick. As a result, Taco Bell is changing their slogan from 'Think outside the bun' to 'Puke outside the store.'"[2]

This was a crisis in need of an immediate damage-control response. Unfortunately, the response was a bit too immediate.

Don't Eat the Onions!

Although Taco Bell executives weren't sure exactly what was causing the E. coli outbreak, as soon as they were alerted that people were getting sick after eating in their restaurants, they acted and spoke out quickly. When the first incident happened on November 30, 2006, in a Taco Bell restaurant in New Jersey, company officials closed the location and worked aggressively with local health officials to figure out what was causing people to become violently ill. Taco Bell clearly wanted to demonstrate their commitment and ability to identify the problem—so much so that in their haste they incorrectly blamed "green onions" for the problem, when in fact it was later learned that Taco Bell's E. coli outbreak was caused by lettuce grown in California.

As is often the case in a crisis or scandal, timing matters a lot. The Taco Bell incident took place on the heels of a national E. coli/spinach scare in the fall of 2006. In that case two elderly women in Wisconsin and Nebraska as well as a small child in Idaho died. The public was already afraid. They were aware that this E. coli "thing" was out there. But what exactly was it? Where was it? What food was safe and what wasn't?

According to Gene Grabowski, a public relations and communication executive based in Washington who formerly served as vice president of communications and marketing for the Grocery Manufacturers of America: "There are so many food safety issues now that it is safe to say that this [the E. coli outbreak] is one big running story. We can measure and detect all kinds of food safety issues that we couldn't 30 years ago, and with the greater ability to measure, the more things we're going to find."[3]

So, when the Taco Bell incidents in New Jersey occurred, the media was all over them because the E. coli outbreak angle was already firmly set in the public's mind. Consumers knew that there was something seriously wrong with certain green vegetables and, according to Grabowski, the extensive nature of 24/7 nonstop media coverage made dealing with this crisis that much more difficult and complex: "Consumers who are frightened that their families may be at risk are not open-minded. They want quick solutions. The second problem is journalism: There is a premium on news that is alarming, entertaining and exciting and not a premium on stories that are reflective and put things in perspective. The true weighing of facts is drowned out by stories that emphasize risk."[4]

Grabowski has it exactly right. Today's mainstream media, which go well beyond the print tabloids or the television magazine programs popular in the 1990s like *Inside Edition* or *A Current Affair*, are obsessed with scaring the hell out of people. Fear makes for great television and sells a lot of newspapers.

Add to that the fact that instantaneous reporting on the Internet, with its catchy headlines, digital video, and almost instantaneous spreading has made crisis communication extremely problematic and challenging. It is not an impossible job, but it can't be compared to crisis communication of even the 1980s or early 1990s. The media/information environment is different and requires a very different skill set as well as a corporate and organizational mindset to respond appropriately, if that organization hopes to have any chance of surviving.

The Good

To Taco Bell's credit, company officials understood how important it was to have their president, Greg Creed, out front from the beginning. They also spent millions of dollars on an aggressive series of print and electronic ads attempting to reassure jittery consumers by letting them know that Taco Bell was being proactive in finding the cause of the outbreak and ultimately dealing with it.

According to Taco Bell public relations director Rob Poetsch, "Our approach in this entire situation has been to respond as quickly as we can and provide information to our customers and media as quickly as it becomes available."[5]

As for Taco Bell's overall crisis communication strategy, it is very clear that they used Johnson & Johnson's Tylenol model from 1982 in establishing the guiding principals of their actions. In Taco Bell's case, this meant that as soon as they got information, they disclosed it to key audiences, in this case customers and the media. It was essential that they worked closely with government and regulatory authorities to figure out how best to handle this potential public health crisis.

Further, by putting their president out there immediately, they were attempting to emulate what Johnson & Johnson did with their CEO, James Burke, who was the most visible and consistent presence on behalf of the company, as opposed to using public relations assistants or subordinates.

Taco Bell did an adequate job in communicating during the two weeks of intense media coverage around their E. coli scare. In fact, Peter Morrissey, a professor of communication at Boston University (who formerly worked on J&J's crisis communication team), praised Taco Bell's efforts by again comparing them to Johnson & Johnson. "Both [cases] are about credibility, trust and leadership, and those absolutely apply today as much as they did then," he said. "Technology has changed, and the means of communication is faster, but you still have to show leadership and decisiveness and do the right thing quickly—regardless of the consequences."[6]

Of course the real-time, international and national media coverage that accompanies such a crisis today requires a more comprehensive response than the communication experts at Johnson & Johnson needed almost twenty years ago after the Tylenol scare. But in any age, responding quickly and yet accurately to a crisis is a factor that must be included in a crisis communication plan.

The Bad

Within days of the November 30, 2006, New Jersey Taco Bell incident, Poetsch acknowledged that onions were not in fact the cause of the E. coli problem. He noted that this incorrect information was based on "preliminary testing" done without having conclusive evidence.[7]

Further, Poetsch later said that it was Taco Bell's concern over customer health and safety that drove the green onion statements: "We didn't want to risk anyone else becoming ill. Imagine if we had that information and waited four or five days and the test results confirmed it and we hadn't taken action? All the action we took was clearly customer-centric and focused on food safety. That was the driving force behind all our decisions and communications."[8]

Interestingly, Poetsch and his colleagues at Taco Bell seemed to be saying that in some cases it is better to be fast than to be accurate—that it is more essential to demonstrate action than to be cautious and thorough, even if the information you put out there distorts reality. Let's face it, when it comes to certain crises, you are, in some ways, damned if you do and damned if you don't.

The quandary of course is that if you wait too long to respond, you create an entire set of difficult communication problems with those who will feel the lack of response is a sign of arrogant detachment. But if you respond too quickly and say something that turns out to be untrue, that's a whole other set of problems that will hurt your credibility.

The Fix

Technology, along with the new post-9/11 mentality that reminds us how vulnerable we all are, adds an additional degree of challenge to handling this type of crisis that causes confusion and anxiety among the general public. To successfully meet the goal of restoring consumer/client confidence and trust, business leaders must be fully prepared to immediately deal with a worst-case scenario—even when they don't know what to say.

According to Professor Morrissey: "We are in a period of higher uncertainty, so today when something like this happens, you need decisive leadership. You need a plan in place if anything should happen and work through the details of how you're going to respond because otherwise, in the line of fire, you're not going to respond in a reasonable, intelligent way. Today, things happen too quickly to allow time for a forensic review of the facts before responding."[9]

So what's your plan if a crisis hits and you need to face your stakeholders and/or the media with scant information? Many will demand "the facts." Yet these so-called facts or at least the pieces of information that you possess are sometimes incomplete, incorrect, and very fluid.

One important lesson to remember is that the information you have will rarely if ever be totally complete. Of course it depends on the nature of the information in question and the situation you face, but you must always be cautious about releasing unconfirmed information as if it were fact, while at the same time you should avoid shutting down completely or delaying your public communication until you are 100 percent sure of the facts. A delicate balance must be struck between being able to respond, while trying to be as accurate as possible.

To do this effectively in the early hours of a crisis, you should quickly and directly face your stakeholders and the media—never hide. But until you have confirmed facts, face the public with confidence, saying something like the following over and over again until the facts are all in:

"The preliminary information we have at this time, tells us . . ."

"We don't have enough information at this time to make a statement, but when we get that information we will make an official announcement."

"This is what we know right now, but the situation is fluid and the information may change."

Period. If you don't know the answer to a particular question or don't have the information at hand, then say so. Don't fudge. Don't feel compelled to predict or to respond to hypothetical questions. Sometimes less information is best. But under no circumstances should you respond by saying "No comment."

The *New York Times*

COVERING UP FOR JAYSON BLAIR

What were they thinking?

When it was discovered that a reporter had routinely made up facts and plagiarized articles, the top editors and executives at the *New York Times* were thinking they could deny, cover up, and escape responsibility and blame.

The Lesson

When a scandal hits (particularly when it's self-inflicted), the goal should be to minimize the damage—not to escape it. Apologize, take full responsibility, and communicate whatever actions you will take to make sure such things won't happen again.

Throughout its 154-year history, the *New York Times* has employed some of the most talented reporters and editors in the field and has had its pick of young wannabe journalists with the most impressive credentials. As one reporter has noted: "There is no tougher job to get in the world of journalism than a writing gig at the New York Times. Tens of thousands of hot-shot reporters around the country dream of working at the Grey Lady, without ever getting so much as an interview."[1] Certainly, the Times is still considered the place to work in the world of print journalism.

Yet, in 1999 the *New York Times* top editorial executives decided that Jayson Blair—a young African American intern with a seriously spotty track record at best, with very limited journalistic experience—should be hired and put on the fast track to reporting stardom. The Times was looking to diversify its newsroom and, like most established media organizations, was playing catchup, since most of its reporters were white men. The paper had a very small number of African American reporters and embarked on an aggressive affirmative action program. With this laudable intent, the top editors and execs at this bastion of journalistic integrity found themselves facing an international communication crisis.

Jayson Blair Fiasco

Jayson Blair was an unqualified beneficiary of this corporate initiative to diversify. When the *New York Times* hired Blair as an intern in 1998 he already had a history of problems during his brief journalistic career as an intern at the *Centreville Times,* where he "was typically unreliable, disappeared at crucial times and missed deadlines."[2]

As an intern at the *Times,* Blair's performance was not impressive. He racked up a series of lapses that created an obvious credibility gap. Yet his mentors, including executive editor Howell Raines and managing editor Gerald Boyd, decided to promote him from intern to reporter and then to full-time reporter. He then became a national reporter and finally landed a prestigious assignment on what was called the "D.C. Sniper Team," leading a group of colleagues to investigate and report on the highly publicized series of shootings in the D.C. area. In a front-page *New York Times* exclusive, Blair reported that when suspect John Muhammad was about to confess, the U.S. attorney forced an end to the interrogation. Blair attributed the information to five unnamed law enforcement sources, whom his editors never asked him to identify. The story drew immediate criticism from federal officials who claimed the information was blatantly wrong. The *Times* would eventually admit that the report was "flawed."[3]

Despite Blair's consistent pattern of shoddy reporting, highly questionable research efforts, and consistent faking of his stories, his preferential treatment continued for several years. Even though he was using a credit card of one of his superiors while supposedly on assignment, Blair submitted few receipts for air and car travel, hotel rooms, or anything connected with a five-month, twenty-city reporting stretch. Blair was slapped on the wrist a couple of times by his bosses and told not to repeat certain actions, but after a short leave from the paper, Blair was back. Execs at the paper felt that communication problems among senior editors, as well as a lack of complaints from the public about his inaccurate facts, allowed him to continue in his favored position.[4] They were right about the lack of communication, but did nothing to resolve it.

Clearly, the desire of top editors to promote a black reporter—regardless of his transgressions—blinded them to early and continuous warning signs of trouble. And, more relevant to our discussion, the fallout of the eventual crisis must be laid directly at the feet of those top editors.

The Crisis

Even though Jayson Blair was ultimately forced to resign from the *Times* on May 1, 2003, the damage was already done. Despite the many lessons that might be learned from an examination of Jayson Blair, remarkably, he is not the one with a communication problem. The responsibility for the eventual scandal is shared by his supervising editors, particularly Raines and Boyd, who failed to address their protégé's problems, and by the upper management at the *New York Times* for their failure to directly and honestly deal with the resulting fallout once Blair's history of faulty reporting was uncovered. It is the actions of these people that turned an internal problem with a rogue reporter into a full-blown crisis on the front pages of national and international papers and on cable news stations.

The problems with Blair were known in-house for years. That's when a crisis plan should have been in place and enacted. An internal *New York Times* investigation found that thirty-six of the seventy-three articles that Jayson Blair had written for the paper had serious problems. "They ranged from factual errors to plagiarism to pure fabrication. In some cases he purported to file stories from cities without actually traveling to them."[5] This finding surprised no one in the organization. Many staff editors had their suspicions about Blair all along. Danielle Newman, an editor under Blair, told a *Newsweek* reporter: "When Jayson was initially hired, people were really upset. . . . We said we just didn't think he was qualified. . . . We definitely had our suspicions about his reporting, but what could we do?"[6] In April 2002, during Blair's employment, Jonathan Landman, the metro editor at the *Times*, put in writing what these staffers were thinking and feeling. In an e-mail to top executives at the newspaper, Landman bluntly stated: "We have to stop Jayson from writing for the *Times*. Right now."[7] Nothing changed.

Clearly, top editors at the *New York Times* had created a professional climate that discouraged dissent and ignored it when it was voiced. A corporate policy that encouraged higher-ups to address the concerns of trusted employees and to deal directly with problematic employees in a responsible and timely fashion would likely have minimized the PR fallout of this case.

But nothing of this sort happened in the Jayson Blair case. The complaints about Blair were ignored for four years. Not only wasn't Blair (who later was found to have serious psychological issues and a longstanding substance abuse problem) stopped from making a mockery of journalistic standards, he was promoted and his transgressions swept under the rug by top managers. It is a strategy for disaster in any organization.

It is significant to note that it was not the *New York Times* editors who brought the transgressions of Jayson Blair to the attention of their readers. That would have to some extent lessened the fallout. As we've learned in this book, proactive, self-revelation of errors is often helpful. Instead, the paper found itself in an unwanted media spotlight when a Texas newspaper reporter revealed that Blair had made up major aspects of a story about the family of U.S. soldier Jessica Lynch. The *Times* was now in a defensive position and in need of a crisis communication plan.

When the "flawed" reporting and promotion of this *Times* reporter was announced, many concluded that the problem was rooted in preferential treatment based on race. As professional journalists, what else could have been the editors' compelling reason to allow a young, inexperienced, and reckless reporter with such a checkered track record to gain more and more editorial responsibility and occupy a significant amount of prime journalistic real estate, including the front page of the *New York Times?* Some have argued that only one conclusion could be drawn: The color of Jayson Blair's skin was the determining factor in how he and his work was managed and supervised. Could it really be that the *New York Times* was so committed to promoting black reporters in the name of diversity that top editors ignored the fact that this black man fabricated facts, created quotes, and made up events? Could it be that Blair's supervisors were so dedicated to this goal that they would ignore the brewing crisis and expose the *Times* to the biggest and most publicized embarrassment and scandal in the paper's century-and-a-half history?

To the public who had trusted the *New York Times*, the answers to these questions would determine their own response to this crisis.

The Paper's Response to the Crisis

The *Times* had a reputation for high journalistic standards. The public expected the information they reported to be truthful and exact. To protect this reputation, *Times* execs chose to follow a common, but almost always ineffective, communication plan: deny, cover up, and shift the blame to someone else.

The breach of trust—and Blair as main culprit—was the first issue to be dealt with. In a 7,500-word account published in their own paper on May 11, 2003, the New York Times attempted to explain how the Blair fiasco transpired. In this extremely lengthy examination of the problem, Times editors pointed the finger of blame largely at one person—Jayson Blair. The Times editors took little responsibility for allowing Blair to fabricate and falsify dozens of articles. Instead, they painted themselves as victims.

Some, like *Washington Post* columnist Richard Cohen, weren't fooled: "a close reading of the Times' own account of what went wrong suggests that the paper itself does not fully comprehend what happened. It was not, as some outside observers have said, that no newspaper can fully protect itself against a liar. It was rather that the paper should have known it had a liar on its hands and, despite obvious warnings, did little about it. . . . The answer appears to be precisely what the Times denies: favoritism based on race."[8]

When first pressed about what role Blair's race and the New York Times' effort to diversify its newsroom and promote a "star" reporter played in the situation, editors denied that any of these factors were major contributors. News accounts reported: "Both executive editor Howell Raines and managing editor Gerald Boyd have bristled when such a thing was suggested to them. Raines called the affair simply 'a tragedy for Jayson Blair,' and Boyd asserted, 'It's not an issue about diversity, but about a reporter who had issues that allowed him to deceive.' "[9]

It was in fact the vehement denials by Raines and Boyd and their laissez-faire management style toward Jayson Blair regarding his four-year record of out-of-control and fake reporting that really fueled this scandal for the Times. It seemed clear to any reasonable person that race had to be a significant factor in the promotions of Jayson Blair. Any time a double standard for employees exists, it is a prescription for serious problems internally and for a potential public relations crisis in the outside world.

This case of corporate leaders being blinded to the bigger picture by one particular goal is complicated further by its irony. While the Blair fiasco was going on, the *Times* ran a comprehensive fourteen-part series entitled "How Race Is Lived in America," which examined racial attitudes and experiences. This, while at the same time failing miserably to deal honestly and directly with a racial double standard in its own news room. This from a newspaper where top editors failed to reprimand, if not stop (and indeed promote) an out-of-control reporter because he was a minority. Leaders in such visible positions cannot separate their words from their actions and they cannot hide the truth forever.

In this case, the Jayson Blair embarrassment was not about one bad reporter; as one *New York Times* writer told reporter Eric Boehlert: "This really is a story about race."[10] Overlooking well-documented inaccuracies and erratic behavior and promoting incompetence in the name of "diversity" is a far more serious action than simply mishandling a young hire—especially while the paper is publishing articles analyzing the issue of race discrimination in America. By putting their own agenda to attract and retain black journalists above the goals and objectives of the company they worked for, to the point of ignoring input from other employees familiar with the potential disaster Blair represented, Raines and Boyd compromised the integrity and reputation of their employer and lost the trust of the people they were supposed to serve.

The response of the *Times* executives to this attempt to hide the truth created a second (and perhaps more damaging) crisis. According to reporter Roger Clegg: "As is typically the case with scandals, it's not the original misdeed itself that is so damning, but the cover-up. Bad enough to have hired and then kept on a corrupt reporter. But to deny that the reporter was there because of a corrupt system—that is the real scandal."[11]

Reaction from the New York Times staffers was mixed. Everyone knew that a significant price had to be paid for the scandal and that saying that Jayson Blair was largely responsible for the paper's transgressions was not going to cut it. When a crisis or scandal like this occurs—and is allowed to fester and spread—the responsibility and the blame should be directed upward to the highest organizational levels, not as far down as you can push it.

On June 6, 2003, both Raines and Boyd resigned as top editors at the New York Times. Lena Williams, the Times' Newspaper Guild representative, acknowledged that the staff believed the two editors had been "unapproachable as managers and that they bore the ultimate responsibility for the scandal."[12]

Boyd and Raines weren't the only ones to take a hit in the Jayson Blair case. The reputation of the New York Times was also severely damaged. The Times would forever be tied to its bungling of one of the worst cases of journalist plagiarism in history.

The causes of this reputational black eye were largely avoidable: When it was first apparent that Blair was an incompetent journalist, his superiors should not have looked the other way and engaged in a dangerous and risky game of benign neglect. When the "flaws" in Blair's articles were discovered, the Times itself should have reported the errors to their readers rather than try to hide the facts, hoping no other media outlet would break the story. When it was obvious to any thinking person that Blair was benefiting from a double standard based on race, the Times should not have tried to deny it. And when the mess was made public, the Times should not have attempted to place the lion's share of responsibility and blame on Jayson Blair.

Simply put, as is the case with many of the crises explored in this book, the Jayson Blair scandal should have never gotten this bad. It could have been minimized and contained if the

Times had an organizational crisis communication plan in place to deal with problem employees in-house before they became national scandals. And once the problem went public and became a national story, the top executives at the *Times* should have known better than to even try using the tactics of denial and blame—tactics the paper itself so frequently and rightly pounce on and expose when those in the government or corporate sector try to do the same.

Don't Let This Happen to You

When it comes to crises, some are the product of larger forces that are often beyond anyone's control—9/11, Hurricane Katrina, and the West Virginia mine collapse, for example. Yet, there are other crises that are the product of organizational weakness and managerial ineptitude and neglect. The Jayson Blair case is one of those crises that clearly could have been avoided. And then, once it occurred, it could have been minimized and managed, but ultimately blew up because of the action or inaction of those in charge.

Let's all learn these lessons from this entirely avoidable crisis:

1. Pay attention to the warning signs of trouble within your organization. When you hear that mistakes have been made or when a pattern of incompetence emerges, address the situation in a direct and serious fashion. If you do not, the problem can move from an internal issue to an exploding external crisis, if not outright scandal. The *New York Times*' top editors did in fact ignore clear and consistent signals and warnings that Jayson Blair was troubled. It went on for four years. Concerns about Blair were put in writing from several high-level *Times* editors, including Jonathan Landman, but again, not only wasn't the issue dealt with through a reprimand or even firing, he was promoted, which sent all the wrong signals. Simple lesson: take care of your own business, because if you don't, someone else will.

2. Promote an organizational environment that allows for candid feedback. It appears that the culture promoted by executive editor Raines didn't allow for this kind of internal dialogue. Some employees did express their concerns to superiors, but if such feedback wasn't wholly embraced and taken seriously, the communication plan needs to be altered. Just having a feedback channel isn't enough. So, it seems that the internal complaints did not reach up to Raines; if a better internal communication system were in place between the rank-and-file staff and the upper level executives, Raines may have gained a better grasp of Blair's potential liability.

3. Using race or any other criteria beyond performance and merit is risky business. *New York Times* top management had decided that diversity was a goal and that a double standard measuring Jayson Blair's journalistic performance would be established. It wasn't an official policy, but clearly that is the way they acted. Further, by creating this race-based double standard, when Blair's transgressions were exposed by a Texas newspaper, it left *New York Times* top editors in a position to deny that race was a factor. Such contradiction only fueled the controversy into a full-blown scandal. A simple lesson: you can seek diversity, but everyone in your organization must be held to the same standard or performance, because, in the end, if things go wrong, it is hard to justify any other managerial approach.

4. When serious mistakes are made, responsibility and sometimes blame should move up the organization, not down. The *New York Times*' efforts to put responsibility and blame largely on Jayson Blair's shoulders didn't cut it. Again, it only fueled the controversy and ultimately forced top *New York Times* editors Raines and Boyd to step down. If they had accepted responsibility for Blair's actions early on, they might have been able to survive. An important lesson to remember is that when things go wrong, responsibility moves up.

5. Your response when things go wrong should be concise and to the point. Apologize, take full responsibility, and announce whatever actions you will take to make sure such things won't happen again. The *New York Times*'s 7,500-word explanation about the Jayson Blair debacle was certainly laudable (if not concise), and for a time placed our attention on one lowly reporter and his mistakes. But in all those words, again, *Times* editors failed to take full responsibility for their action or inaction. It's not how many words you use that matters, but rather how contrite and honest you are.

Your goal when a controversy occurs is to minimize the damage. Once the Jayson Blair story broke, there was no way the *New York Times* was going to avoid being embarrassed in public. But if the *Times* top editors had conducted themselves differently, they could have minimized the damage and potentially shortened the duration of the negative publicity. Sometimes in an effort to avoid a controversy and make a potential crisis go away, organizational leaders act in ways that perpetuate the problem by being less than forthright, appearing to engage in a cover-up.

Once an organization's reputation has been damaged, efforts must be redoubled to develop a comprehensive and realistic plan to ensure the same mistakes are not repeated. The Jayson Blair story must be told over and over again inside the *Times*. All reporters and editors regardless of their level of experience must be reminded of what the standard of conduct should be as well as the consequences of failing to meet those standards. Rather than pretend that the embarrassing or scandalous event never happened, leaders in that organization must embrace and use the painful experience to do everything possible to ensure that it doesn't happen again, because those who forget the past are likely to repeat those same mistakes in the future.

In spite of everything I've said in this chapter about how the *New York Times'* top leadership failed to deal with the Jayson Blair situation, I read the *New York Times* every day. I still consider it one of the finest and most comprehensive newspapers in the country. But at the same time, along with millions of others who read the *Times*, the Blair situation is still in the back of my mind. I wonder now if what I am reading is as accurate and factual as it could or should be. In the end, all an individual organization has is its reputation. Clearly the *New York Times* hasn't gone away and won't in the foreseeable future, but its reputation has taken a serious hit.

The Duke "Rape" Case

A RUSH TO INJUSTICE

What were they thinking? ──────────────

District Attorney Michael Nifong thought he could play fast and loose with the facts and, along with the Duke administration, pandered to what he perceived to be public opinion.

The Lesson ──────────────

Don't jump to judgment or manipulate the truth.

By all accounts, Durham County North Carolina District Attorney Michael Nifong was a media neophyte who was politically desperate to win voter approval in his 2006 reelection campaign. So when a black stripper claimed that she was raped by a group of well-to-do white Duke University lacrosse players in March 2006 at a team party, Nifong pounced. He smelled an irresistible opportunity for a publicity-hungry politician in the middle of a tough campaign.

Pandering to the Public and the Press

At a candidate forum during the controversy, Nifong (whose constituency included a significant African American voting bloc) boldly proclaimed that he would never allow Durham to become the county in North Carolina infamous for a "bunch of hooligans . . . raping a black girl."

But let's go back, to earlier in this story. Nifong had never been elected to the D.A. post. He had been appointed in 2005 and was now in a tough primary. He needed an issue—a cause—a way to graphically demonstrate that he was a crusading, progressive prosecutor that black voters could count on to stand up for them. The stripper—who would change her account of what happened at that lacrosse party on several occasions, gave Nifong what he thought he was looking for. Nifong boldly courted the local and national media that had descended on Durham County to cover a case with all the elements of a salacious and white-hot news story.

The media fell in step, with pronouncements such as "Black Stripper Raped by White Jocks from Elite Southern School." This was a headline writer's dream and great fodder for 24/7 cable news outlets. On paper it looked like a case of a woman—a black woman—taking a job as an exotic dancer, struggling to get by, who was victimized by a group of privileged white jocks just because they felt entitled. Mike Nifong saw an opportunity to use the media to pander to his constituents and apparently never considered his occupational and ethical guidelines, nor the consequences.

Soon it became clear that D.A. Nifong had a case that was based on seriously faulty evidence, but that didn't stop him from continuing his crusade against the Duke lacrosse players. He ignored evidence; he hid evidence; he withheld evidence. He failed to turn over critically important DNA test results that "identified genetic matter from several young men—but no members of the lacrosse team—in the accuser's underwear and body."[1]

That evidence clearly indicated that the three Duke men who were charged with rape—Collin Finnerty of Garden City, Long Island; Reade Seligmann of Essex Fells, New Jersey; and David Evans of Bethesda, Maryland—were not guilty. Nifong also ignored the pleas of Reade Seligmann and his attorneys, who tried to present evidence that Seligmann was nowhere near the lacrosse party when the alleged assault took place.

Nifong also withheld critical evidence from the defendants and their lawyers that he knew he was legally and ethically bound to disclose. Mike Nifong did these and other disgraceful things while holding countless press conferences and appearing

in numerous media interviews railing against the Duke defendants and clearly getting well ahead of, and in fact contradicting,
the evidence he had access to.

Because of Nifong's aggressive and reckless prosecution of
the Duke lacrosse players, the national media attention grew. In
fact, I was asked to do media commentary on Court TV analyzing the implications of the D.A.'s manipulating and misusing the
power of the media to prosecute a case before the general public, particularly one so volatile because of its connection to race
and class and the violent nature of the allegations involved.

But Court TV was only one network focusing on the Duke
case. Every major news organization, from ABC, CBS, and NBC,
as well as the FOX News Channel, MSNBC, and CNN, was all
over it. It was a naturally enduring and sensational media story.
It had all the elements to be a ratings bonanza. It was a dramatic and powerful story and everyone wanted to find out how
it would end. Mike Nifong knew that and did everything he
could to milk it for all it was worth. The D.A. was a lightning
rod—a media magnet—a prosecutor in a high-profile case
who said outrageous things on camera. He was a prosecutor
who seemed to love the spotlight and was convinced that the
intense media attention he was attracting would boost his
political prospects.

Duke's Rush to Judgment

In the midst of a crisis, some organizations become paranoid
and don't act quickly enough. They miss opportunities and their
leaders fail to be proactive. They are then seen as weak and in-
decisive as well as unconcerned and lacking compassion. (Think
Exxon CEO Lawrence Rawl in the *Exxon Valdez* oil tanker accident.) However, in the midst of the crisis at Duke University,
campus leaders went in the opposite direction, following
Nifong's lead. They acted in a rash and irresponsible, not to men-

tion unfair, manner—to hell with due process and forget about "innocent until proven guilty."

Duke University President Richard Brodhead was getting pressure internally at the university to act. The faculty at Duke got involved, particularly a group called "The Gang of 88," which consisted of eighty-eight faculty members and staff who amazingly drafted and signed a public statement concluding that the three Duke lacrosse payers were guilty and demanding that they be punished. Again, all of this occurred before the evidence was even considered and after the accuser had changed her account several times.

According to a *New York Post* editorial on June 19, 2007, the faculty public statement also "hailed the 'collective noise'" that led Mike Nifong to file dubious legal charges.[2] The public statement of the Gang of 88 rhetorically asked, "What does a social disaster look like?" The editorial went on to include that the purported rape was proof of the "racism, sexism, sexual violence and homophobia" on the Duke campus.[3]

It was in this environment that the Duke University administration felt compelled to act. Before any evidence could be examined and decisions reached as to the guilt or innocence of the Duke players, President Brodhead and his administration's game plan clearly was to distance the school from anyone and anything having to do with this scandal—the entire lacrosse team, the players, the head coach, and, in fact, it seemed the sport of lacrosse itself. Lacrosse, perceived as an upper-class sport played mainly be white men, was somehow tainted by these unsubstantiated allegations. This need to cast out these students and the lacrosse program grew out of fear or some misguided sense that any action, no matter how irrational or unfair, was better than deliberately and methodically considering all the options and ultimately being accused of stonewalling, whitewashing, or not dealing directly with the players accused.

Duke University suspended the three lacrosse players before they were even officially charged. They cancelled the entire lacrosse season and pressured the team's coach, Mike Pressler, to resign. Duke President Brodhead apparently decided that someone had to be the fall guy in this crisis and it wasn't going to be him. Rather, it was better to have Duke's lacrosse coach of sixteen years fall on his sword.

Pressler would later write a fascinating book about the whole experience, *It's Not about the Truth*. According to Pressler, the book's title came from one of many meetings he had with President Brodhead, who told him that the university had to suspend the players and cancel the season because ultimately "it's not about the truth." Apparently this was a reference to the university president's believing that his job was to protect the larger university's reputation even if the facts and the evidence contradicted what he was doing.

Ironically, the so-called social disaster in this case was the way the Duke faculty as well as the administration grossly mishandled this most sensitive and volatile of public situations. They thought they were using the media to get out a message that they were sensitive to a minority woman who alleged that she was sexually violated by elite, white Duke jocks. Rather, the message sent to many was that, together with D.A. Mike Nifong, the Duke faculty and administrators were reactionary cowards who rushed to judgment and ignored the "truth" in order to pander to what they thought most constituents, especially blacks, wanted.

The Case Unravels

As the case proceeded, the dancer involved continually changed her account of what happened that night and who at the party had assaulted her. Ultimately, Mike Nifong felt compelled to drop the rape charges, but continued to pursue lesser charges of sexual assault and kidnapping against the three student athletes.

According to accused Reade Seligmann, who hails from Essex Fells, New Jersey, and went to Duke on a lacrosse scholarship, "At that point it felt almost like a sick joke, like we were being toyed with, like he was doing it maliciously against us."[4]

Later, North Carolina Attorney General Ray Cooper's office would ultimately dismiss all the charges against the Duke players after conducting its own independent investigation and calling Nifong's prosecution a "tragic rush to accuse."

In the end, Duke University would reach an undisclosed financial agreement with the three players accused. In a joint statement, the players responded in this dignified fashion: "The events of the last year tore the Duke community apart, and forcibly separated us from the university we love. We were the victims of a rogue prosecutor concerned only with winning an election, and others determined to railroad three Duke lacrosse players and to diminish the reputation of Duke University."[5] The players said their goal was ultimately to bring the Duke family back together again.

Of course Brodhead too would like nothing more than to leave behind the negative publicity wrought by his bungling of this incident, but that is unlikely to happen for a long time—particularly given the way he continues to make mistakes in his communications with the public. In late September 2007, a full year-and-a-half after the accusation was first hurled at the lacrosse players, Brodhead finally apologized for not better supporting the players falsely accused: "the fact is that we did not get it right, causing the families to feel abandoned when they were most in need of support. This was a mistake. I take responsibility for it and I apologize for it."[6]

These well-spoken words—they do not try to defuse the blame, make excuses, or deny—would have meant something if they had come a year earlier. This would have been a classic example of getting it right, if the words had been spoken when they were needed. Instead they came far too late to communicate any sincere sentiment. Timing was crucial in managing this crisis well. Did the university's lawyers tell Brodhead that an apology at the time of the trial was risky in terms of the legal process and might imply some level of guilt or culpability? Maybe. But regardless of the reason for the extended delay, this "apology" came across as a lame effort to patch things up and put the event behind him. It won't work.

Knowing When to Shut Up

Mike Nifong too would find that he could not put this "mistake" behind him. Ultimately, Nifong would not only lose his position as Durham County D.A., but also be disbarred as a lawyer. In the words of Lane Williams, chairman of a three-person disciplinary committee of the North Carolina State Bar Association: "This matter has been a fiasco. There is no doubt about it." Lane called Nifong's outrageous public statements to the media and his attempt to curry favor with minority voters a "selfish" prosecutorial crusade.[7] My then MSNBC colleague, senior legal analyst Susan Filan, said this about the case: "Mike Nifong had many chances to escape his fate, yet he never chose to do the right thing. Not once."[8]

Finally, in a teary statement before Chairman Williams in his disciplinary committee, a disgraced Nifong offered these words; "To the extent that my actions have caused pain to the Finnertys, Seligmanns, and Evanses, I apologize."[9]

Nifong continued by saying: "To the extent that my actions have brought disrespect, disrepute to the Bar, to my community, I apologize." He continued with: "much of the evidence against me is justified, the accusation that I am a liar is not justified."[10] Regarding his inflammatory and unsubstantiated public comments to the media, including his referring to the Duke athletes as "hooligans," Nifong, who said at the time that he had not watched himself on TV during the crisis, offered this analysis: "I saw a clip [from a previous broadcast] this week that I had not seen before. It made me cringe. It did not come across at all like what I was trying to do. . . . Maybe if I had seen some of these things sooner, I'd have shut up sooner."[11]

But Nifong didn't shut up. He continued to press on and played the media card as hard as he could in the face of countless warnings and signals that he was on shaky and dangerous ground. He was in a world he understood little if nothing about. Simply put, he was playing with fire.

Further, many saw Nifong's tears at his much publicized disciplinary hearing as tears for himself and his career. Joe Chesire, attorney for Dave Evans, spoke for some when he said, "Nifong's tepid apology is too little far too late."[12]

An Amateur Playing in the Major League

Other than political expediency and overreaching ambition, what else might explain Mike Nifong's bumbling of this sensitive and high-profile case? My sense is that like many people who are in prominent positions, Nifong had an overblown sense of his ability to manage and deal with the media. He was no longer dealing with the local print or electronic press of Durham County, North Carolina. Nifong was dealing in the big leagues with major national television networks and national publications like the *New York Times* and *Washington Post*. Tabloids around the country had a field day with the salacious details and the outrageous sound bytes that he offered.

Mike Nifong, from all indications, had no media coaching or training and never really thought through what would happen if he entered into a high-profile, crisis-driven situation. He relied on his own counsel like so many who overestimate their abilities in a field that is far outside of the one they are trained in.

Savvy leaders, particularly in the media-dominated age of instantaneous "news," must realize that the skills and tools required to deal and communicate effectively—especially when on the hot seat or in the line of fire—may be beyond their experience and expertise. Your key to successfully facing the media in a high-profile situation is in building a team of crisis communication professionals whose skill set compliments and adds to yours. Your opinion matters, but is limited and sometimes myopic. Nifong never asked himself the tough questions he would likely face from the media and/or key constituencies. His approach wasn't challenged by a close, yet independent, circle of advisors who would dare to tell him things he didn't want to hear. He didn't seek evaluations of his media appearances.

But the biggest mistake Nifong made was one of hubris and arrogance. His headlong prosecutorial style matched his communication style. As Susan Filan said, Nifong "never chose to do the right thing."[13] Doing the right thing sometimes means taking a hit—acknowledging your mistakes—even if you don't think you're totally wrong. It is about realizing how others could legitimately perceive your actions as ill-advised or, worse, dangerous.

Of all his mistakes and indiscretions in the Duke case, it was Nifong's ignorance as to the impact of his public statements that seemed the most egregious. When Nifong called the Duke players "hooligans" and injected race into this case in front of the national media, the stakes went up dramatically. His comments made him and his words a huge target. There is a very basic rule when you are in an official government position like prosecutor in a high-visibility case with intense media attention—no name-calling. But Nifong was highly quotable. He provided great and unexpected copy because prosecutors rarely call those they accuse of crimes "hooligans" or make public statements that include the race of the alleged victim and/or the accused. Using such language is inflammatory and dangerous. Nifong should have communicated in a more reserved and credible fashion. He should have stuck to the "facts" as he knew them and realized that the kind of pretrial publicity he was generating hurt both his reputation and his case. He should have remembered what any informed citizen or first-year law student knows: Those who are accused of a crime are innocent until proven guilty.

Nifong thought he was helping his political career, but that couldn't have been further from the truth. As the ethics committee of the North Carolina Bar Association prepared to discipline and ultimately disbar Mike Nifong, his attorney Dudley Witt attempted to explain his client's intentions as well as his mistakes by offering this analysis: "[Mike Nifong] was an 'old-school prosecutor' who had never dealt with the media and never had a DNA report other than from the state laboratory."[14]

Basic Lessons

Susan Filan, who prosecuted numerous high-profile, media-driven cases before she joined MSNBC and NBC News as a legal analyst, offered profound words as well as a lesson to all public servants who find themselves tempted to play with media fire. These words have significance also for professionals in other fields who may find themselves under the gun or have their backs against the wall in some sort of crisis. Filan says, "Let this case serve as a cautionary tale to all prosecutors who handle cases which receive media attention:

1. Don't go 'Hollywood.' Remember, your job is to keep the public informed, to try your case in the courtroom, not the press, and to make sure those you accuse get a fair trial.

2. Don't play fast and loose with the evidence.

3. Play by the rules.

4. Prosecute mightily and fairly in the courtroom and speak carefully and thoughtfully to the press."[15]

If Mike Nifong had considered any of this advice before he led this charade, which made this case a major crisis that he was wholly unequipped to handle, it is highly likely that his actions would not be profiled in this book.

Alberto Gonzales

PAYING THE PRICE
FOR PLAYING WITH WORDS

What were they thinking?

Former United States Attorney General
Alberto Gonzales was thinking that as the
nation's highest-ranking law enforcement officer
he could make a critical executive decision for
inappropriate political reasons, be less than
totally honest about it, and then try to hide
that fact with legalese and doublespeak.

The Lesson

Strong leaders must take full responsibility for
poor executive decisions and carefully prepare
how to face the media so they don't fan the
flames of their own fyneral pyre.

Alberto Gonzales was considered by many to be a decent, hard-working, and dedicated lawyer who felt quite comfortable being a judge. Yet, when he was appointed as U.S. attorney general, the country's top law enforcement officer, the skills and tools required for this job appeared well beyond Gonzales's grasp.

This was especially the case when it came to dealing with the media in a pressure-filled, potentially controversial situation. Case in point: The mass firing of eight United States attorneys by the attorney general's office for reasons that many believed to be politically motivated and directed by the Bush White House in the spring of 2007.

U.S. attorneys are appointed by the president and report to the attorney general. As White House appointees, they "serve at the pleasure of the president," yet as prosecutors their job is to uphold the law and try corruption and other criminal cases in

an objective, impartial, and professional fashion. U.S. attorneys
are not hired to do the bidding of any political party or the person occupying the White House.

But when eight U.S. attorneys were fired all at once, many
questioned the attorney general's actions. It was suspected that
some U.S. attorneys were fired for not more aggressively prose-
cuting certain Democratic political figures in their jurisdictions
and for not trying particular cases that could potentially benefit
the Republican Party. Alberto Gonzales was asked by Congress to
testify before the U.S. House Judiciary Committee as well as the
U.S. Senate and to clarify his role in the firings. He was questioned about the firings, and soon was being challenged as to as
to how honest and straightforward he was being regarding his
own involvement in the firing process.

In addition, Gonzales agreed to do an interview on March
25, 2007, with Pete Williams of NBC News, who was a former
top Republican White House operative. Both in the House testimony and the Williams interview, Gonzales demonstrated how
poorly equipped he was to communicate in a clear, confident,
and candid fashion when under pressure.

Bungled Opportunities

Consider this account in the *New York Times* from May 11, 2007,
reporting on Gonzales's testimony before the House Judiciary
Committee:[1]

Representative John Conyers Jr., Democrat of Michigan and
chairman of the panel, seemed to voice the most frustration over
Mr. Gonzales's testimony, saying, "Tell us, just tell us how the
U.S. attorney termination list came to be, and who suggested
putting most of these U.S. attorneys on the list and why."

Mr. Gonzales repeated his assertion that the list represented
"the consensus recommendation of the senior leadership of
the department."

"OK, in other words, you don't know," Conyers said.

The New York Times article went on to say:

Mr. Gonzales at times expressed contrition for his mishandling of the dismissals, including his earlier misstatements about the process, but insisted he had acted correctly. "What I have concluded is that although the process was not as rigorous or as structured as it should have been, and while reasonable people might decide things differently, my decision to ask for the resignations of these U.S. attorneys was not based on improper reasons and therefore the decision should stand."

Several members of the House Judiciary Committee were publicly frustrated with Gonzales's testimony. In fact, it was his lack of responsiveness to direct and reasonable questions regarding highly publicized and controversial actions that caused many members to push for a "no confidence" vote regarding the attorney general. Many Democrats as well as some Republicans publicly went after Gonzales for his contradictory and confusing public comments.

Gonzales's own allies were turning against him because of his frustrating lack of direct, candid communication. It was as if he was communicating in some moot court experience, where splitting legal hairs and not admitting any criminal wrongdoing or mistakes was the only goal that mattered. This was an avoidable and dumb mistake and he wound up alienating his most important stakeholders because of it. This in turn would ultimately make him more expendable to the Bush White House.

Consider this commentary from an article written in the Los Angeles Times by David Iglesias, who was the U.S. Attorney for New Mexico from October 2001 to February 2007 (and a supporter of Alberto Gonzales), and who was on the list of U.S. attorneys to be fired:

I once said that I found Gonzales to be a personal inspiration. No one can deny him his life's story, which is the American dream writ large. It began in Humble, Texas, born of impoverished Mexican American parents. He, like me, is a veteran of the U.S. military. He went to some of the best schools in America, including Harvard Law. Yet, somewhere along the line, he drank the loyalty Kool-Aid. Watching him testify before the Senate and House was painful for me. He had been a trailblazer for the Latino community, and then, in the space of a few hours of tortured testimony, he became just another morally rudderless political operative.[2]

Iglesias's stinging rebuke and other similar statements should have made Gonzales see how he was being perceived and characterized by credible sources, yet it seemed to have no effect on Gonzales, who would continue to speak in a counterproductive fashion, digging a deeper hole for himself that ultimately he would not be able to climb out of.

Feeling the pressure to respond to his challengers—to clear the air and hopefully clear his name—Gonzales agreed to an interview with Pete Williams of NBC News, who had covered the Justice Department for years. Based on his subsequent performance, it seemed that Alberto Gonzales had no coherent or credible plan for how to deal with the interview. Following is a representative exchange:[3]

Pete Williams: Can you answer some of the questions that have come up over the weekend? As you know, there was a— an e-mail that came out Friday night that showed that ten days before the firings there was a meeting in your office which you attended to discuss the firings. And yet when you talked to us here at the Justice Department two weeks ago, you said you were not involved in any discussions about the firings. Can you—can you explain what seems like a contradiction?

Gonzales: Let—let me just say—a wise senator recently told me that when you say something that is either being misunderstood or can be misunderstood, you need to try to correct the record and make the record clear. Let me try to be more precise about my involvement. When I said on March 13th that I wasn't involved, what I meant was that I—I had not been involved, was not involved in the deliberations over whether or not United States attorneys should resign.

As the NBC News interview went on, it would get worse for Gonzales. At a certain point Gonzales said:

I don't recall being involved. Let me—let me be more—more precise because I know that—with respect to this particular topic, people parse carefully the words that I use. [LAUGHTER] And—and I wanna be careful about what I say. And, of course, at the end of the day, I will have the opportunity to present my story to the Congress, as will other DOJ officials—Department of Justice officials.

Gonzales went on to talk about how D. Kyle Sampson, one of his top aides, was conducting a performance audit of U.S. attorneys and was reporting back to the attorney general. Gonzales seemed to be shifting the responsibility to one of his aides. In our other case studies, we've seen how in a crisis this can be a fatal mistake. It looks weak and appears as if you are denying responsibility. That is not what people are looking for. They want to see a leader step up and lead. Take the hit. Be accountable, especially when the shit hits the fan.

Alberto Gonzales's efforts to shift responsibility and blame became more apparent as the interview continued:

Williams: So the list came to you toward the end [of the process] for you to sign off on. But you were not involved in deciding who should be on or off the list during the process.

Gonzales: I was not involved in the deliberations during the process as to who—who should or should not be—asked to resign. I depended on the people who knew about how those United States attorneys—were performing—people within the department—who—who would have personal knowledge of—about these individuals, who would have, based upon their experience, would know what—what would be the appropriate standards that a United States attorney should be asked to—to achieve.

It seemed that the attorney general had walked himself into a corner that Williams recognized when he followed up with: "Given that, then how can you be certain that none of these U.S. attorneys were put on that list for improper reasons?"

Gonzales responded with an answer that would come back to haunt him.

Gonzales: What I can say is this: I know the reasons why I asked you—these United States attorneys to leave. And it—it was not for improper reasons. It was not to interfere with the public corruption case. It was not for partisan reasons.

Williams: To put this question another way—if you didn't review their performance during this process, then how can you be certain that they were fired for performance reasons?

Alberto Gonzales had to know that he was in serious trouble, and he began to stammer on the nationally televised broadcast.

Gonzales: I—I've given—I've given the answer to the question, Pete. I know—I know the reasons why I made the decision. Again, there's nothing in the documents to support the allegation that there was anything improper here. And there is an internal—department review to answer that question, to reassure the—the American people that there was nothing improper that happened here.

Gonzales was unraveling on national network news. He was literally thinking and then talking out loud and in turn reacting to how he thought his comments might be negatively received. Under the glare of the lights, the camera was recording this dreadful stream of consciousness from Gonzales that would be watched by millions and ridiculed by many.

The Problems and the Solutions

Like many Americans, Alberto Gonzales worked hard to climb up the professional ladder. And also like too many Americans on the top rungs of that ladder, he was unprepared as to how to conduct himself when controversy hit. In Gonzales's case, he struggled with several communication problems, all of which had surprisingly simple solutions.

1. BE PREPARED. Lack of preparation before facing the media is a common problem contributing to the downfall of a number of high-profile people discussed in this book. Gonzales joins the

ranks of those who thought they were savvy enough to wing an important interview and then found themselves mired in mud. When facing Pete Williams on NBC News, Gonzales acted as if he was engaged in a private conversation with a trusted colleague or close friend or associate instead of being grilled by seasoned and appropriately adversarial journalist.

In a crisis, journalists, no matter how polite they may be, should never be considered a friend. They have a job to do and they are going to do it whether it hurts you or not. So be prepared.

Certainly, Gonzales should have practiced for the interview and received constructive feedback by responding to mock questions and seeing how the experience felt. Instead, he wound up going to bat in the ninth inning of the seventh game of a World Series without ever taking a few warm-up swings.

Gonzales should have been advised that such hesitating and evasive answers were likely to be seen as less than candid and credible. He needed to understand that his credibility was on the line and that he had to take some responsibility for what went wrong in the process of firing these eight U.S. attorneys. The advice needed to come not from the lawyers on his staff but from experienced experts in public relations and crisis communication. He needed to be more audience-focused and what I call "other-centered" in order to step out of his executive branch position and try to imagine how an average citizen (not a group of legal subordinates) might perceive his comments.

If he had done this preparation, Gonzales could have learned basic ways to better answer questions without sounding so defensive. Instead, he made classic communication faux pas such as when he said, "There's nothing in the documents to support the allegation that there was anything improper here." This no doubt recalled to the public Al Gore's "No controlling legal authority" statement.

When under pressure, leaders must frame their comments in a more affirmative fashion and highlight what they *are* doing—not what they *aren't* doing. A denial of wrongdoing using language such as "nothing in the documents support the allegation . . ." translates to "you can't prove anything." And then by denying "that there was anything improper here," he reminds the listener of the negative charge—focusing attention on the act of wrongdoing. (Think—President Nixon's "I am not a crook" denial during the Watergate scandal.)

A more positive framing would have sounded like this: "Everything we did was totally appropriate. I am confident that our internal review will conclude that the process worked the way it is supposed to." And asking the interviewer, even before the first question, to make such a statement, can be helpful. It is proactive, gets your message out, helps you partially dictate the discussion.

It is obvious that Gonzales never received the kind of direct and honest feedback that would have helped him better understand how others might perceive him. That's unfortunate because things might have been different in the end if Alberto Gonzales had gotten this type of coaching for this high-stakes media interview and congressional testimony.

2. DON'T PARSE YOUR WORDS. Gonzales seemed to do exactly what he said he feared others would do when analyzing his words—parsing. That is, twisting the meaning of words to manipulate the truth.

His own use of this deceptive communication approach was brought to the public's attention in a March 26, 2007, broadcast of *Countdown with Keith Olbermann* on MSNBC. Olbermann used Gonzales's interview with Williams as fodder to portray Gonzales as a bumbling and less-than-honest public official who had exacerbated the scandal through his own words. Admittedly, Olbermann is a critic of the Bush administration. But still, Gonzalez supplied the material!

Olbermann ran this sound byte of Gonzales's interview: "When I said on March 13th that I wasn't involved, what I meant was that I—I had not been involved, was not involved in the deliberations over whether or not United States attorneys should resign."[4]

So there it was. Gonzales's words coming back to haunt him and Olbermann, who can be sarcastic and biting in his commentary, said, "So it depends on what your definition of *involved* is?" Viewers knew that Gonzales's parsing of the word "involved" was being compared to former President Bill Clinton's words regarding whether he had sex with White House intern Monica Lewinsky. In that case, Clinton said, "It depends on what the meaning of the word *is* is." Such legal doubletalk and parsing of words hurt Bill Clinton then and it clearly hurt Alberto Gonzales in the spring of 2007.

With his legal training at Harvard and his years as a successful attorney, Gonzales convinced himself that he could make the American people buy his revisionist definition of "involved." Instead, he insulted our intelligence and underestimated our ability to recognize doublespeak when we hear it.

Once the words are out of your mouth, you can't take them back. You can't redefine them. You can't claim that's not what you meant to say. More reason to prepare carefully in advance.

3. STICK TO THE TRUTH. Another problem for Gonzales was that he thought his version of the truth would be accepted without question. He never calculated that his former top aides as well as White House staffers would have a very different version of events and would share that version under oath before Congress and later before millions through the mass media.

While Gonzales was insisting that the firings were in no way politically motivated (again, denying the charges), others like Chief of Staff Kyle Sampson and former White House aide Monica Goodling (who had been given immunity by Congress to testify) told a very different story. Goodling apparently was the point person between the White House and the attorney general's office and was charged with coordinating with Gonzales's office to execute the firings.

According to a May 24, 2007, New York Times article entitled "Witness for the Prosecutors":

In her testimony to the House Judiciary Committee, Ms. Goodling removed all doubt about whether partisan politics infected the Justice Department's treatment of federal prosecutors. She admitted that she investigated the party affiliations, and even campaign contributions, of applicants for prosecutor, and other nonpolitical jobs. "I know I crossed the line," she said of her actions, which may have violated federal law. Her admission that partisan politics was used to hire people only makes it more likely that it was also used to fire people.

Ms. Goodling appeared to be straining to make her testimony helpful to Mr. Gonzales, but when backed into a corner, she conceded that he had lied about his role in the scandal. At a press conference in March, he said he had not seen any memos or participated in any discussions about the firings. But Ms. Goodling made clear that he was briefed and attended a key meeting.[5]

The truth is the truth. Once you stray into falsehoods when responding to a crisis, you're bound to go down. Ethics aside, in these modern times, there are just far too many records of everything you say and do. Gone are the days when you could get yourself out of a jam that you rightly belong in by saying, "I never did that."

Unfortunately for Alberto Gonzales, despite his life of hard work and impressive accomplishments, history will remember him as the U.S. attorney general who bumbled and fumbled and tried to play games with words in front of the U.S. Congress and in critical media interviews. In the end, he sealed his own fate by being woefully unprepared to face the scrutiny of the media, by playing with words, and by bending the truth.

When Gonzales publicly announced his resignation from office effective September 17, 2007, he did so in a terse statement, taking no questions and giving no reason for stepping down. Apparently, in spite of everything that Alberto Gonzales faced and the myriad of mistakes he made when communicating under pressure, the way he left office clearly indicates that he learned very little, and his reputation will be greatly tarnished because of that.

NFL Boss
Roger Goodell

SCORING BIG POINTS

UNDER PRESSURE

What were they thinking?

Unlike Bud Selig of Major League Baseball, National Football League Commissioner Roger Goodell believed that he had to face the media and the American public (especially football fans) and candidly address the scandals that the NFL's stars were embroiled in—even if it acknowledged what many already perceived.

The Lesson

The media and the public respect honest and forthright information; on the other hand, they are brutal to those who try to hide, stonewall, or deny what we already believe to be true.

In the first few months of his first year as the National Football League commissioner, Roger Goodell demonstrated the kind of solid and highly credible media savvy that is often lacking with corporate executives who are under significant pressure—particularly those in professional sports. In 2007 Goodell faced a series of major scandals in the NFL, including the Michael Vick dog-fighting debacle, Pacman Jones's endless stream of criminal problems, and the New England Patriots/Bill Belichick "videogate" cheating scandal.

In every case, Commissioner Goodell was a stand-up leader. He didn't duck any of these challenges. He made tough decisions and handed down stiff penalties. He didn't wait to communicate; he was proactive, and when he got the opportunity to speak with the media on a national stage on NBC's *Sunday Night*

Football, he took every question and challenge head-on. That's good crisis communication in action.

Costas and Goodell

During Goodell's interview with NBC's Bob Costas before the September 16, 2007, game between the New England Patriots and San Diego Chargers, Costas was on his game. He asked very tough questions of Goodell, who didn't flinch. Goodell stayed cool, calm, and under control at all times. Costas, who is as tough and knowledgeable an interviewer as there is in sports, never threw Goodell off point. Goodell was not just disciplined and "on message," he was candid and highly responsive.

Costas asked Goodell about the penalties and fines he handed down to the Patriots, including a $500,000 personal fine to Bill Belichick, a $250,000 fine against the club, and the forfeit of a first-round draft choice in the next year's draft if they make the playoffs (which was pretty much a lock). Costas cited NBC's Cris Collinsworth's commentary before the Goodell interview suggesting that Belichick should have been suspended for several games, particularly the next Jets game (against whom the Patriots had "spied" in the first place) and the first playoff game.

Without missing a beat, Goodell responded: "I don't agree with that and I respect Cris a great deal. But, I don't think that's appropriate here. My job here, Bob, is to make sure that all thirty-two teams are operating within the same rules [and] on a level playing field. That's what I tried to do here with this penalty—is to make sure that all teams are playing by the same rules."[1]

Goodell's answer was direct and straightforward, concise and to the point. He didn't get defensive and didn't take any cheap shots at Collinsworth. His body language never changed—he never showed anger or frustration. He respected Collinsworth's opinion, but he simply disagreed. Goodell did what few media performers are able to do, which is to disagree without being disagreeable. Further, Goodell was prepared and disciplined enough to go back to his main message, which is that all thirty-two NFL teams must operate within the same rules.

No matter what Costas asked Goodell, after the commissioner's initial response, he found his way back to his main point. Some might call that spin, but I call it great media communication. Goodell was able to reframe the discussion while still being credible. Someone as good as Costas is often able to bait sports executives and others into saying stupid things they wish never came out of their mouths. That's because most people, when dealing with the media, have absolutely no game plan, or if they do, they don't have the discipline or awareness to stick with that regardless of the situation. Roger Goodell did, and it paid off.

Later in the NBC interview, Costas pressed Goodell by saying there was sentiment that he was easier on Coach Belichick than on players, like Pacman Jones and Michael Vick. Again, Goodell never lost his cool. He just responded: "I understand this job's going to come with criticism, Bob. I heard you earlier in the week and Peter King [of *Sports Illustrated*] earlier in the week talking about a second-round draft choice being an extremely strong statement. I understand that and people are going to have a difference of opinions. I listened today and I heard a lot of people who thought it was too strong. That's part of my job. What I have to do is make sure that I maintain the integrity of the NFL and allowing each team to be on the field playing by the same rules is a critical point for me."[2]

Goodell once again returned to his main message. Not ignoring the question, but not being a slave to it, either. He didn't get testy about the criticism; he just said it was part of the job. Further he reminded Costas that the NBC broadcaster himself said that the commissioner's penalty was "an extremely strong statement." This technique of giving the interviewer's words right back to him or her takes some steam out of an interviewer, even one as tough as Costas.

As a leader who had to make tough decisions, Goodell didn't take any crap—unlike Major League Baseball Commissioner Bud Selig (who bumbled his way with his eyes closed through the ongoing steroid scandals involving sluggers like Barry Bonds and previously Mark McGwire and Sammy Sosa), or the lame executives running Madison Square Garden profiled in this book (who condoned and were in denial about the blatantly sexist and racist comments made by New York Knicks general manager and head coach Isiah Thomas). Goodell wasn't afraid to make the tough decisions, even when it came to icons and heroes in his sport like Bill Belichick.

Anyone, be it a sports executive, a CEO of a major corporation, a school principal, or a university president, can learn a great deal by watching those seven and a half minutes of Roger Goodell taking everything Bob Costas threw at him and standing tall by being candid, forthright, and highly prepared. Goodell never mentions anyone else, never tries to shift blame onto an underling (à la the New York Times and its story on Jayson Blair). Twice Goodell refers to "my job," showing us that he's the one in charge. In this instance, the media was Roger Goodell's friend. Not because that was Costas's intent, but because of Goodell's performance.

Such confidence and strong leadership requires that an executive be able to perform well when dealing with the media under heavy pressure. That's what Goodell did in that Sunday night interview with Costas.

The Media Response to Goodell

There are several benefits to leading in a direct and clear fashion and communicating via the media in such a proactive and assertive fashion. In Roger Goodell's case, he was praised by many sportswriters and television commentators, whether or not they agreed with his decisions. Reporter Eric McHugh, for example, had this to say: "Goodell, in a letter to the Patriots, said the team had engaged in a 'calculated and deliberate attempt' to circumvent the rules. All in all, an embarrassing episode for a franchise whose brand used to be squeaky clean."

Vic Carucci, the national editor of NFL.com, noted: "The commissioner has had a pretty hard hammer, especially on issues that threaten the credibility of the game. And that applies as much to Michael Vick and Pacman Jones as it would to violating the rules for coaches. Commissioner Goodell holds coaches to a higher standard."[3]

In USA Today, columnist Jon Saraceno also praised Goodell for taking such a clear position on the "videogate" scandal and seizing the opportunity to send a strong message about the NFL and its effort to raise the ethical bar:

> Last spring, Commissioner Roger Goodell made it abundantly clear with his repeated "It's all about the shield" edicts. Well, "Dirty Tricks" Belichick, possessor of a Nixonian-like paranoia regarding perceived enemies of state, has managed to stomp on and muddy the league's red, white, and blue logo in a way no player ever could.
>
> From a punishment perspective, that should have left him in no better position than a passel of Pacman Joneses, Michael Vicks, or Tank Johnsons. You know what happened to them when they went afoul of Commissioner Crackdown. Goodell has set an Olympic-height character bar for every employee; Belichick flopped straight into it.
>
> Thus far, offending players have paid a steep price for no-nos. We found out Goodell—whose hiring was approved by ownership—had the stomach for doing the right thing when it came to one of the NFL's most successful franchises and coaches. He sent a zero-tolerance message to every owner regarding the violation of NFL policy.[4]

The case of Roger Goodell and his handling of "videogate" and other high-profile controversies isn't just about sports.* It's about society and what behavior is and is not acceptable. Goodell has become a role model for many organizational leaders and the way he communicated has set the bar for all of us. The other benefit of this kind of straightforward communication (even when it hurts) is to the organization you serve. The NFL is a better organization because of the commissioner's leadership.

Unfortunately, the way Roger Goodell handled three high-profile incidents involving Pacman Jones, Michael Vick, and Bill Belichick is atypical. Too many executives who have the opportunity to turn such embarrassing incidents around and speak publicly—especially in the media—in a smart, thoughtful, and forthright fashion wind up badly missing the mark. Often these executives make the crisis much worse. Let's use Major League Baseball as an example.

Major League Baseball

Major League Baseball Commissioner Bud Selig made embarrassing errors in two highly publicized scandals: the MLB's failure to deal with and communicate in a strong and decisive fashion the moment the Bay Area Laboratory Co-operative (BALCO) steroid scandal erupted in 2003; and Selig's own bumbling and awkward performance in connection with Barry Bond's suspected steroid use and much-publicized run to break the home run record of the legendary Hank Aaron.

Once the media picked up the BALCO story and demanded answers, Selig appointed former U.S. Senator George Mitchell to investigate the multiple steroids allegations around Bonds and other Major League Baseball players. Before finally concluding at the end of 2007, the investigation stalled and was thwarted by several forces. The long-awaited Mitchell report was released to

---

*Later, when Goodell made the ill-advised decision to destroy videotape in the Bill Belichick/New England Patriots scandal, saying that there was nothing of significance on the tape, he would be criticized by many, including sportswriters who had previously praised him for his initial reaction to the "videogate" incident.

the public on December 13, 2007. All the time, baseball's boss Bud Selig had little if anything to say. Unlike Roger Goodell's proactive and strong approach, Selig's inept crisis leadership hurt Major League Baseball's reputation and invoked intense criticism from commentators across the country. Sport reporters Mark Fainaru-Wada and Lance Williams of the *San Francisco Chronicle* noted:

> After a summer defined by Barry Bonds' pursuit of the career homerun mark and Commissioner Bud Selig's equivocations over a suspected drug cheat capturing the most hallowed record in sports, baseball seemed poised to emerge from its steroid crisis.
>
> Instead, four years after the BALCO scandal erupted, the game appears headed deeper into the drug abyss. With new reports revealing the use of performance-enhancing drugs by two high-profile players, as well as continuing steroid investigations, the game's looming pennant races and postseason are at risk of being overshadowed by further doping revelations.[5]

In a *Newsday.com* column titled "Selig Is Aloof, Silent Witness to Bond's 755th," Joe Gergen stated:

> The man in charge of the sport acted with all the zest of a notary public. It was an element of his job, he decided, to acknowledge the transaction that lifted Barry Bonds to the top pedestal of baseball achievement, alongside Henry Aaron. But by his presence, Bud Selig determined only that No. 755 was official; he didn't have to approve it.
>
> Unlike the 42,497 paying customers at Petco Park Saturday night, the commissioner neither booed nor applauded when the controversial Giants slugger ended a 2-for-18 slump and an eight-day homerun drought by slamming a 2-and-1 pitch by Clay Hensley over the leftfield fence in the second inning of the Padres' 3–2, 12-inning victory. He [Selig] would be a witness to history, not a willing participant.
>
> Selig offered no token gift nor even a handshake to the player who inevitably will surpass his good friend, Aaron, and add the career record to his single-season mark of 73 set in 2001. Instead, the commissioner issued a statement from the Padres' owners box high above the field. It was as spare a document as could be crafted on short notice.

"Congratulations to Barry Bonds as he ties major league baseball's homerun record," it said. "No matter what anybody thinks of the controversy surrounding this event, Mr. Bonds' achievement is noteworthy and remarkable."[6]

On the night that Bonds actually tied Aaron's 755 home runs, Commissioner Selig's behavior once again sent mixed signals. *Newsday.com* described it in this way:

Baseball commissioner Bud Selig headed home to Milwaukee on Sunday and is likely to miss Barry Bonds' next three games.

Selig was at Petco Park when Bonds hit his 755th homer Saturday night, tying Hank Aaron's record. Selig attended the start of Sunday's game, when Bonds didn't play, then headed home.

In his absence, Major League Baseball will be represented at AT&T Park by executive vice president Jimmie Lee Solomon for the first two games of the homestand and then Hall of Famer Frank Robinson.

Selig, close friends with Aaron, stood with his hands in his pockets as Bonds' family and friends cheered during Saturday's homerun trot.

The distance the commissioner's office has put between itself and Bonds was clear at the news conference. Six years ago, when Bonds tied Mark McGwire's season record with his 70th homer, the background was MLB logos. On Saturday night, the backdrop was a large Giants' symbol.[7]

Again, unlike NFL Commissioner Roger Goodell, Bud Selig seemed incapable or unwilling to take a strong stand on baseball's most embarrassing and serious ongoing scandal—suspected steroid abuse by some of its biggest stars and sluggers including Barry Bonds, Mark McGwire, Sammy Sosa, and Jason Giambi. Selig postured, equivocated conveniently, delegated, and avoided media interviews.

It is clear that the media and communication strategy used by Bud Selig and Major League Baseball's leadership was hamstrung by their inability to be decisive and proactive. Selig's crisis communication strategy cannot be separated from the actions of those in charge.

One might ask why it is so difficult for many business leaders to communicate proactively when things go wrong. First, it's hard. It is sometimes easier to look the other way. Making touchy calls and communicating decisively can make some people uncomfortable. Some leaders have a "things will take care of themselves" philosophy; but again, wishful thinking is no leadership plan.

Emulating a True Leader

Unlike Selig's run-and-hide communication style, Roger Goodell's confidence and clarity when facing the media regarding the much-publicized incidents involving NFL stars was based on a solid foundation of a well-planned crisis communication model and his own consistent action. No media or crisis communication plan can be effective unless a leader's words and actions are in sync.

A quick summary of Goodell's strengths shows that his impressive media presence was no accident. This is a crisis communicator who works hard to get it right. To emulate Goodell, be sure to:

1. Be candid, forthright, and highly prepared.

2. Deliver a bottom-line message and be disciplined enough to stick to it.

3. Be direct and straightforward.

4. Disagree without being disagreeable.

5. Avoid being defensive or taking cheap shots.

6. Stand or sit tall. Master your body language so it communicates your sense of confidence.

7. Channel your anger or frustration into productive passion and conviction.

8. Answer questions directly without becoming a slave to them.

9. Expect and calmly deal with criticism.

10. Take responsibility; don't shift the blame onto others.

This is the Goodell model that communication coaches, such as myself, will be talking about for years to come.

FEMA Fails during Katrina

TALK ABOUT "CLUELESS"

What were they thinking? _____

President Bush was thinking that he could distance himself and ignore the clear signs of an impending disaster and then not suffer the consequences of being detached and oblivious to the severity of the problem.

The Lesson _____

A leader who is not fully engaged and informed in order to communicate effectively during an emergency or crisis is a dangerous leader indeed.

"I feel somewhat abandoned," said FEMA chief Michael Brown to a congressional committee on February 10, 2006, regarding his perception that he was taking the brunt of the blame for the colossal failure of the federal government to deal effectively in response to Hurricane Katrina.[1]

In his explosive testimony, Brown said, "It's nice to appear before a committee as a private citizen and not be constrained by talking points."[2] Brown had taken a big hit for being the point person (or the scapegoat, depending upon your point of view) for the federal government's slow and feeble response to Hurricane Katrina.

Further, Brown became a laughingstock for many in part because of President George Bush's odd characterization of Brown's job performance in the face of what was seen as a universal failure on the part of FEMA. "Brownie, you're doing a heckuva job," said the president on September 2, 2005, three days after Katrina hit and two days after the New Orleans levees failed and the city was flooded. Thousands were displaced and, as the president spoke, many were stranded without food or water. Apparently the president had limited knowledge of what was going on in New Orleans and therefore he tried to pass off the responsibility for managing the crisis, making his communication with the hurricane victims and with all Americans dismally inadequate.

Out of Touch

President Bush's highest approval ratings were the product of his ability to demonstrate compassion and empathy after 9/11. Many Americans, even those who disagreed with Bush's policies and politics, sensed the president's human qualities in the days after 9/11. His physical and emotional presence at Ground Zero on September 14, walking through the rubble of the Twin Towers and speaking to heroic rescue workers with a bullhorn in hand, was powerful on many levels. It characterized what any great leader must do in the face of a crisis of unimaginable proportions.

But the way President Bush handled the Ground Zero impromptu speech and the way he handled Katrina in New Orleans are two very different stories. His poorly timed and frankly absurd characterization of Michael Brown's performance as the head of FEMA during and after Hurricane Katrina became symbolic of President Bush's denial of how bad the Katrina crisis was and how poorly his administration, as well as government at every level, performed and ultimately failed to protect American citizens, most of whom were poor and black and left to fend for themselves.

This perception was captured in a photo of Bush aboard Air Force One, on his way from Crawford, Texas, to Washington, D.C. Looking down at the devastation and heartache in New Orleans, he shows no particular expression and flies on by. Bush appeared pathetically out of touch. Apparently the president's advisors told him that it wouldn't be good for him or his image if he actually landed in New Orleans and was photographed amid the death and destruction or if he tired to deal directly with suffering and angry citizens who might confront him on the failure of FEMA. Ironically, by trying to so tightly control the images put out by the media and to avoid a public relations fiasco on the ground in New Orleans, a much more serious mistake in crisis communication was made—President Bush was not only seen as out of touch with Katrina's havoc, but thanks to that Air Force One fly-over photo-op, he was seen as uncaring and insensitive. (Later the president would visit New Orleans and walk what was left of the streets, but it would be seen by many as too little, way too late.)

It is with this powerful image in mind that we were stunned and disappointed with President Bush's inability and/or unwillingness to handle the crisis of Hurricane Katrina the way he handled the terrorist attacks of 9/11. According to Paul Krugman in an opinion column for the *New York Times* entitled "Heck of a Job, Bushie," "Mr. Bush was apparently oblivious to the first major domestic emergency since 9/11. According to *Newsweek*, aides to Mr. Bush finally decided, days after Hurricane Katrina struck, that they had to show him a DVD of TV newscasts to get him to appreciate the seriousness of the situation."[3]

When it comes to crisis communication, great leaders don't have to be especially articulate or charismatic. They don't have to be great orators. But great leaders must be actively engaged, involved, and informed so that when they speak it is in a clear and credible fashion. Strong leaders communicate to key stakeholders and audiences that they are on top of the crisis and in control of the situation. This is the area in which President Bush was weakest—communicating a sense of intellectual curiosity and emotional involvement in a crisis.

Sticking to the Facts

In responding to questions about Hurricane Katrina, President Bush would say several times that he didn't know that the levees in New Orleans were in serious trouble. He seemed to say that no one could have known that before it happened. But the facts show that was simply not the case. So the president's defense seemed to be that he either really did not know what he should have known or did not remember what he had been told by his advisors. Either way, Bush appeared to be less than truthful and sometimes clueless, which in a crisis only makes things worse.

This became clear when an explosive videotape was uncovered by the *Associated Press* that highlighted an August 28, 2005, meeting with in-depth discussions between the president and his top Homeland Security and White House aides as Hurricane Katrina approached New Orleans.

According to a *New York Daily News* story entitled "W Knew Kat Was Big One: Vid Debunks Pres Denial," President Bush and Homeland Security chief Michael Chertoff "were painstakingly briefed before Hurricane Katrina on worst-case scenarios—contradicting Bush's later assertions that no one could have guessed New Orleans' levees could fail."[4]

Ironically, on the day before Hurricane Katrina hit, FEMA chief Michael Brown told Bush and Chertoff that because the Superdome in New Orleans was twelve feet below sea level, it was highly susceptible to flooding. Brown also said: "We are going to need everything that we can possibly muster, not only in this state and in the region, but the nation to respond to this event."[5]

President Bush's response was indeed unusual given the circumstance described by news reporter Seth Borenstein: "Brown and his hurricane team are seen [in the videotape of the August 28 meeting] as sounding the alarm of an impending disaster. In contrast, President Bush and Homeland Security Secretary

Michael Chertoff appear impassive the day before Katrina struck as officials predicted that the levees around New Orleans could fail. The president asked no questions."[6]

Then, after being told that the levees would likely fail and that New Orleans was about to be seriously flooded, Bush told Louisiana and New Orleans government and emergency officials right before Katrina hit that we are "fully prepared." Again, that was simply not the case. What kind of crisis communication plan was that? Why would the nation's leader not be direct, honest, and proactive with such important information?

New York Post conservative media columnist John Podhoritz, who is not one to often criticize President Bush, wrote of the president's reassuring New Orleans and Louisiana officials: "The president made his assertion on the basis of things he had been told by Brown and others, but the videotape does suggest a kind of leadership by assertion or by wishful thinking."[7] To repeat: Wishful thinking is not a strategic plan.

Consider this chronology of events entitled, "What Did Bush Know and When Did He Know It?" printed in the New York Daily News, featuring a picture of one of thousands of New Orleans homes destroyed by the floods which the New Orleans levees couldn't stop:

> Sunday, August 28 Brown warns President Bush by video-conference to expect a "catastrophe."
>
> Monday, August 29 Katrina hits. Brown tells Deputy Chief of Staff Joe Hagin in the evening that the levees were breached and calls it "our worst nightmare."
>
> Tuesday, August 30 Bush plays golf and says New Orleans "dodged the bullet."
>
> Thursday, September 1 Bush says no one anticipated the levees failing.
>
> Friday, September 2 Bush tours area and says, "Brownie, you're doing a heckuva job."[8]

Over and over, President Bush made it clear that he was disengaged from the facts and therefore lacked any real genuine sense of urgency leading up to or immediately after Hurricane Katrina.

Passing the Buck

When a crisis occurs, great leaders not only take charge, but take full responsibility in the spirit of Harry Truman: "The buck stops here." In reaction to the botched federal response to Hurricane Katrina, there was an effort by the president and his White House aides to make sure that the buck stopped as far away from them as possible. The Bush White House tried to shift the blame away from the president and his Homeland Security Chief Michael Chertoff and on to FEMA head Michael Brown (this after the laughable "Brownie, you're doing a heckuva job" comment by the president).

Brown was an easy target because of his often surly and combative public communication style that was graphically displayed in his acrimonious congressional testimony. In fact, it was Brown's style, if not his actual performance, leading up to and in the aftermath of Hurricane Katrina that was so weak and problematic. He antagonized members of Congress unnecessarily with his angry and defensive responses to difficult but legitimate questions. According to Republican Congressman Chris Shays of Connecticut: "I'm happy you left, because that kind of . . . look in the lights like a deer tells me that you weren't capable to do the job." At several points Brown turned red in the face and slapped the table in front of him saying "so I guess you want me to be the superhero, to step in there and take everyone out of New Orleans." Congressman Shays responded: "What I wanted you to do was do your job and coordinate."[9] Communication style matters greatly in a crisis and Michael Brown's style was anything but controlled, confident, and most of all compassionate (à la Rudy Giuliani in connection with 9/11) given the suffering of so many innocent Americans because of the failure of government.

So the pass-the-buck approach was employed twice in this case. Bush passed off responsibility to Brown, and Brown fought back to deflect the blame. Neither Bush nor Brown has ever accepted the responsibility for the government's embarrassing response both before and after Hurricane Katrina hit New Orleans. In fact, they found another easy target to point to—the local and state government officials in New Orleans and Louisiana. In any crisis, there is no end to the number of people who can be blamed when the leaders at the top of the company or organization refuse to be held accountable.

Lessons Looking Back

When top-level leaders fail to communicate effectively in times of crisis, many people who look to them for information, advice, and comfort are hurt and disappointed. But in retrospect, these cases give all of us an opportunity to examine what went wrong and use our findings to improve our own crisis communication strategy or approach. Let's look at a few of the lessons that can be drawn from the way Hurricane Katrina was handled by President Bush, FEMA director Michael Browne, and others who should have known better:

1. It is essential to listen to those around you, particularly advisors who are bringing you "bad news," no matter how difficult it may be. All effective communication plans involve the participation of a variety of knowledgeable people whose expertise is trusted, acknowledged, and put to use when a crisis strikes. But if top leaders refuse to listen to those people or to take their recommendations seriously, the communication plan is bound to fail. The video of the meeting one day before Katrina hit shows a president clearly disengaged from his top advisors and seemingly uninterested in the details. Therefore, the catastrophe that followed was not unexpected.

2. Once a crisis actually does occur, a leader must understand the degree or severity of the problem. The idea that the president had to be shown a DVD of television news reports that graphically described and demonstrated the suffering of people in New Orleans is hard to imagine. But it did happen—don't let this happen to you. Consider the worst-case scenario while hoping for the best.

3. Wishful thinking is not a substitute for a legitimate crisis communication strategy. As I've emphasized: anticipate and prepare for the worst and then hope for the best. As seen in other chapters, such as the ones relating the serious communication mistakes made during the Virginia Tech shootings and the West Virginia coal mine collapse, proactively warning people of a possible disaster is indeed a most difficult task for any leader, especially when there is the possibility of causing undue fear or panic. But holding back critical information has the potential to cause even greater chaos, confusion, and even death for those who look to you for leadership and direction. A comprehensive crisis communication plan must include a specific process for warning people of potential trouble.

4. Leaders must measure their words very carefully in the aftermath of a crisis when under the glare of intense media attention. When the president said to FEMA director Michael Brown: "Brownie, you're doing a heckuva job," it is safe to assume that he never realized how that one line would come to characterize just how out of touch he really was with the failure of the federal government's response to Katrina. Praising Brown publicly in the midst of abject failure caused many Americans to question the president's judgment and credibility. It was a comment that reinforced the deeply held perception of many that President Bush was dangerously disconnected from reality—the kiss of death for any leader in a crisis.

5. Don't engage in revisionist history. In other chapters in *What Were They Thinking?* we see over and over how this mistake damages reputations. For example, when EPA administrator Christie Whitman claimed that she never said the air directly around the fallen Twin Towers in New York City was safe to breathe, we were reminded of George Bush claiming that no one could have anticipated the levees collapsing. Both statements were eventually proven to be clearly untrue. In a world dominated by video cameras, electronic recordings, and the omnipresent media, whatever you say will become part of the permanent public record. So think carefully before speaking.

6. A leader must keep his or her eye on the bigger picture. In this case, President Bush's obsession with anti-terrorism after 9/11 made it appear that he had little if any interest in natural disasters, which is why FEMA seemed so poorly prepared to respond when it mattered most. A leader must see the forest from the trees, which cannot be done if one is obsessed with the condition of an individual tree. Leaders who become blinded by a single-minded focus on a particular topic, issue, or problem are tremendously vulnerable when a crisis, controversy, or serious challenge confronts them and their organization from a direction they never expected.

7. Those being scapegoated cannot become so obsessed with clearing their name that they lose sight of the larger crisis. Of course, strong leaders don't skulk around looking for someone else to blame, but when this happens (as it often does), the needs of the people you serve must remain your top priority. It was Michael Brown's televised testimony before Congress that crystallized for millions of Americans the image of a government bureaucrat who just didn't seem to get it—that the hearings weren't about him, but about those who suffered from Katrina and the failure of the feds. Brown was consumed with defending himself and so even in the face of undeniable failure he insisted: "I know what I'm doing, and I think I do a pretty darn good job of it."[10]

8. It is essential that a leader demonstrate genuine compassion and concern when people are suffering. This is what the president did at Ground Zero right after 9/11 and what he didn't do when he was flying over New Orleans on Air Force One looking down on the destruction and suffering. The difference in his emotional response made all the difference in the way his leadership skills were perceived by the American public.

The powerful and genuine 9/14 Ground Zero "bullhorn" response by President Bush to the tragedy of 9/11 aside, his bungled response to Hurricane Katrina is indicative of a larger Bush problem. His handling of a variety of scandals and controversies shows an alarming pattern of weak and nonexistent communication skills. A pattern emerges of a leader who is simply not intellectually or, it seems, emotionally curious about significant events going on around him. We can easily see the damage his poor crisis communication and leadership skills have caused to his image when dealing with the issues surrounding national and international events such as the firing of U.S. Attorney Alberto Gonzales, the NSA wire tapping controversy, and the problems associated with the war in Iraq, the Abu Ghraib scandal and his premature pronouncement of "Mission Accomplished!" in connection with "winning" the war in Iraq.

A leader who is not fully intellectually and emotionally engaged to the degree required in order to communicate effectively and with genuine empathy and compassion during an emergency or crisis is a dangerous leader indeed.

NOTES

Johnson & Johnson's Tylenol Scare

1. Kathleen Fearn-Banks, *Crisis Communications: A Casebook Approach* (Mahwah, NJ: Lawrence Erlbaum Associates, Inc., 2006), 93.

The *Exxon Valdez* Oil Tanker Spill

1. Sean Kelly, "Exxon Quits Conservation Group Claiming Unfairness in Alaska Oil Spill," *Washington Post,* October 28, 1989, A3, *http://proquest.umi.com/pqdweb?did=73907419&sid=2&Fmt=3&clientId=3470&RQT=309&VName=PQD*; Ken Wells and Charles McCoy, "Out of Control: How Unpreparedness Turned the Alaska Spill into Ecological Debacle," *Wall Street Journal,* April 3, 1989, 1, http://proquest.umi.com/pqdweb?did=27474061&sid=1&Fmt=3&clientId=3470&RQT=309&VName=PQD.
2. Wells and McCoy, "Out of Control," 1.
3. John Holusha, "Public-Relations Problem: Experts See Failings in Handling of Spill," *New York Times,* April 21, 1989, D1, http://selectnytimes.com/search/restricted/article?res=FA0710FB3B550C728EDDAD08.
4. Ibid.
5. James Lukaszewski, "Exxon Valdez: The Great Crisis Management Paradox," *E911.com,* 1993, http:/www.e911.com/monos/m008.html.
6. Natalie Phillips, "Former Exxon Chief Revises Story on Spill," *Washington Post,* May 21, 1994, A3, http://proquest.umi.com/pqdweb?did=72247487&sid=1&Fmt=3&clientId=3470&RQT=309&VName=PQD.
7. Wells and McCoy, "Out of Control," 1.

The New York Knicks

1. Thomas Zambito, "Former Coach Backs Knicks' Accuser's Claims," *New York Daily News,* September 18, 2007, http://www.nydailynews.com/sports/basketball/knicks/2007/09/18/2007–09–18_former_coach_backs_knicks_accusers_claim.html.
2. Katie Cornell, "Witness: Thomas Accuser Was Nearly Fired," *New York Post,* September 19, 2007, https://www.nypost.com/seven/09192007/news/regionalnews/dolan_just_fired_away.ht.
3. Christina Boyle, "Dolan's Other 'Frat' House: He Ran Cablevision Like a Wild Child, Say Former Employees," *New York Daily News,* September 23, 2007, 7.
4. Jane Ridley, "James Dolan's Indifference Shows Anything Goes at MSG," *New York Daily News,* September 19, 2007, http://www.

nydailynews.com/sports/basketball/knicks/2007/09/19/2007–09–19_james_dolans_indifference_shows_anything.html.

5. Boyle, "Dolan's Other 'Frat' House," 7.

6. Cornell, "Witness."

7. Thomas Zambito and Corky Siemaszko. "Sleaze Play in Stephon Marbury's Back Seat," *New York Daily News,* September 13, 2007, 5.

8. Ridley, "James Dolan's Indifference Shows Anything Goes at MSG."

9. Andrea Peyser, "Please End This Game of Ugly Ball," *New York Post,* September 19, 2007, 5.

Chaos in a West Virginia Coal Mine

1. Howard Kurtz, "Was the Media's Credibility Buried?" *Washington Post,* January 9, 2006, http://www.washingtonpost.com/wp-dyn/content/article/2006/01/08/AR2006010801225_pf.html.

2. Marisa Guthrie, "Mother Lode of Misinformation," *New York Daily News,* January 5, 2006, 75.

The Church's Pedophilia Scandal

1. John McLaughlin, "Shaking the Cathedral." *Star-Ledger,* June 24, 1993, 25.

2. "Clergy Child Molesters." *ncrnews.org,* n.d., http://www.multiline.com.au/~johnm/ethics/ethicscontents.htm.

3. Jason Berry, "The Bishop and the Boy," *Rolling Stone,* June 20, 2002, http://www.bishop-accountability.org/news/2002_06_20_Berry_ThePriest.htm.

4. Denise Noe, "Pedophile Priest: The Crimes of Father Geoghan," *Crime Magazine,* Dec. 1, 2003, http://crimemagazine.com/03/geoghan,1201.htm.

5. Andrew Greeley, "Priestly Silence on Pedophilia," *New York Times,* March 13, 1992, http://www.bishop-accountability.org/resources/resource-files/timeline/1992–03–13-Greeley-Priestly%20Silence.htm.

6. Rorie Sherman, "Legal Spotlight on Priests Who Are Pedophiles," *National Journal,* April 4, 1988, 30.

Dick Cheney

1. "White House Under Fire over Cheney Shooting: Texas Ranch Owner Revealed Story to Media Nearly a Day after Incident," *MSNBC.com,* February 13, 2006, http://www.msnbc.msn.com/id/11312757/.

2. "White House Shoots Foot," *NYtimes.com,* February 14, 2006, http://www.commondreams.org/views06/0214–26.htm.

3. Ibid.

4. David Sanger. "Political Memo; Handling of Accident Creates Tension between White House Staffs," *New York Times,* February 15, 2006, A18.

5. "Controversy Swirls Around Cheney. Reid: Delay in Information Shows 'Secret Nature' of Administration," *CBSnews.com,* February

15, 2006, http://www.cbsnews.com/stories/2006/02/14/national/main1313525.shtml.

6. Sanger, "Political Memo," A18.
7. Full disclosure: From 2003 to 2006, I appeared on a regular basis as a media analyst on the FOX News Channel.
8. "Cheney: 'One of the Worst Days of My Life'; Vice President Defends Handling of Hunting Accident," *CNN.com*, February 16, 2006, http://www.cnn.com/2006politics/02/15/cheney/index.html.
9. Mark Barabak, "Dick Cheney's Quail Hunting Shot an Indelible Scene, Analysts Say," *SFGate.com*, February 26, 2006, http://sfgate.com/cgi-bin/article.cgi?file=/c/a/2006/02/26/MNGEEHCNJ41.DTL.
10. Ibid.

The Glen Ridge Rape Case

1. Bernard Lefkowitz, *Our Guys* (New York: Vintage Books, 1998), 4.
2. Ibid., 30.
3. Ibid., 272.

The Death of Pat Tillman

1. "Tillman Killed in Afghanistan: Former Cardinals Safety Walked Away from NFL to Join Army Rangers," *CNN.com*, April 23, 2004, http://sportsillustrated.cnn.com/2004/football/nfl/04/23/tillman.killed/index.html.
2. Ibid.
3. Ibid.
4. Ibid.
5. Scott Lindlaw and Martha Mendoza, "General Admitted Doubt on Tillman: But He Cleared Enemy Fire Story," *Washington Post*, August 4, 2007, http://www.washingtonpost.com/wp-dyn/content/article/2007/08/03/AR2007080301868.html.
6. Ibid.
7. Steve Coll, "Barrage of Bullets Drowned Out Cries of Comrades," *Washington Post*. December 5, 2004, A01.
8. Ibid.
9. "Soldier: Army Ordered Me Not to Tell the Truth about Tillman," *CNN.com*, April 25, 2007, http://www.cnn.com/2007/POLITICS/04/24/tillman.hearing/index.html.
10. Ibid.
11. Erica Werner, "Rumsfeld: No Cover-Up in Tillman Death," *Time.com*, August 2, 2007, http://www.Time.com/time/printout/0,8816,1648848,00.html.
12. Ibid.
13. Ibid.
14. Ibid.
15. Ibid.
16. Kathy Gill, "The Pat Tillman Story," *About.com*, September 28, 2005, http://uspolitics.about.com/b/a/206237.htm?terms=The+Pat%20Tillman%20story.

17. "Soldier: Army Ordered Me Not to Tell the Truth about Tillman," *CNN.com.*
18. Gill, "The Pat Tillman Story."
19. Werner, "Rumsfeld: No Cover-Up in Tillman Death."

Rudy Giuliani

1. Andrew Kirtzman, *Rudy Giuliani: Emperor of the City: The Story of America's Mayor* (New York: Harper Paperbacks, 2001), 293.
2. Wayne Barret and Dan Collins, *Grand Illusion: The Untold Story of Rudy Giuliani and 9/11* (New York: Harper Paperbacks, 2007), 14–15.
3. Kirtzman, *Rudy Giuliani,* 301, 302.
4. Ibid., 303.
5. Ibid., 304.
6. Nancy Gibbs, "Rudy Giuliani, Mayor of the World, is TIME's 2001 Person of the Year," *Time.com,* December 31, 2001, http://www.time.com/time/magazine/article/0,10987,1001567,00.html.
7. Kirtzman, *Rudy Giuliani: Emperor of the City,* 305.
8. Ibid., 260.
9. Ibid., 261.
10. Ibid., 267.
11. Ibid., 306.
12. Ibid., 304.
13. Barret and Collins, *Grand Illusion: The Untold Story of Rudy Giuliani and 9/11,* 24.
14. Ibid., 25.

Christie Whitman and the EPA

1. David Saltonstall, "Whitman Piles Blame on Rudy," *New York Daily News,* September 8, 2006, 6–7.
2. Ibid.
3. Ibid.
4. Ibid.
5. Ibid.
6. Jane Kay, "9.11.01: Two Years Later Ground Zero Air Quality Was 'Brutal' for Months: UC Davis Scientist Concurs that EPA Reports Misled the Public," *San Francisco Chronicle,* September 9, 2003, http://sfgate.com/cgi-bin/article.cgi?f=/c/a/2003/09/10/MN266317.DTL.
7. Ibid.
8. Ibid.
9. "The Dust at Ground Zero—Katie Couric Reports How It Affected Ground Zero First Responders," *60 Minutes.* CBS News, September 10, 2006, http://www.cbsnews.com/stories/2006/09/07/60minutes/main1982332_page2.shtml.
10. Ibid.
11. Juan Gonzalez, "Christie Won't Clear Air on Mess at Ground Zero," *New York Daily News,* May 16, 2007, 14.
12. Ibid.

13. Ibid.

14. Ibid.

15. "Cluck, Cluck, Cluck, Cluck," *New York Daily News*, May 17, 2007, 26.

16. Juan Gonzalez, "Ex-EPA Head Finally Faces 9/11 Heat—Agrees to Congressional Hearing on WTC Air Quality," *New York Daily News*, May 19, 2007, http://www.nydailynews.com/news/2007/05/19/ 2007–05–19_exepa_head_finally_faces_911_heat.html.

Prudential's Terror Threat

1. Full disclosure: Prudential is a longtime supporter of public television programming that I have anchored.

2. Eric Battenberg, "What to Tell Employees? Communicating a Terrorist Threat," *The Public Relations Strategist*, Fall 2004, 4.

3. Ibid.

4. "Terror Threat Info May Be Dated," *cbsnews.com*, August 3, 2004, http://www.cbsnews.com/stories/2004/08/03/national/main 633663.shtml.

5. Battenberg, "What to Tell Employees?" 4.

Virginia Tech

1. "Virginia Tech President Defends Security Response," *CNN.com*, April 18, 2007, http://www.cnn.com/2007/US/04/17/campus .security/index.html?eref=rss_topstories.

2. "Tech's Response Questioned," *Roanoke Times*, April 17, 2007, http://www.roanoke.com/vtshootingaccounts/wb/113341.

3. "University Alerted Students via E-mail," *CNN.com*, April 16, 2007, http://www.cnn.com/2007/US/04/16/university.emails/index .html.

4. Ibid.

5. "Virginia Tech President Defends Security Response."

6. "Tech's Response Questioned."

7. Bruce Blythe, "Virginia Tech Shootings: Crisis Magnifies the Significance of Small Weaknesses," *Crisis Management International*, April 18, 2007, http://www.cmiatl.com/news_article73.html.

8. Ibid.

9. "Tech's Response Questioned."

10. Blythe, "Virginia Tech Shootings."

11. Vincent Bove, "Virginia Tech Tragedy: A Crisis of Leadership," *The Sentinel*, July 15, 2007, http://vincentbove.blogspot.com/2007/06/ virginia-tech-tragedy-crisis-of_30.html.

12. Ibid.

13. Ian Urbina, "Virginia Tech Criticized for Actions in Shooting," *New York Times*, August 30, 2007, A1.

Don Imus

1. Brooks Barnes and Emily Steel and Sarah McBride, "Unhorsed Jockey—Behind the Fall of Imus," *Wall Street Journal*, April 13, 2007,

http://online.wsj.com/public/article/SB117641076468168180-TfMzyqKQiK1gcJfwRly50NRZTEo_20080411.html.

2. Ibid.

3. David Carr, "The Media Equation: With Imus, They Keep Coming Back," *New York Times*, April 9, 2007, http://select.nytimes.com/search/restricted/article?res=FB0912F63F5B0C7A8CDDAD0894DF404482.

4. Barnes and Steel and McBride, "Unhorsed Jockey—Behind the Fall of Imus."

5. Ibid.

6. Ibid.

7. Clem Price (Executive Producer), "Inside Trenton," PBS Channel Thirteen/WNET, September 9, 2007.

8. "Richards Says Anger, Not Racism, Sparked Tirade," MSNBC.com, November 22, 2006, http://www.msnbc.msn.com/id/15816126/.

Jon Corzine

1. Tom Hester, Jr., "N.J. Governor Releases Seat Belt Ad—New Jersey Governor's Seat Belt Warning for Memorial Day Weekend: 'I Should Be Dead,'" *abcnews.com*, May 24, 2007, http://www.abcnews.go.com/US/wireStory?id=3207752.

2. Joe Donahue, "Corzine Ordered to Release His Katz Communication," *The Star-Ledger*, August 4, 2007, 13.

3. "Katz Out of the Bag: Corzine's Ex Spilled the Beans," *New York Post*, June 6, 2007, 1.

4. Cindy Adams, "Jon's Ex Tells All," *New York Post*, June 6, 2007, 7.

5. Donahue, "Corzine Ordered to Release His Katz Communication," 13.

6. Ibid.

7. Steve Adubato, "Corzine Must Face the 'Katz Issue,'" *Stand & Deliver*, 2007, Stand-deliver.com/syndicated/2007/070524.asp.

Jet Blue Airways

1. Bob Meadows, Michelle York, and Diane Herbst, "Trapped on the Tarmac," *People*, March 5, 2007, 71–72.

2. Jeff Bailey, "Long Delays Hurt Image of Jet Blue," *New York Times*, February 17, 2007, http://www.nytimes.com/2007/02/17/business/17air.html?ex=1329368400&en=3ae37894f1a0910a&ei=5090&partner=rssuserland&emc=rss.

3. Susan Todd and Joe Perone, "Humbled Jet Blue Picks Itself Up Off the Tarmac: A Week after Its Meltdown in Ice Storm, It Initiates a Program of Guarantees," *The Star-Ledger*, February 21, 2007, 1.

4. Ibid.

5. "The David Letterman Show," *CBS*, transcribed by Broadcast Monitors, February 20, 2007.

Big Mouth Bill O'Reilly

1. Full disclosure: At the time of writing this book, I am under contract as a media analyst at MSNBC, a longtime competitor of FOX News

Channel, where I had previously appeared as a regular guest-expert on media issues.

2. Howard Kurtz, "O'Reilly, Accuser Air Their Cases: Fox News Channel Host Sees Career Threat in Harassment Suit," *Washington Post,* October 15, 2004, http://www.washingtonpost.com/wp-dyn/articles/A34312-2004Oct15.html.

3. Marvin Kitman, *The Man Who Would Not Shut Up: The Rise of Bill O'Reilly* (New York: St. Martin's Press, 2007), 252.

4. Jonathan Wald, "O'Reilly Harassment Charges Head to Court," *CNN.com,* October 21, 2004, http://www.cnn.com/2004/LAW/10/20/oreilly.suit/index.html.

5. Ibid.

6. Kurtz, "O'Reilly, Accuser Air Their Cases."

7. "O'Reilly Hit with Sex Harass Suit," *The Smoking Gun,* Oct. 13, 2006, http://www.thesmokinggun.com/archive/1013043mackris1.html.

8. Ibid.

9. Kurtz, "O'Reilly, Accuser Air Their Cases."

10. Joe Hagan and Sheelah Kolhatkar, "Revolt of Fox's Hens," *New York Observer,* Oct. 24, 2004, http://www.observer.com/node/49947.

11. Ibid.

12. Peter Johnson, "Media Mix: Lots of Ways to Spin the O'Reilly Story," *USA Today,* Oct. 17, 2004, http://www.usatoday.com/life/columnist/mediamix/2004-10-17-media-mix_x.htm.

13. Ibid.

14. Howard Kurtz, "Bill O'Reilly, Producer Settle Harassment Suit: Fox Host Agrees to Drop Extortion Claim," *Washington Post,* October 29, 2004, http://www.washingtonpost.com/wp-dyn/articles/A7578-2004Oct28.html.

Taco Bell's *E. Coli* Scare

1. Chris Cobb, "The Taco Bell E. Coli Outbreak—Calming Public Fears during Food-Borne Illness Scares," *Public Relations Society of America (PRSA),* January 10, 2007, http://www.prsa.org/supportfiles/news/viewNews.cfm?pNewsID=789.

2. Ibid.

3. Ibid.

4. Ibid.

5. Joe Malinconico, "Slowly but Surely, Jersey Consumers Return to Taco Bell," *The Star-Ledger,* December 29, 2006, 27.

6. Cobb, "The Taco Bell E. Coli Outbreak."

7. Ibid.

8. Ibid.

9. Ibid.

The *New York Times*

1. Nicholas Stix, "The Jayson Blair Case: At the *New York Times,* the Spin Cycle Never Ends," *Geocities.com,* May 23, 2003, http://geocities.com/nstix/blairi.html.

2. Ibid.

3. Ibid.

4. "*New York Times*: Reporter Routinely Faked Articles: Probe Alleges Made Up Quotes, Plagiarism in at Least 26 Stories," *CNN.com*, May 11, 2003, http://www.cnn.com/2003/US/Northeast/05/10/ny.times.reporter/.

5. Eric Boehlert, "The Forbidden Truth about Jayson Blair," *Salon.com*, May 15, 2003, http://dir.salon.com/story/news/feature/2003/05/15/nytimes/index.html.

6. Stix, "The Jayson Blair Case."

7. "*New York Times*: Reporter Routinely Faked Articles."

8. Stix, "The Jayson Blair Case."

9. Roger Clegg, "The Gray Lady and the Black Reporter: The Scandal behind the Scandal," *National Review*, May 13, 2003, http://www.nationalreview.com/clegg/clegg051303.asp.

10. Boehlert, "The Forbidden Truth about Jayson Blair."

11. Clegg, "The Gray Lady and the Black Reporter."

12. Rose Arce and Shannon Troetel, "Top New York Times Editors Quit," *CNN.com*, Mar. 1, 2004, http://www.cnn.com/2003/US/Northeast/06/05/nytimes.resigns/.

The Duke "Rape" Case

1. Aaron Beard, "Duke Case Prosecutor Disbarred," *The Star-Ledger*, June 17, 2007, 8.

2. "Nifong's Enablers." *New York Post*, June 19, 2007, 28.

3. Ibid.

4. "Mike Nifong on Trial," *CNN Saturday Morning News Transcript*, June 16, 2007, http://transcripts.cnn.com/TRANSCRIPTS/0706/16/smn.01.html.

5. Aaron Beard, "Judge: Disbarred D.A. Must Leave Now," *WashingtonPost.com*, June 19, 2007, http://www.washingtonpost.com/wp-dyn/content/article/2007/06/18/AR2007061800771.html.

6. Aaron Beard, "President Says He's Sorry for Duke 'Mistake,'" *The Record*, September 30, 2007, A12.

7. Beard, "Duke Case Prosecutor Disbarred."

8. Susan Filan, "Nifong's Punishment Is Extreme, Appropriate—Let This Case Serve as a Cautionary Tale to All Prosecutors Who Handle Cases Which Receive Media Attention," MSNBC, June 17, 2007, http://www.msnbc.msn.com/id/19275010.

9. Mandy Locke and Joseph Neff, "Nifong Says He'll Quit As District Attorney," *News & Observer*, June 15, 2007, http://www.newsobserver.com/news/crime_safety/duke_lacrosse/nifong/story/605101.html.

10. Ibid.

11. Ibid.

12. Ibid.

13. Filan, "Nifong's Punishment Is Extreme, Appropriate."

14. Duff Wilson, "Hearing Ends in Disbarment for Prosecutor in Duke

Case," *New York Times*, June 16, 2007, http://select.nytimes.com/
search/restricted/article?res=FA0612FF395B0C748DDDAF0894DF4
04482.

15. Filan, "Nifong's Punishment is Extreme, Appropriate."

Alberto Gonzales

1. David Johnson, "House Democrats Push Gonzales," *New York Times*,
   May 11, 2007, http://select.nytimes.com/search/restricted/article?
   res=F40E13F93F550C728DDDAC0894DF404482.
2. David Iglesias, " 'Cowboy up' Alberto Gonzales," *Los Angeles Times*,
   May 23, 2007, http://www.latimes.com/news/opinion/la-oe-
   iglesias23may23,0,2188119.story?coll=la-opinion-center.
3. Pete Williams, "Gonzales: Firings Were Not Improper," *NBC News*,
   May 27, 2007, www.msnbc.msn.com/id/17801927/print/1/
   displaymode/1098.
4. Izzy Povich (Executive Producer). *Countdown with Keith Olbermann*
   [television broadcast], Secaucus, NJ: MSNBC, Mar. 26, 2007.
5. "Witness for the Prosecutors," *New York Times*, May 24, 2007,
   http://select.nytimes.com/search/restricted/article?res=FA0915FF3
   D540C778EDDAC0894DF404482.

NFL Boss Roger Goodell

1. Bob Costas and Roger Goodell (interview), *Sunday Night Football*,
   NBC, New York. September 16, 2007.
2. Ibid.
3. Eric McHugh, "His Legacy Is Suddenly in Danger," *The Patriot Ledger*,
   September 14, 2007, http://www.patriotledger.com/articles/2007/
   09/14/sports/sports01.txt.
4. Jon Saraceno, "Belichick Got His Due—But Was Due More," *USA
   Today*, September 14, 2007, http://www.usatoday.com/sports/
   columnist/saraceno/2007-09-13-saraceno-col_N.htm.
5. Mark Fainaru-Wada and Lance Williams, "Bonds Exits Limelight, But
   Baseball's Steroid Headaches Go On," *San Francisco Chronicle*, September 8, 2007, http://www.sfgate.com/cgi-bin/article.cgi?f=/c/a/
   2007/09/08/ MNOMS19MV.DTL&hw=Balco&sn=006&sc=433.
6. Joe Gergen, "Selig Is Aloof, Silent Witness to Bonds' 755th," *News-
   day.com*, Aug. 6, 2007, http://www.newsday.com/sports/
   columnists/ny-spgerg065322470aug06,0,2333066,print.column.
7. "Selig Likely to Miss Bonds' Next Three Games: Commissioner Will
   Send Representative in His Place; Giant Needs 1 for Record,"
   MSNBC.com, Aug. 6, 2007, http://www.msnbc.msn.com/id/
   20127817/.

FEMA Fails during Katrina

1. Andy Soltis, "FEMA'S Ex Storms Over White House," *New York Post*,
   February 11, 2006, 8.
2. Ken Bazinet and James Gordon Meek, "Brownie's Revenge," *New York
   Daily News*, February 11, 2006, 6.

3. Paul Krugman, "Heck of a Job, Bushie," *New York Times.* December 30, 2005, http://select.nytimes.com/search/restricted/article?res= F40F17F638540C738FDDAB0994DD404482.

4. Bill Hutchinson, "W Knew Kat Was Big One: Vid Debunks Pres Denial," *New York Daily News,* March 2, 2006, 7.

5. Ibid.

6. Seth Borenstein, "Rethinking Brown as FEMA Scapegoat: Experts Say Fault Lies with Chertoff, Bush," *The Star-Ledger,* March 3, 2006, 10.

7. John Podhoretz, "Brownie's Revenge: Media Now Loves Ex-FEMA Chief," *New York Post,* February 11, 2006, 33.

8. "What Did Bush Know and When Did He Know It?," *New York Daily News,* February 11, 2006.

9. Bazinet and Meek, "Brownie's Revenge," 6.

10. Ibid.

ABOUT THE AUTHOR

Steve Adubato, Ph.D., is a four-time Emmy Award–winning anchor for Thirteen/WNET (PBS), media analyst for MSNBC, MSNBC.com, and TODAYshow.com contributor who often appears on the *TODAY Show* as a media expert. He also provides contributing political commentary on 77-WABC, the country's top-rated talk radio station. Previously, Steve has appeared on such networks as the FOX News Channel, CNN, NBC 4 in New York, CBS 2 in New York, and Court TV as a media and political expert. Dr. Adubato is a distinguished visiting lecturer at Rutgers University, Montclair State University, and Seton Hall University and a much sought after speaker on the subjects of crisis communication, leadership, and the role of the media in American society. He is a *Star-Ledger* columnist and the author of two books, *Speak from the Heart: Be Yourself and Get Results* (Simon & Schuster) and *Make the Connection: Improve Your Communication at Work and at Home* (Rutgers University Press). He is the founder and CEO of Stand & Deliver (www.stand-deliver.com), a leadership and communication executive coaching and professional development firm. Steve lives with his wife and three sons in northern New Jersey.